D0742447

JACOBIN AND JUNTO

JACOBIN AND JUNTO

OR

EARLY AMERICAN POLITICS
AS VIEWED IN THE DIARY OF
DR. NATHANIEL AMES
1758—1822

BY

CHARLES WARREN

BENJAMIN BLOM  New York/London 1968

First Published 1931
Reissued 1968
by Benjamin Blom, Inc. Bronx, New York 10452
and 56 Doughty Street London, W.C. 1

Library of Congress Catalog Card Number 68-21232

Printed in the United States of America

CONTENTS

INTRODUCTION: A JACOBIN DIARY 3

I. COLLEGE, COUNTRY LIFE, AND REVOLUTION . . . 15

II. JACOBINS AND MONOCRATS 42

III. JOHN ADAMS, COCKADES, AND LIBELS 71

IV. THE GAG LAW, LIBERTY POLES, AND TAXES . . . 97

V. JAIL BREAKERS AND JACOBINS 127

VI. JEFFERSON, THE ESSEX JUNTO, AND THE LAW CRAFT 146

VII. A POLITICAL MURDER 183

VIII. EMBARGO DAYS AND A POLITICAL FUNERAL . . . 215

IX. THE WAR OF 1812 AND THE BOSTON REBELS . . 245

X. THE GREAT CHURCH FIGHT 286

XI. PERSONAL LIFE, 1796–1822 312

JACOBIN AND JUNTO

INTRODUCTION

A JACOBIN DIARY

NEVER in American annals has there been a period when men "took their politics so hard" as in the twenty-five years between the framing of the Constitution and the end of the War of 1812. Households, families, communities, trades, and professions were split on political lines, in hot and abusive enmity, according as they held Federalist or Antifederalist views. Men patronized the taverns, shops, stage lines, banks, and other enterprises which were conducted by their party associates; they even regarded the political complexion of their doctors. Many lawsuits were argued on partisan lines, ruled on by partisan judges, and decided by partisan juries. Politics gave rise to murders, and entered into the trials for the crime. Churchgoers were divided on political lines, and men accepted only the preaching of those clergymen whose political beliefs coincided with their own. Politics entered even into the conduct of funerals. Moreover, the field of politics was a mire of scandal, libel, and scurrility; and political opponents belabored each other with epithets of the most opprobrious and contemptuous character. Ordinary daily life became a welter of acrid taunts, malignant personal attack, and vituperation. In those years the American people showed a capacity for passionate and sentimental expression, and for violence of speech and action, which was strangely out of keeping with the usual reticence of the Anglo-Saxon.

Of that era in the Nation's hot-blooded youth a vivid picture is presented in the writings of two brothers [1] who lived in the old country town of Dedham in Massachusetts: Fisher Ames, the squire, and Nathaniel Ames, the doctor — the one a conservative, aristocrat, and Federalist, the other a radical, democrat, and Antifederalist, each imbued with strong passions and gifted with a sharp and witty tongue and a pungent pen. [2] These two men personified in their actions, and embodied in their writings, all the conflicting politics of their day. Fisher Ames, the younger of the brothers, is well known in history as an orator and statesman, a man of personal charm and brilliant ability, whose early death was deplored by his party associates as a National calamity, and whose printed essays and published letters have long been regarded as literary models of political exposition and invective.

The elder brother, Dr. Nathaniel Ames, wrote no essays for publication, and no letters for posterity; but he was the more picturesque, original, and entertaining character. He kept, moreover, a private diary which commented on the politics and personalities of his era — from 1758 to 1822 — in an intimately individual manner that is equalled by no other American writing, unless it be the pugnacious, self-stripping diary of John Quincy Adams. [3] Certain it is that

---

[1] There were several brothers in the Ames family, but the writings of only two are mentioned in this book.

[2] See "Squire Ames and Doctor Ames," by Samuel Eliot Morison, in the *New England Quarterly* (1928), vol. I.

[3] The Diary of Dr. Nathaniel Ames, written in current almanacs of the day, is in the possession of the Dedham Historical Society, through whose courtesy use is made of it in this book. Portions of it were published without editorial commentary in the *Dedham Historical Register* (1890–1903), vols. I–XIV.

The eccentricities of Dr. Ames in the matters of abbreviations, lack of punctuation, and unsystematic use of capital letters have made it necessary to depart somewhat from an exact reproduction of the form of many of his Diary entries, in order to make them more easily intelligible to the reader, but in no instance has the phraseology been altered.

no man ever recorded his likes and dislikes in a more acute and unrestrained fashion than did Nathaniel Ames.

The father of these two interesting sons, Nathaniel Ames, Senior, was a physician, an innkeeper, and the author of the earliest successful American almanac — *Ames' Almanac* (which preceded Benjamin Franklin's *Poor Richard's Almanac* by seven years and which was published from 1726 to 1775). The son Nathaniel, born in 1741, was brought up amidst the news-mongering conviviality of a Colonial tavern, in the family of the leading doctor of the town, and under the literary influence of the pithy and practical phrases of the old almanac-maker. Graduating from Harvard College, and adopting his father's profession of medicine, he early developed into a man of quaint personality. From his father he inherited wit, acuteness, and breadth of interest. That he was no ordinary man, even in his youthful days, may be seen from the following striking admonition which he wrote in his Diary in 1758, at the age of seventeen years, when he was a freshman:

Cambridge, Septr. 20th, 1758. They who see this in future time may know that it is the covering of an old Almanack 1758. And do not despise old times too much, for remember that 2 or 3 centurys from the time of seeing this, you will be counted old-times folks as much as you count us to be so now. Many People in these times think the Consummation very nigh; much more may you think so — and do not think yourselves so much wiser than we are as to make yourselves proud, for the last day is at hand in which you must give an account of what you have been about in this state of probation, and very likely you are more given to vice than we are, and we than the last century folks. If you have more arts than we have that you yourself have found out, impute it not to our inability that we could not find them out, for if we had only those very arts that we have now, when we first came to settle in N. America, very like we should have found out those very things which you have the honor to be the Inventors of. Dinner is ready; I must leave off.

The Diary is an amazing self-revelation of a man of tenacious, unreasoning, elemental hatreds as well as devotions; a man of quick temper and gruff manners, of easily aroused suspicions and passions; yet on the other hand a man of eminently keen humor, clear perception, and widely practised common sense; a man of varied interests, an able physician, and a progressive citizen, alert to the improvements of his day; devoted equally to the practice of his profession and to the culture of his crops and garden; an omnivorous reader of scientific, historical, astronomical, and agricultural books. All this his Diary portrays in phrases of a rare pungency and quaint wit and in entries that, in view of wide range of subjects, are of surprising shrewdness and originality. Though in 1779 he began his entries thus modestly: "What amazing sagacity will posterity discover in these my memorandums! I should despise myself if I had any other views than to facilitate my own recollections," nevertheless the heading of his Diary for 1799 more adequately expressed its scope: "Domestical, political, obstetrical, clerical, clinical, etc., economical, etc., meteorological, chymical" — to which he might have added "agricultural, poetical, historical, local."

The life of Nathaniel Ames the younger, from his graduation at Harvard College in 1761 through the years of unrest prior to and during the Revolutionary War, was full of interest and activity as a citizen and as a physician. It is, however, for its astoundingly illuminating portrayal of the political conditions in this country in the years between 1794 and 1815 that the Diary is of intense interest as an historical document. History recorded from day to day may be less intelligible, less philosophic, and more

biased than history compiled by studious comparison of
authorities and sources, years after the events, but it is
unquestionably more vivid and picturesque. In the tem-
pestuous politics of those days — an era when political
conditions were more heated and violent than at any other
period in our history (save possibly immediately prior to
the Civil War) — Dr. Ames took a most active part. He
was a bitter partisan Antifederalist, a "Jacobin of Jacobins" — "Grumbleton the Jacobinite" (as a fellow-towns-
man termed him). He lived in a town which was always a
stronghold of the Antifederalist party — although in 1797
he noted: "A Royal or Monarchical party of high Federal
public servants grow very bold! Here, too!!" His political
enmities were indeed so violent as to interfere seriously
with his professional success, and the following significant
entry in his Diary disclosed the fact that his own family
evidently regretted his activities: "*Sept. 16, 1798.* I cannot think it as obnoxious for any other profession as the
clerical to be conversant in politics. Is it for a physician?
Ha! Yes, says my wife!" Fortunately for posterity, however, Dr. Ames, disregarding his wife's views, continued to
mix in politics and to record in his Diary all his extreme
political prejudices and his views of his opponents, with
that absolute freedom of epithet which so characterized
the spirit of those heated times. Few men ever delighted
more in vigorous denunciation of those who disagreed with
them; and few ever originated more novel and pungent
phrases in which to voice their pugnacity than did Dr.
Nathaniel Ames. "The prigarchy," he called the Federalist party. "Pettifogarchy" was one of his favorite terms,
referring to the vast preponderance of lawyers in that
party; and he wrote to the local Dedham paper as to "a
vile tool of Federalism which is the genuine quintessence of
Pettifogism." In 1802 he commented on a letter from

Thomas Paine, which "sets lawyers and Federal Tories roaring and vomiting black." The Boston-Salem-Beverly group of Federalists — Theophilus Parsons, George Cabot, Timothy Pickering, Stephen Higginson, and John Lowell — known as the Essex Junto was his particular bugbear — the "insolent British Junto," as he called it. "Traitors in Congress, wretches that would gag us," he termed those who voted for the Alien and Sedition Laws in 1798. "Devilism reigns!" he exclaimed, when the Federalist party came into ascendency in 1808. "Lobster princes," he termed the Boston merchants of 1812. In 1805, in describing a new Federal newspaper, the *Repertory*, he deplored the fact that "the filth and spume of all the entongueing tools of Federal attorneys far outdoes the spitting under B. Russell." He delighted in noting other writings in which the Federalists had been termed "monarchical aristocrats," "British bootlickers," "arch-traitors," "malignant," "scurrilous," "debauchers of liberty," "British sycophants."

On the other hand, no man in the Federalist party denounced the Antifederalists with more sincerity and intensity of feeling than did Nathaniel Ames' own brother, Fisher Ames. In his published letters and essays the latter employed every term of execration which a brilliant literary imagination could evolve. He spoke of the Antifederalist clubs as "Jacobins born in sin, impure offspring of Genêt, sons of darkness." He called them "trumpeters of sedition," "sans culottes," and their policies "the contagion of licentious Jacobinism." In a single essay in the *Boston Gazette*, in 1799, he called his opponents "mobocracy," "toads," "serpents," "malignant," "despicable, "ignorant." In the next essay, he spoke of their leaders as "knaves, cold-thinking villains," and defended an "open avowal of contempt and detestation of the Jacobins." Regarding his brother Nathaniel as a Jacobin, he wrote in a semi-humorous, but yet bitter, strain: "I am still puny and tender . . . my constitution is like that of Federalism — too feeble for a full allowance of even water gruel; and like that, all the doctor I have is a Jacobin. The Lord, you say, have mercy on me, a sinner!"

The dissensions produced in family circles by the politics of the day have never been more strikingly and entertainingly illustrated than in the many entries of his Diary in which Dr. Nathaniel pilloried his brother Fisher. Although the two brothers lived in the same town, — Fisher dying at the age of fifty in 1808, and Nathaniel living to the ripe age of eighty-one and dying in 1822, — nevertheless, during the common years of their life, they were at swords' points on every possible question. In the first place, Fisher Ames was a lawyer, and Dr. Nathaniel Ames hated lawyers with a good round hatred; for lawyers, as a class, belonged almost exclusively to the detested Federalist party. Hence, among the liveliest entries in the Diary were those in which the members of the bar were denounced as "pettifogs," "aristocrats," "blackguard hedgehogs," and the Bar Association was termed a "Conclave of Jesuits or Junto of the Dogs of the Law"; and the political activities of the legal profession in 1803 were thus referred to: "The Order of Lawyers are barking destruction at all that won't submit to their domination, under the guise of Federalism"; and "Jefferson, 'tho bred a Lawyer, despises the narrow spirit of Pettyfogism, therefore the Lawyers hate him." In local politics the two brothers fought each other bitterly; and when each party was contesting for political supremacy in the town Nathaniel wrote of the "tools of F. A.," saying: "Every exertion made by the Feds. to obtain voters, every bribe of treating, carriages, and arts of delusion practiced. Egg rum was administered

at F. Ames' office. His men and wagon loaded with lumber
of unprincipled wretches who would sell their Lord for 30
glasses of egg rum." In Congress, Fisher Ames represented
and advocated everything which Nathaniel abhorred as
traitorous and unrighteous; and in 1797 Dr. Ames noted,
regarding a Federal appointment just given to his brother:
"F. Ames, Bushrod Washington and Alfred Moore appointed to hold a treaty with the Cherokee Indians to extinguish titles to Tennessee lands. What a fine thing to be
a Federal man or Hedgehog, i. e., to black our Saviours,
the French, and praise our enemies, the English!!!" In
1803 Dr. Ames entered in his Diary: "F. A., under sign of
Fabricius in *Centinel*, Ben Russell's, July, tries to black the
brightest traits in Jefferson's administration — the purchase of Louisiana for reasonable sum of money instead of
war, blood, and wealth of all the States; but plain truth in
the *Chronicle* beats him down and still he goes on barking,
after beat, like other Lawyers." In 1796 Dr. Ames refused
to continue his subscription to a local newspaper because
it seemed to be controlled by Fisher and his party views;
and he noted: "*Minerva*, Dedham Gazette, published this
morning and wholly dictated by F. A. to another political
enquiry and make public servants Lords"; and in 1798 he
noted that he had written the editor "to send no more such
stuff," as the paper was "of a base, British, aristocratical
complexion." He refused to become one of the organizers
of the local bank in 1804, because of its control by his political opponents; and he noted in his Diary: "Sundry
mechanics of Dedham meet with a Lawyer at their head to
confer on the subject of a Bank in Dedham, and subscribe,
it is said, to a fund. . . . As I am decided to take no part in
conference with those who excommunicated me in December, 1802, and abused me, viz: F. A. and Deacon Bullard,
and feel indignation to find the Eastern States fettered

down in chains of Pettyfogism, I think I shall keep aloof yet awhile, especially as T. Gay, Jr., and J. Richardson seem the only puppets played off on this occasion by the man behind the curtain." The term "excommunication" referred to the fact that divisions on political lines had occurred even in church and parish affairs; and in a series of amusingly abusive entries in 1802 Nathaniel accused his brother Fisher of successfully manœuvring to drive him out of the church: "Parish meeting led by F. A. to my excommunication. F. A. wishing to shut me out of meeting so as to enjoy my pew, he harangued them so pathetically about pious forefathers that he crammed the Priest down their throats, tail foremost . . . duped by a Lawyer. . . . Civil and ecclesiastical oppression, intrigue, triumphant harangueing, arrogating, blackguarding in Parish meeting beat the people out of their senses, made them defeat their own wishes, and drum good citizens out of the meeting, playing the rogue's march. . . . Parish meeting yield to yoke of F. Ames to ordain Bates, 16 March, entail discord on the Parish; many, discontented, join Episcopal Church. . . . Every infamous slander against seceders is raised to justify themselves in their oppression and tyranny that drove us to withdraw. This is common to unprincipled mortals!" And in 1803 Dr. Nathaniel made the following highly original comment on his brother's control of the church: "Bo't of Elijah Fisher a heap of dung, at 20 dollars — and in casting away on my clover, F. Ames came and stormed at my presumption to my men, in buying dung without his leave, when I did not know he arrogated all the dung as well as religion in Dedham. After turning me out of the House of God, I expected he would allow me to grovel in dung!"

Political rancor, however, could go no farther than upon the death of Fisher Ames, July 4, 1808, when, because the funeral was to be held publicly in Boston, under the charge of a committee composed of leading Federalists, Dr. Nathaniel Ames refused to attend, and recorded in his Diary: "In the afternoon came George Cabot to allure me into a sanction of ridiculous pomp of pretended apotheosis. But none of the relations will attend. . . . But making a farce of a funeral will rebound upon their heads, unless perhaps it may be the introduction of a Fashion to make political funerals."

With Dr. Ames, all men were either heroes or villains, angels or devils, and the statesmen and politicians whom he favored or opposed were painted by him in no neutral colors. George Washington fell like Lucifer, in Dr. Ames' opinion, when he signed the Jay Treaty with England in 1795; and the Diary had this caustic comment: "Washington now defies the whole Sovereign (People) that made him what he is — and can unmake him again. Better his hand had been cut off when his glory was at its height, before he blasted all his laurels." John Adams was Dr. Ames' chief devil — "an aristocratic lawyer in favor of British dignities, manners, and Government," and "a monarchist." In the presidential campaign of 1800, Adams and Alexander Hamilton were thus referred to in the Diary: "Fine times when murderers and adulterers are best candidates for highest offices!" Jefferson and Burr, on the other hand, were termed "the old Patriots — triumphant over the treason of the last four years"; and Dr. Ames hailed Jefferson's election as the sign of "the eradication of hierarchy, oppression, superstition and tyranny"; Jefferson's reëlection in 1804 he regarded as "the regeneration of the United States." The attitude of the Boston Federalists during the era of the Embargo Acts and the War of 1812 met with Dr. Ames' severest denunciation. In 1808, when John Quincy Adams and many others thought that New England was preparing to advocate secession from the Union, on account of the Embargo Laws, he noted: "Beyond conception, almost, is the impudence of the pettifog faction in sedition and slander against the best administration of government ever blessing men. They, the Pettyfogs, have already raised rebellion, murder, and treason, in some parts in July and August. . . . Both natural and political atmosphere hazy, drizzling with pestilent drops of maritime or mercantile sedition and slander of the best administration of government, trying to extricate maritime enterprises from piratical fangs of two lawless belligerents, England and France." In August, 1808, he noted a convention of Republicans in the county as "necessary to combat the pulpit, the bar and host of superstition, vanity, pride, and selfish wretches under foreign influence, that never had a conception of searching out principles or seeking the truth, and will neither read, see nor hear anything contrary to their own narrow prejudices, wholly actuated by the impulse of the moment." In February he wrote of the votes of various Massachusetts towns at "seditious Federal meetings, belching rebellious resolves against President Jefferson and Congress for embargo." In 1811 he noted, "Here we have plenty of apeish miscreants and English agents that excite sedition and rebellion against the best of government in our own country," and "Boston Feds. as seditious rebels." In 1812, on the declaration of war with England, he noted, July 23: "Boston Junto, outrageous, seditious, hiss Seaver and other Congress members in streets of Boston"; February 5, 1813: "Embargo excites Boston Lobster-princes and their dupes to the edge of rebellion." In September, 1814, he stated that in the country at large there was "more union, against British brutality, except in Boston where the Junto are on the verge of rebellion," and December 17,

1814, he referred to the famous Hartford Convention: "No news yet from the Rebel Convention or Conspiracy."

Such, in general, were the views of this pugnacious personality as they will be more fully illuminated by the extracts from his Diary given in the succeeding chapters. The controversy over Jay's treaty; the British and French factions of John Adams' administration; the sedition trials under the "Gag Laws" or Alien and Sedition Acts; the Jacobins of 1798 and 1799; the triumph and "reign" of Thomas Jefferson; the struggles of Boston Federalism against the Embargo; the charges of treason and disunion against the Boston Junto; the Selfridge murder in 1807; the local views of the progress of the War of 1812; the mixture of politics and religion in the Massachusetts churches — all these episodes were incisively portrayed in miniature in the Diary, in a manner which no general book of history can rival, and with little need for elaborate commentary. In fact, the Diary might well be entitled "Jacobin Days in America."

To complete the picture of the man as well as of the times in which lived, the first chapter of this book is devoted to Nathaniel Ames' entries depicting life at Harvard College and in a country town prior to the War of the Revolution, as well as his political views before and during that War — entries which, while not as startling as in his later years, present a youth of a singular individuality.

I

COLLEGE, COUNTRY LIFE, AND REVOLUTION

IN THE fall of 1757, Nathaniel Ames, this son of a country doctor, innkeeper, and almanac-maker, entered Harvard College (then comprising about one hundred and fifty students) as a freshman member of the Class of 1761; and in the following January, 1758, being then seventeen years of age, he began his Diary. His early entries were chiefly concerned with attendance at lectures, and showed little evidence of the humor and incisive personal comment which appeared later. On February 27, 1758, however, he piously recorded: "Performed all the Duties of Day." In the next month, other occupations began to appear: "*March 18.* Fit with the Sophomores. *19.* Went to meeting all day. *20.* Had another fight with the Sophomores. *23.* Bottled Cyder. *31.* Sent a letter to my father." On May 4 an entry of "The Class was placed, last Tuesday" recorded the quaint custom then prevailing under which the order of the undergraduates' names followed more or less the social rank of their families in the community. Ames was ranked 20 in a class numbering 39 at graduation.[1] The remainder of his freshman year was occupied with the following diversions:

> *May 22.* Went a fishing with 13 of my class mates. Got away from Cambridge wharf at 12 o'clock, catch'd 3 cods besides dog fish, skates and sculpins; arrived at Nantasket

[1] It may be noted that among Ames' college contemporaries John Adams of the Class of 1755 was No. 14 out of 24, Joseph Warren of the Class of 1759 was No. 25 out of 35, John Pickering of the Class of 1761 was No. 29 out of 39, and Elbridge Gerry of the Class of 1762 was No. 26 out of 47.

at 8 o'clock at night. Lodg'd at a tavern, got off in the morning between 7 & 8 o'clock, passed Holloway's prize. Arrived at the Castle at 2 o'clock. . . . Came from the Castle to Charlestown from whence we walked on foot to Cambridge, which we were obliged to do, the tide being so low we could not come up Cambridge River.

June 1. Ye 1st Division of our Class declaimed.

12. A crew went out a fishing.

13. Went in swimming.

14. They came from fishing.

23. Declaimed this morning, left off my wigg.

26. President's grass mowed.

30. Valedictory Day, I waited on the orator. Tom Went-worth was orator.

July 1. Finished the President's hay.[1]

His sophomore year began with the following entries: "*Sept. 1.* Did nothing only read the Customs. *2.* Began Homer. *6.* Read the Customs to the Freshmen. *12.* Hooper shook a Freshman." These ancient "customs" were perhaps more interesting than anything else connected with the undergraduate life of those days. Among them were the following: that "no Freshman shall wear his hat in the College yard unless it rains, hails or snows, provided he be on foot and have not both hands full"; that "no undergraduate shall wear his hat in the College yard when any of the Governors of the College are there"; that "no Freshman shall speak to a Senior with his hat on"; that a freshman should be obliged to go on errands for any of his seniors except in study hour or after nine in the evening; that a freshman should immediately open his door "without inquiring who is there when any person

---

[1] These last entries refer to the old custom by which the grass around the President's house, "Wadsworth House," and in the "Tutors' Lot" (where the Widener Library now stands) was mowed by freshmen, and also to the custom by which the freshmen were bound to wait on and do errands for the upper classmen.

knocks except in study time"; that no scholar should call up or down, to or from, any chamber in the college, or play football or any other game in the yard, or throw anything across it; that freshmen should "furnish batts, balls and footballs for the use of the students to be kept at the Battery." Finally, as most of the Customs sought to regulate the conduct of the freshmen, it was made incumbent upon their traditional enemies, the sophomores, to publish these Customs to the freshmen in the chapel, "at which time the Freshmen are enjoined to keep their places in their seats and attend with decency to the reading."

In October Ames was much concerned with the making and first wearing of the "surtout," the distinctive sophomore apparel, as the following entry showed: "*Sept. 30.* Went to Molly Kingsbery yesterday to get her to make my Gowne, but now, [*October 8th*] she hath disappointed me. *Oct. 6.* Went to Boston. Surtout. Transports from Halifax. *7.* Broke my buckle in the Play Place. *12.* Went to Boston, got my gowne. *17.* The President prayed, 1st time since I came. *25.* Wore my surtout 1st time." In connection with the entries as to his "surtout," it may be noted that extravagance of expenditure in college had increased so greatly at about this time that, in 1754, the Overseers had passed a vote reciting that the "costly habits" of many of the scholars "not only tends to discourage persons from giving their children a college education but is also inconsistent with the gravity and demeanor proper to be observed in this society," and urging a law (which was later adopted) that no scholar should wear gold or silver lace or brocade, that candidates for a degree appear in black, dark blue, or gray clothes, and that "no one wear any silk night gowns."

In December the meetings of his club engaged Ames' attention: "*Dec. 9.* Went Whitfield. Club, Hooper's Chamber. *14.* Had some cold pig, catch'd cold. *15.* Class met, a new committee, I not one of them. *18.* Juniors disputed forensically, we did not dispute. *21.* Had a dance at Bradford's Chamber, my chum at Boston all night. *22.* Freshman began to declaim. *26.* Began 3rd book of Euclid. *31.* Club at my chamber, Saturday night."

In the year 1759 social and theatrical events played a considerable part in his life: [1]

Feb. 1. Small shock of an earthquake, this night.
2. Measels thick about.
9. Vacancy [vacation] prolonged 3 weeks on account of the measels.
April 20. Went see *The Drummer* acted at How's.
21. *The Orphan* acted, ye 13th inst.
24. Begun Locke, My Chum bottled Cyder.
27. Went to Boston and Castle, got my new coat.
May 1. Went Boston to see the soldiers.
3. Our Court sets.   A famous dance at How's.
5. Joyned the Tea Club.
June 11. Went a fishing, took breakfast at ye Lighthouse.
20. *The Recruiting Officer* acted by ourselves, then public.
July 6. *The Revenge* acted, my Father came.
15. Advanced a seat in ye meeting house.
18. Commencement very hot.
Sept. 7. *Cato* acted this evening.
10. A bear seen.   Men hunt him.
11. Bear killed, a dance this evening.
15. Made tea for Club.
Oct. 19. Did not declaim.   Joyn'd a new Club.
22. Disputed on *Status futurus patet lumine natura.*
Nov. 23. Went to Boston.   *The Revenge* acted at Bowman's.
27. Disputed on *Bruta non cogitant.*

---

[1] Already, as a freshman, Ames displayed considerable interest in the drama, and recorded, June 22, 1758, "*Roman Father*, a play"; July 3, "*Cato*, a play acted at Warren's chamber"; July 6, "*Cato* to perfection"; July 11, "*Cato* more perfect than before."

Early entries in 1760 were:

Jan. 25. Went Balch'es Lecture. Had a sort of a Frolick with Whitwell, Gay, Steward, etc.

Feb. 13. Father Flynt [1] died at 5 o'clock.

19. Flynt interred. An oration by Lovel.

24. A Funeral Sermon by Appleton.

March 15. Examination in the chapel.

18. Winthrop's private lecture for our Class.

20. Alarm'd this morning about 4 o'clock with cry that Boston was half burnt up. With that I got up, and looking out at my window beheld a blaze big enough to terrify any Heart of common Resolution, considering such valuable combustibles fed it — All College up by five. I went to Boston about 9 o'clock and there beheld a most shocking sight! Nigh 300 Houses consumed by Fire! It began at the Brazen Head and spread away to the Bunch of Grapes Tavern in King Street, then over to Fort Hill; burnt the Fort and blew up the magazine, then it also burnt a ship, several sloops and boats. By far the largest fire ever known in New England. It was seen above 30 miles from Boston.[2]

Entries during the next few months showed the discipline administered to college men of the period.[3]

[1] The "Father Flynt" referred to was the famous Henry Flynt, who died at the age of eighty-four and who was a tutor at Harvard for fifty-five years. Soon after his resignation in 1754 a vote was passed that tutors should remain no longer than eight years in the college.

[2] The Brazen Head Tavern was on the east side of Washington Street about opposite Williams Court. The Bunch of Grapes Tavern was on the west corner of State [King] and Kilby Streets.

[3] College discipline was of the strictest kind, for, as Josiah Quincy said in his history of the University: "The changes which occurred in the morals and manners of New England about the middle of the Eighteenth Century unavoidably affected the College. 'Profane cursing and swearing', habits of frequenting taverns and alehouses, the practice of using wine, beer and distilled liquors, by undergraduates, in their rooms, greatly increased. Tutors were insulted and combinations to perpetuate unlawful acts were more frequent." The number of acts which the students were forbidden to do were far greater than the studies to which they were constrained; and to each enjoined act was annexed a pecuniary penalty for its violation. Thus there were fines for absence from and tardiness at prayers and lectures; profanation of the Lord's Day; ill behavior and absence

April 8. *Tancred and Sigismunda* acted, with a Farce at ye
end on't.

June 12. Acted *Tancred and Sigismunda*, for which we are
like to be prosecuted.

Sept. 9. President sick, wherefore much deviltry carried on in
College.

Sept. 29. President prayed this evening.

Oct. 1. Scholars degraded this morning, 2 admonished, 1
punished.

Oct. 10. Kneeland's and Thayer's windows broke last night.

Dec. 22. Gardiner and Barnard admonished, stealing wood.

For some reason Ames omitted to note that he was one
of the scholars "degraded." The faculty records, however,
contain the following illustration of the manner in which
college discipline was severely maintained: "On Sept. 30,
ten students 'were punish'd one shilling and 6*d.* each, for
making tumultuous and indecent noises in the College.'"

Agreed, also, at the same meeting that as Mr. Thayer had
made Complaint that all the above named students (Huntington
excepted) had greatly insulted him when endeavoring to still
their tumultuous Noises, agreeable to one of the College Laws,
That they therefore be all of them sent for before us . . . accordingly when convened after a full examination of them, we found
'em guilty according to the Complaint, but judging so, in different Degrees. Therefore came into the following Votes 1:
That Palmer and Rand be publickly admonish'd in the Chapel.
That the Rest of Them, besides being admonish'd, be degraded
in their several Classes in the following manner, viz. Ames
fourteen places . . .

from public worship, and going to meeting before bell ringing, neglecting to repeat the sermon, or irreverent behavior; absence from Cambridge without leave;
lodging strangers or entertaining persons of ill character; frequenting taverns;
profane cursing; playing cards, or games for money; lying; opening doors by
picklocks; going upon the top of the college, or cutting off the lead; tumultuous
noises; refusing to give evidence; rudeness at meals; keeping guns; going skating;
firing guns or pistols in the college yard, etc. The fines imposed varied from one
penny to two pounds; ten shillings, five shillings, three shillings, and one and
sixpence being the most general amounts.

On December 30, 1760, Ames recorded: "King George III proclaimed in Boston." The entries in 1761 show a varied life; and a sense of crude humor:

Jan. 26. A dance at Dean's. Ladies were, first Miss Balches, Miss Ponds, Miss Dexter, Miss Debby.

Feb. 1. Went Boston to public concert, took 20 pounds.

16. Begun to recite Wat's Astronomy.

23. Bill Turner here serenading.

26. Lost 2 Pistareens at cards last evening.

28. Club at Palmer's tonight.

March 14. Scholars return from frolic at Dedham.

26. First game of Bat and Ball.

30. Town's engine come.

31. College Cuz-john set on fire to exercise the new engine and show the Town People dexterity in its management. This melancholy accident happened 1/2 past 9 o'clock.

Lively accounts of more college discipline are seen in the following entries:

April 15. Dependents on the favors of the President and Tutors sign an agreement to inform of any scholar that is guilty of profanity.

18. Palmer and others punished for swearing.

May 4. Daniel Oliver degraded to the bottom of the Class. Hunt next to him and Brig'r White degraded 13 for being found guilty of the riot mentioned against him the first day of April.

May 19. Joseph Cabot rusticated. As soon as the President said he was rusticated, he took his hat and went out of the chapel without staying to hear the President's speech out. After prayer, he bulrags the Tutors at a high rate and leaves College. His mother faints at the news.

May 20. Chapel rob'd of the Cushing and Bible cloths.

June 3. New cushions to the Chapel.

The end of Ames' college career and the celebration of the Commencement season were noted by entries which have a very modern sound.

June 19. The last Friday that we are ever to be punished.

20. Valedictory Oration pronounced by S. Hooper.

30. Restored to my former place.[1]

July 15. Commencement, many Dedhamites present.

16. A dance in Town House, Cambridge.

17. A genteel set down at Prentices'. Prentices' account for trouble and a few things taken by negroes on my account came to about 34 pounds. When Seth [his brother] takes his degree, get all things from Boston that you can and give his landlord cautions for what to charge for and what not, and don't pay him for things which were not allowed to be delivered.

18. Devouring the remains of Commencement.

It is to be recalled that at this time the Harvard Commencement Day was not only a holiday through the Province, but also the scene of considerable disorder, gambling, and dissipation in Cambridge. This condition was a source of great trouble to the governing boards of the college. In 1760 dancing was forbidden in any college building during the week, and no undergraduates were allowed to give any entertainment after dinner on Commencement Day. The President was deputed to inspect all literary performances and expunge exceptionable parts; and he was particularly enjoined "to put an end to the practice of addressing the female sex." In some respects, however, the regulations were much laxer than in modern times. Thus, in 1759, the Corporation passed a law that "it shall be no offence if any scholar shall at Commencement make and entertain guests at his chambers with punch." Two years later it extended this liberty so that "it should be no offence if the scholars, in a sober manner, entertain one another and strangers with punch, which as it is now usually made, is no intoxi-

---

[1] The faculty records, under date of June 30, 1761, read: "Ames, Sen'r. who stands degraded in his Class as on p. 119, was, upon a very humble confession of his crime restor'd to his original place in his Class."

cating liquor"—a law the truth of the declaratory portion of which seems very doubtful.[1]

At graduation, Nathaniel Ames' class consisted of thirty-nine members, among whom were John Pickering, later Chief Justice of the New Hampshire Supreme Court and United States District Judge, and Samuel Sewall, later Hancock Professor of Hebrew at Harvard. Many other famous men were his college contemporaries — in the Class of 1759 were General Joseph Warren of Bunker Hill fame, and Jonathan Trumbull, the great war Governor of Connecticut and later United States Senator; in the Class of 1760 was John Lowell, who in 1799, as United States District Judge, pronounced a sentence on Ames for contempt of court; and in the Class of 1762 were Francis Dana, later Chief Justice of Massachusetts, and Elbridge Gerry, later Vice President of the United States.

Upon graduation, Nathaniel Ames returned to his home town of Dedham, and within a month he entered upon his chosen profession, as noted in his Diary, August, 1761: "Began the practice of physician by bleeding a taylor in the foot." Three years later he succeeded to much of the practice of his father, upon the latter's death in 1764. That

---

[1] It may be of interest to note later entries in Ames' Diary as to certain subsequent Commencements which he attended. Thus, in 1763 Ames described Commencement as follows: "*July 20.* Went Commencement. . . . Solemnity began with an oration in Latin saluting the audience, then came on a Disputation in Latin, then an English Oration on the Advantages of a Liberal Education, which concluded the forenoon exercise. Afternoon begun with a Disputation by the Masters, after that a Dialogue in English. Then they descended to take their degrees, then the Valedictory oration, then the President concluded with a Prayer. N. B. Masters Respondents do not repeat the Syllogisms. *July 21.* Gay evening in Cambridge. *July 22.* Returned to Dedham." In 1766 he recorded: "*July 18.* Came home from Commencement, satisfied"; and in 1768 he noted: "*July 20.* Went Commencement and saw no very extraordinary performances, nor indeed many of my ancient acquaintances, so that with me the entertainment grows more diffident every year" — this last being a most characteristically modern touch. In 1776 he noted: "No Commencement. College Made Barracks."

he regarded highly the honor of his profession and resented the kind of competition which he had to meet in the town from the low character of some of those who passed as physicians was amusingly shown in a number of caustic entries in his Diary. Thus, in 1765, he wrote:

> Some of them commence Quacks and call themselves Doctors, having seen a man that saw another man cured of a very foul gunshot by hot oil of Turpentine, and heard their Grandmother say that Carduus Tea will vomit, and Fisingers are very cooling; or, perhaps having exercised their skill on passive beasts, at length have the Audacity to practice their Butchery on the Human Race, and upon the slightest Occasion, or oftener none at all, absent themselves from Public Worship to be thought Men of Business; thus, without one Qualification necessary for a Physician, they become famous water gruel doctors.

And in frequent other passages of his Diary he referred to the obstacles which beset the path of professional practice:

> *Sept. 3, 1764.* Several Quacks threaten coming to Dedham.
> *Dec. 23, 1765.* If the Art of Physick consisted in the knowledge only of medicines and their virtues, then every apothecary would be the best physician.
> *Feb. 11, 1766.* Doctor Lincoln called here to apologize for stooping so low as to practice with a certain quack named Ephraim Ware, who came as soon as my father died, and endeavors to succeed him, in the practice of Physick in Dedham.
> *June 16.* What security is there against the slanderous tongues of ill-minded men who seek all opportunity to slur and destroy a man's character, where conscious innocence is his only support? What a stock of patience need I have, calmly to bear the false and slanderous report of having put a little Hybernian into a salivation in a pleurisy, not being able to draw off any blood in V. S., altho' she bled 3 times as freely as I desire any person to in the same circumstances.

On July 11, 1764, he suffered a severe loss in the death of his ingenious and talented father, as to whom he wrote in his Diary:

July 11, 1764. My Father's noble and generous soul took his flight into the region of spirits.

July 13. Now leaning on my Father's coffin, I could not help writing the last words he ever said to me: "Natty, Natty, is it not very hard that I cannot have one Trial?"

After his father's death he continued to edit the Ames' Almanacs each year until 1775. They proved, however, a source of considerable annoyance, since he was forced coincidently to run the tavern which his father had kept and to settle his paternal estate, with a mother and brothers who were not always in agreement with him. As to these difficulties he wrote: "*September 4, 1766.* Laid aside astronomy and thought of publishing an Almanack. I was deeply engaged in calculating for an Almanack for 1767 and broke off by the importunity of my mother, to settle the estate, they met agreeing to take care of the Tavern whilst I could make an Almanac. So that my character will be spoiled and I deprived of the only means of getting a living in this world; wherefore I pray God to take my soul into the next scene of Being, where I hope to know everything intuitively for which I now grope about by the dim light of Reason." When still a youth he began to write for the newspapers in a tart style, which, throughout his life, kept him in epistolary hot water. As early as September 24, 1766, he noted: "Never let me write again to the Printers of Boston newspapers, for they are all Knaves, Liars, Villains, to serve their Interest, and when they appear most friendly have most of the Devil in their Hearts."

Colonial life in a country town in Massachusetts in the middle of the eighteenth century, however, was not wholly

a sober and serious affair; and Dr. Ames depicted its lighter
side with a vivacious, picturesque, and humorous pen.
Thus, he retained his youthful fondness for plays throughout his life. Shortly after he returned from college he
noted that, on August 1, 1761, he went to Providence and
"saw Douglass acted with *Harlequin*," and, the next night,
"*The Distressed Mother*"; two months later he "went to
Battles [in Roxbury] in the evening, acted a play, rebuked
for it by our parents"; and November 14, "proposed to act
a play in Dedham"; two years later, November 13, 1764,
"undertake to act '*The Orphan*.'" On April 20, 1772, he
recorded: "The Farce called *The Toy Shop* was acted . . .
before a numerous audience of the most respectable Inhabitants of the First Parish in Dedham both male and
female." Ames himself wrote a Prologue for this occasion,
the last lines of which were:

> Here, though no Theatres our Land adorn,
> This work they left their children then unborn;
> We then, their offspring, diffident presume
> To make a present Theatre of this room.
> And tho' the piece we've chose fine thoughts displays,
> 'Tis not so striking as some other plays.
> Yet, if our undertaking you approve,
> Some leisure Night we'll all your passions move.
> We'll make you laugh or shed the generous tear,
> With plays yon virgins need not blush to hear;
> Or be as solemn, let it not alarm one,
> As the dull Priest who steals his weekly sermon.
> Of this, whatever People may conjecture,
> You'll safely call it but an Evening Lecture.

As a postscript to this entry Ames noted, "The guests
were invited to come to 'An Evening Lecture'" — a sly
reference to the fact that play-acting in public had been
forbidden by statute in 1750, in which it had been recited
that theatrical entertainments "not only occasion great

and unnecessary expense, and discourage industry and frugality, but otherwise tend generally to increase immorality, impiety, and a contempt for religion." [1] The colonists continued to witness plays, however, under the disguise of "lectures," "moral lectures," and "entertainments."

In 1762 the demolition of the old parish church and the raising of the new structure were thus graphically described:

> *June 6, 1762.* Mr. Haven preached a pretty affecting funeral sermon for the Old Meeting House. Snivelling women.
>
> *June 7.* Parish Meeting this morning. They pulled down the old Meeting House, and great was the fall thereof. A good number of Spectators — both Sexes. In the evening, the youth frolic heartily.
>
> *June 20.* Thursday, Mr. Haven preached at his door to the people in the yard.
>
> *June 28.* Began to raise the new Meeting House, four days about it.
>
> *July 18.* First sermon in the new Meeting House.

Social parties and cards were not absent from the life of the town, and in the year after he left college Dr. Ames noted:

> *Nov. 11.* Leonard Fisher, Scollay, Hunt, Sherburne, Andrew Oliver, Balch, Seth, and myself agree to spend the evening with the same lady. This evening had a very pretty and genteel Ball for Dedham.

---

[1] An interesting entry is found in the Diary, November 20, 1764: "Scholars punished at College for acting over the great and last day, in a very shocking manner, personating the Jude, eternal Devil, etc."

In 1756 a "Concert Hall" was built in Boston, where dances and plays were given to such an extent that in 1779 another bill was introduced into the legislature for "suppressing theatrical entertainments, horse racing, gaming, and such other diversions as are productive of idleness, dissipation, and a general depravity of manners." As late as 1792, Otway's *Venice Preserved* and *Hamlet, Romeo and Juliet*, and other plays were produced at "New Exhibition Hall," as "a moral lecture in five parts," and the first theatre in Boston was not opened until 1794.

The company consisted of the above-mentioned Gentlemen, and the Ladies were as follows: *Imprimis* and before all was the adorable P. S., next P. Balch, Elis Day, Miss Hilly Newfoundland and *mea Soror*, held at Mrs. Steward's, to whom we very impolitely gave no warning of our coming, but were received very graciously.

Nov. 12. We all . . . spent the chief of the day in playing Bragg. Very unlucky at dinner, for, attempting to move the table nearer the fire, we overset a fine boiled dish and broke several things. Just before night, we all (except Seth) went up to Robin's and had a very good supper and spent most of the night in playing Bragg, a very enticing game. We breakfasted and spent ye forenoon at Bragg still; then at 12 o'clock we set out for our respective homes, but some of us went with very bad luck, for after Leonard had parted from us we had no horse to carry us home that was ever in a chaise. However, we tryed one, but not succeeding were obliged to get an old tired one, who as I was riding down a hill gave me a complete fall without any bones broken. We made out, with walking half the way, to get home in 5 hours which was but 3 miles. And the horse being so tired Oliver could not go to Cambridge but spent Sunday in Dedham. A. M., I went to Roxbury, P. M. Oliver went to Battles. In the evening acted a play — rebuked for it by our parents.

It is possible that the events of November 12 had some connection with a pessimistic entry which he made in his Diary at the end of the year, December 29, 1762: "Went over to old Brown's *cum Puellis*, etc. Alas! How have I spent the year past! Grant, ye Powers, it may not be my last!"

Husking bees were a favorite form of amusement in country towns at that period — and perhaps not as innocent amusements as poets and romancers have sometimes depicted them; for Cotton Mather, in his *Advice From the Watch Tower*, as early as 1713, spoke of the "riots that have too often accompanied our huskings," and remarked:

"May the joy of Harvest no longer be prostituted into vicious purposes. Husbandmen and Householders, let the night of your pleasure be turned into fear lest your children take their leave of God and Piety." And this description may seem warranted by Dr. Ames' entry of October 14, 1766:

> Made an husking entertainment. Possibly this leafe may last a century and fall into the hands of some inquisitive Person for whose Entertainment I will inform him that now there is a custom amongst us of making an Entertainment at husking of Indian Corne whereto all the neighboring Swains are invited, and after the Corn is finished they, like the Hottentots, give three cheers or huzzas, but cannot carry in the husks without a Rhum bottle. They feign great exertion, but do nothing until the Rhum enlivens them, when all is done in a trice; then, after a hearty meal about 10 at night, they go to their pastimes.[1]

Another form of entertainment in the same year — a house-raising — apparently bored him, for he noted:

> *June 17, 1766.* Went to raising of Michael Metcalf's house by invitation of Capt. Battle and Mr. Haven, etc.; but the scene was very tedious and the consciousness of my not being invited by Mr. Metcalf makes me record this Resolution never to go again in such circumstances; not but that Metcalf used me genteely, yet 'twas sinking.

And he apparently preferred the town club, which he joined in this year:

> *March 21, 1766.* The Sociable Club, consisting of Rev. S. West, Manasseh Cutler, Nat Fisher, Seth Ames, James Jerauld and myself met at Deacon Ellis, the first time.
> *March 28.* Said Club, called Free Brothers, by vote met at Ellis'.

[1] On April 7, 1771, Ames noted: "Haven preached against Ebriety and Bundling."

Seven years later Dr. Ames depicted his life as a lonely one:

> *Nov. 25, 1773.* Annual Thanksgiving, which I celebrated with much thankfulness on a little boiled rice, at home alone. Then came in my Brother William, who had good provision sent him from his Mother, and dined here at my House upon it, of which I could not so much as taste. Mrs. Whiting, my Housekeeper, prevented my having provisions of my own cooked and went among her relations to dine, leaving me to cook for myself.
>
> *Dec. 5, 1773.* Altho' I went to Meeting all day, could not attend to the Sermon, but roved on my solitary situation, and that of my absent.

Accordingly, it was not surprising that in 1775, on the outbreak of the Revolutionary War, he was married, at the age of thirty-four, to Meletiah Shuttleworth, daughter of one of the town's prominent citizens. And at the same time he gave up keeping his father's tavern and confined himself largely to medicine and farming.

Such, briefly, were Nathaniel Ames and his early surroundings. It is, however, for his lively interest in American politics that his Diary is of intense value to all who desire a characteristic picture of our early politics, written from the viewpoint of an overheated partisan. His gift of picturesque expression increased as he grew older. Nevertheless, his entries as to political events in the years before the Revolution throw striking lights upon the manner in which the great things which were stirring in England and in the American colonies impinged upon life in a country town. That a youth of twenty-one should show so great an interest in public affairs of the day illustrates how close home all these events pressed.

The resignation of William Pitt, the elder, first engaged his attention:

Jan. 1762. Mr. Pitt's resignation makes a great noise among the people. Pitt hot for a Spanish War. Parliament non Judicis jumpit. Pitt resigns. Wagers that *Will the Coachman* will get upon the Box in less than a fortnight.

Feb. 20. Pitt not reinstated. Troops against Martineco landed with small opposition.

Feb. 26. Carthagena sunk by an earthquake. Same we had Nov. 1, 1761 here.

March 26. War declared against Spain in England.

April 14. War proclaimed in Boston against Spain.

Sept. 8. News of the reduction of the Havannah which was on the 11th Aug. . . . also of Admiral Saunders attacking ten sail of Men of War (Spanish) that had just put out of Cadiz and taking 8 of 'em and sinking one. Also that our Queen was safely delivered of Twins. What a flood of good news is here.

The end of the Seven Years' War and the Peace of Paris were noted in 1762 and 1763:

Sept. 20, 1762. Public Thanksgiving appointed on account of the late success of his Majestie's arms in taking the rich city of the Havannah.

Nov. 18. Soldiers came home from Halifax and Crown Point.

March 14, 1763. Much wrangling, both public and private, in Church and State.

May 11. Report that a Bishop is come for Oswego, and General Amherst, Viceroy of North America.

Aug. 10. Peace proclaimed.

On October 12, 1763, he noted: "Mr. Benjamin Franklin here"; and with the year 1764 his political entries began to be frequent. As early as August 8 he noted: "Alarming duties and taxes laid on America." When the Stamp Act, enacted in England on March 22, 1765, went into effect on November 1, 1765, the day was marked by the tolling of bells, the display of flags at half-mast on the shipping in the port, and the hanging of the English ministers in effigy.

Dr. Ames gave a striking picture of the manner in which the Act was received:

August 1765. Secretary Oliver appointed Distributor of Stamps for this Province — Secretary looses the Favor of the People by accepting the odious Office of Stamp Distributor. The country incens'd against the Stamp Distributors and begin to hang them in effigy as well as Judges of Admiralty Courts.

Lieutenant Governor [Hutchinson] suspected of being in favor of Stamp Act and has his House destroyed, with some others, viz. Hollowell and William Story.

Oct. 9. A Congress of Commissioners from the House of Representatives of each of the Colonies held at New York, to form an humble, united, loyal Address to his Majestie and Parliament concerning the Stamp Act.

Nov. 1. Stamp Act takes place. Grenville and Rushe hanged in effigy.

Nov. 5. Pope, Devil, and Stamp man exhibited together.

Nov. 19. No stamps distributed in America, but at Hallifax.

Dec. 18. Mr. Oliver oblig'd by the People to resign his office at the Tree of Liberty and makes Oath before Mr. Dana never to act in it.

Dec. 19. News that our proceeding against the Stamp Distributors and Opposition to the Enaction of the Stamp Act meets with the Approbation of the Merchants at home and others in general.

Dec. 20. The Connecticut people far outshine the other Governments in the Cause of Liberty and merit the Blessings of all Posterity.

Dec. 23. Great confusion in State. Some are for having all Business cease till we hear from Parliament, but the far greater Part for proceeding without regard to the Stamp Act. And now, the latter end of December, the Courts of Justice are agreed to open, hear and determine causes as usual. Custom House opened, i. e., for those that protest no Stamp Paper can be obtained. Probate Office with great difficulty opened. His Honor the Lieut. Gov'r, not choosing to act in that office deputes his Brother, Foster Hutchinson.

Many people drink, for want of comfortable Food. Stamp Act has this only happy effect, viz., it unites the Colonies.

Jan. 24, 1766. Divers Letters from England mention our late opposition to the execution of the Stamp Act and applaud us for our Spirit of Freedom, tho' some even now pretend it will take place.

Feb. 11. Ship arrived at Boston, short passage from London, brings good news that Stamp Act suspended. Premature. But by letters brought to General Court from the Agents, there is an agreeable prospect with respect to affairs of America.

Feb. 21. Mr. Pitt, that best of men and true Patriot, engaged in behalf of America.

Although the Stamp Act was repealed on March 18, 1766, the news took time to spread in those days, and did not reach Boston until May 16. On April 30 Ames noted: "Impatient for confirmation of the repeal of Stamp Act, prepared for illuminating." He recorded the "glorious news" and the "public rejoicing" which occurred in Boston on May 19, and the celebration by means of cannon, bells, flags, fireworks, and release of prisoners confined for debt. The Diary then began to record an episode almost unique in American history. After hearing of the repeal, the townspeople of Dedham, led by Ames and others, decided to erect a monument to William Pitt in gratitude for his services in the repeal of the Stamp Act; as early as May 21, a stonecutter was set to work; and on eleven days in May, June, and July, Ames noted, "Stonecutter at work on Pillar of Liberty"; July 14, "Sons of Liberty meet to raise Pillar"; July 22, "Pillar of Liberty erected, vast concourse of People"; July 24, "Public Thanksgiving for Repeal Stamp Act"; July 28, "Pillar of Liberty painted." On February 15, 1767, Ames recorded that he "went to Boston with Mr. Haven and Battle, spoke Pitt's Bust of Mr. Skilling," and February 26, "went Boston, brought the Bust of Pitt for Pillar Liberty." This Dedham Pillar of Liberty was a cube of granite about four feet high, bearing a painted wooden column eight feet high, surmounted by a bust. The granite faces bore these quaint inscriptions, composed by Dr. Ames himself: [1]

THE PILLAR OF LIBERTY
ERECTED BY THE SONS OF LIBERTY
IN THIS VICINITY.
LAUS DEO REGI, ET IMMUNITAT M
    AUTORIBUS Q. MAXIME PATRONO
PITT, QUI REMPUB. RURSUM EVULSIT.
        FAUCIBUS ORCI.
THE PILLAR OF LIBERTY
TO THE HONOR OF WILL^M

                    PITT, ESQ.,
& OTHER PATRIOTS WHO SAVED
AMERICA FRON IMPEMDING SLAVE
RY & CONFIRMED OUR MOST LOYAL
AFFECTION TO KG GEORGE BY PRO
CURING A REPEAL OF THE STAMP ACT
        18TH MARCH, 1766.

The use of the word "patrono" in this inscription is especially remarkable as showing how fully the colonists recognized the position of Pitt as their protector. Not content with this mark of gratitude, Dedham held a town meeting, on December 1, 1766, to consider the subject of a bill then pending in the General Court for the compensation of those who had suffered losses in the riots in Boston the preceding August, when Governor Hutchinson's mansion was sacked. A vote was passed that "the sufferers have no demand upon the Province in point of justice," but

---

[1] Ames' Diary stated, August 6, 1766: "Howard altered erepsit into evulsit." This change was made by Ames himself. See also *Dedham Historical Register* (1890), vol. I, pp. 121, 140, for a picture and description of the original monument; see also, for article on Pitt, *ibid.* (1896), vol. VII, p. 123. The granite monument still exists, but the wooden column and bust have long since disappeared. "Autoribus" was probably originally "fautoribus."

the town representative was instructed to vote for the bill, as a testimony of "unfeigned gratitude to those worthy personages who generously and nobly patronized the British Colonies by promoting the repeal of the Stamp Act and by other good offices, who we understand are desirous that compensation should be made."

Between the year of the repeal of the Stamp Act and 1774 Dr. Ames made few political entries; but it may be noted that the people of the town were sturdily resenting the attempts of Great Britain to tax imports, and the following votes are significant. On November 16, 1767, it was voted "that this Town will in all prudent methods encourage the use of such articles as may be produced or manufactured in the British American Colonies, particularly in this Province, and discourage the use of superfluities imported from abroad, and will not purchase any articles of foreign produce or manufacture when the same articles may be got of the produce of manufacture of the said Colonies — that this Town will strictly adhere to the new Regulations respecting Funerals — that no gloves shall be used on such occasions but such as are manufactured in this Province." On March 5, 1770, the town voted to use no foreign tea nor allow it to be used in their families "until such time as the duty being first taken off, this Town shall by some future vote grant an indulgence to drink tea to such as have not virtue enough to leave off the use of it forever." On December 5, 1774, the town voted to appoint a committee "to see that the engagement to refrain from the use of tea be not violated," and it also voted that "if anyone should be so devoid of patriotism" his name was to be posted in the several parishes as an enemy to his country.

Dr. Ames recorded the "joyful" celebration on March 18, 1767, of the repeal of the Stamp Act; but two years later the Tories apparently raised their heads in the town, for the Diary recorded on May 12, 1769: "The Pillar of Liberty overthrown last night."

The development of armed resistance on the part of the colonists was shown in the ensuing entries:

July 31, 1766. At Commencement, Josiah Quincy made the finest oration in English that I ever heard, his subject was Liberty, the Audience enraptured.

June 7, 1768. The Romney Man of War impress men very arbitrarily, to the scandal of the Sons of Liberty.

July 10. Mob in Boston drub the Commissioners of Customs.

July 14. Mob and Town Meeting in Boston. Commissioners all on board the Man of War with their effects.

June 20. Letter came from Authority at home demanding a categorical answer whether the Court will submit to taxation by Parliament.

July 7. Troops coming to Boston.

Sept. 13. The Town of Boston met, chose a Committee to wait on Governor Bernard with their humble request that he would call a General Court, to which he returned a plausible refusal. Whereupon the Town voted to send to each Town in the Province desiring them to send a Committee Man to meet at Boston, on the 22d inst.

Sept. 22. Town Meeting to chuse Convention Man.

Sept. 28. Troops arrived from Halifax to keep us in order.

Oct. 15. General Gage with a grand Retinue passed, to Boston.

Dec. 16, 1773. India Company's Tea sunk by Persons call'd Narragansett Indians.

Jan. 7, 1774. Title Page verse for next year Almanac composed as I lay in Bed this morning:

Let tyrant Princes distant climes explore
For wealth and power all drench in human gore!
Let fleets and armies make their subjects pine
And cannon's mouths assert their right divine.
Let spaniel Courtiers lick their master's feet
And conscious meanness make them feel they're great.

May 12, 1774. The Act of Parliament for blockading Boston and arrival of General Gage as Governor occasion terrible consternation in all America.

June 21. All business in Boston almost ceases. Boston very much distressed by the tyrannical Port Bill stopping up the Harbour. Ships of War lying off, and soldiers in the Town. All America in consternation!

June 22. Boston People trying for places in the country.

July 14. A Voluntary Fast is observed this day thro' this and some of the neighboring Provinces, at the recommendation of our House of Commons, without the Governor's assent, on which occasion Mr. J. Haven delivered an excellent political sermon in the forenoon and a good pulpit discourse in ye afternoon.

Sept. 1. Gen. Gage seized the Powder in Cambridge Powder House.

Sept. 4. Country alarmed even as far as the Mohawks, who under Johnson set out to the relief of Boston from the Tyranny of Gage.

Sept. 9. Appearance of Civil War.

Oct. 5. Training.

Oct. 18. Inhabitants of this Parish meet to choose military officers for old and young.

Oct. 26. Old men train.

The opening battle of the War of the Revolution appeared in the Diary as follows:

Feb. 1. King's speech to the new Parliament full of acrimony against us.

April 3. Bad news from England.

April 6. The Minute Men of all Dedham train here.

April 14. People move out of Boston for the troops.

April 19. The regular forces sent by the British Government to Boston march out to Lexington and fired on a Company of men and killed six, then immediately marched off to Concord to seize our Province Military Stores, destroyed some flour, 2 cannon, and then upon being attacked by our people, began to retreat, and continued fighting all the way to Charlestown. 30 men lost on our side, many more on theirs. I went and dressed the wounded.

April 20. Six Regulars killed by the Marblehead force.

April 21. Elias Haven of Dedham killed. Israel Everett, Jr., wounded in the Battle.

April 22. Boston besieged by Colonists.
April 23. Connecticut forces gone to Boston siege.
April 24. King's ships and arms taken at New York by our Americans.

Long afterwards he recorded in his Diary, April 19, 1815: "40 years ago, I went to Concord fight, extracted a ball from I. Everett's arm! Dead men and horses strewed along road above Charlestown to Concord." [1] To this battle, over twenty miles distant, Dedham sent the extraordinary number of 242 men (of whom one was killed and one wounded), the town being left "almost literally without a male inhabitant below the age of seventy or above that of sixteen." [2]

After this date the Diary was full of the war. Dr. Ames was on intimate terms with Dr. Joseph Warren, and had several conferences with him in Dedham and Roxbury. On May 25, 1775, "Providence artillery pass by." On May 26, "large cannon from Providence pass by." On June 17, "terrible battle forced our intrenchments at Charlestown"; on June 18, "went Cambridge. Country alarmed. Cannons roar." The arrival of General Washington and General Lee and the investment of Boston en-

[1] In the *Memoirs of Major General William Heath*, p. 15, it is noted, April 20, 1775: "On the morning of the 20th, our General (Heath) ordered Captain John Battle of Dedham, with his company of militia, to pass over the ground which had been the scene of action the preceding day, and bury such of the slain as he should find unburied. The grounds around Cambridge were immediately reconnoitred, and alarm posts assigned to the several corps; and in case the British should come out in superior force and drive the militia from the town, they were ordered to rally and form on the high grounds towards Watertown."

[2] From the First Parish (old Dedham Centre), 84 officers and men; from the Second or South Parish (now Norwood) 60; from the West or Third Parish (now Westwood), 31; and from the Fourth Parish (now Dover), 67. See *Address at the 250th Anniversary of the Founding of the Town of Dedham* (1886), by Erastus Worthington.

It may be noted that the town supported a company of Minute Men, fifty-nine of whom were mustered for a period of thirteen days on April 19, 1775. See *Dedham Historical Register* (1897), vol. VIII, pp. 20, 52.

sued in July; and, as Dedham was on the main turnpike from Rhode Island and Connecticut, on August 8 "rifle men pass"; August 9, "rifle men 300 pass, 3 companies Connecticut men"; September 1, "continual roar of Cannon, Night and Day"; September 2, "Regulars intrench near in spight of our Fire." October 7, "heavy cannon at great distance, supposed R. Island." October 12, "dull time, not even Camp news heard"; November 10, "King proclaimed all Americans rebels." The siege of Boston ended in March, 1776; and Ames on March 30 "went Boston which looks gloomy, all shops shut up." By April 1 "soldiers return home, and Continental Troops march every day to the southward." On April 15, 1776, Dr. Ames noted: "General Washington lodged in Town."[1] In May, 1776, a town meeting was held in Dedham to ascertain views as to independence, and on May 27 it was unanimously voted "that if the Honorable Congress should declare the Colonies independent of Great Britain, they would solemnly engage to support it in that measure with their lives and fortunes." In June, 1776, Dr. Ames noted:

June 12. All Dedham Men gone to intrench on the Coste [coast]. Mr. William Denine has a ship from Petersburg condemned at Halifax altho' she comply'd with all the Acts of Trade of Britain. He also rails at the Congress and calls

[1] The house in which Washington slept, a fine mansion, built by the town's wealthiest citizen, Samuel Dexter (father of the famous lawyer Samuel Dexter), and then occupied by Joshua Henshaw, had been recently the scene of a curious tragedy, the death of a sister of Colonel John Trumbull and wife of Colonel Jedidiah Huntingdon of Connecticut, who had been driven insane by her visit to the army in the summer of 1775. The funeral had been held November 28, 1775, in the Dexter House, and the interment was made in the tomb of Nathaniel Ames the elder. After the funeral those attending dined at the Ames Tavern. See Journal of Colonel John Trumbull, and Diary of Lieutenant Jabez Fitch, *Massachusetts Historical Society Proceedings, 2d Series,* vol. IX; *Dedham Historical Register* (1894), vol. V, p. 155; see also article on Samuel Dexter in *ibid.* (1892), vol. III, p. 46.

them a parcel of Blockheads to permit the exportation of Provisions to all parts, but British and the English Islands, from this Continent, when our non-exportation had begun to distress them amazingly and their Fleet must have returned home, had it not been for this permission; but now they can buy at Statia, and they take more provision-vessels than they know what to do with. I hear that Providence is blockaded by the Country People for their extravagance and extortionate prices on goods and that they ask 3 dollars a bushel for salt; if so, they deserved to be blockaded longer than Boston was.

June 14. Artillery and Militia clear Boston Harbour of enemies.

June 16. Two prizes, ship and brig, brought into Boston. Scotchmen.

June 18. Another prize of Scotchmen, and another.

June 21. Another prize of Highlanders carried into Marblehead.

June 26. Scotchmen dispersed over the country.

After these entries the Diary concerned itself to the end of the war with matters of merely local or personal interest or with mere dry record of scattered military events, without any comment. Nothing could more strikingly show how, after the evacuation of Boston, the war was removed from Massachusetts not only geographically but also mentally. After 1776, the citizens of that State felt the war only through taxes and through occasional losses in its contribution of troops. The newspapers and correspondence with friends kept them informed of the war, as something which was affecting States to the southward; but it did not strike home to the ordinary individual citizen personally. All that Dr. Ames had to say in his Diary about the Declaration of Independence was entered on July 14, 1776: "Independency declared by the Congress"; and two years later, on July 1, 1778: "Fireworks preparing to celebrate the 4th." [1] He noted, on January 10, 1778: "Plan of Confederation agreed on by this Town," thus showing that the Articles of Confederation were in Massachusetts actually passed upon by the towns. On April 5, 1778, he noted: "General Burgoyne passed on his way home"; and on April 19: "News that our Independence is acknowledged by France arrived in vessel sent by French King on purpose." The end of the war and the making of peace were thus briefly noted, October 17, 1781: "Cornwallis surrendered his whole army"; June 2, 1783: "Rejoicing for Peace in Dedham. Fireworks, etc." These entries were entirely prosaic. It required another Revolution to awake in Nathaniel Ames strong political passions and to evoke spicy expression of them.

[1] John Adams wrote from Philadelphia, July 3, 1776, to General James Warren as to the manner in which the signing of the Declaration should be celebrated: "Yesterday the greatest question was decided which was ever debated in America; and a greater perhaps never was or will be decided among men. A resolution was passed without one dissenting Colony: 'that these United Colonies are, and of right ought to be free and independent States.' The day is passed. The second day of July, 1776, will be the most memorable epocha in the history of America. I am apt to believe it will be celebrated by succeeding generations as the great Anniversary Festival. It ought to be commemorated as the day of deliverance, by solemn acts of devotion to Almighty God. It ought to be solemnized with pomp, shows, games, sports, guns, bells, bonfires and illuminations from one end of this Continent to the other, from this time forever. You will think me transported with enthusiasm; but I am not. I am well aware of the toil and blood and treasure that it will cost us to maintain this declaration, and support and defend these States; yet through all the gloom, I can see the rays of light and glory — I can see that the end is worth all the means; and that posterity will triumph although you and I may rue it, which I hope we shall not. I am, etc. John Adams." This letter was printed in the *Columbian Centinel* as early as June 23, 1804; see also *Independent Chronicle*, June 25, 1804; and see a similar letter from Adams to his wife, with some changes of phraseology, *Life and Works of John Adams* (1854) vol. IX, p. 420. General Warren replied, July 17, 1776: "The Declaration came on Saturday and diffused a general joy. Everyone of us feels more important than ever; we now congratulate each other as Freemen. It has really raised our spirits to a tone beneficial to mitigate the malignity of the small pox, and what is of more consequence seems to animate and inspire everyone to support and defend the Independency he feels." *Warren-Adams Letters* (1917), vol. I, p. 261.

II

JACOBINS AND MONOCRATS

FROM the end of the War of the Revolution in 1782, for the next ten years Dr. Nathaniel Ames devoted his whole attention to the practice of his profession, to amusing altercations with his peppery neighbors, and to the cultivation of his farm and garden, new ideas for which he constantly dilated upon in his Diary. He paid little attention to public affairs, and though elected, in 1790 and 1792, as a representative to the legislature from his home town, he considered it of so little moment that he wrote (May 4, 1790): "Chosen again to represent Dedham, and upon their assurance to dispense with my attendance, I accepted. I consider myself as a nominal Representative only, to save the Town from being fined." [1] He was appointed a judge of the Court of Common Pleas in 1792, but refused to qualify. He served, however, as clerk of this Court and of the Court of Sessions for many years from 1793.

The only political event which seems to have engaged Dr. Ames' attention to any extent in his Diary was the Shays Rebellion, as to which he wrote:

[1] The town of Dedham, while of extensive area, was small in population, numbering in 1790 only 1659 persons, in 288 families. It comprised four Congregational parishes and an Episcopal church. It was situated on the mail route established in 1693 from Portsmouth, New Hampshire, to Williamsburg, Virginia, on which mails were carried once a week on horseback. Stagecoaches, after 1769, ran daily through Dedham between Boston and Providence; in 1785 Ebenezer Hazard established a mail-coach service. In 1796 the first newspaper was published in the town — the *Dedham Minerva* (later the *Columbian Minerva*), which continued until 1804.

Jan. 18, 1787. Capt. Fisher marched today against the Rebels.
Jan. 21. Massachusetts Civil War begins. Many oppressions
having been practised, extortion and usury at 12, 20, 30, 40,
and sometimes 50 per cent., but most common 25; now, prevailing taxes called for that bear very unequally upon the
people, and all property accumulating with greater rapidity
than ever known into a few people's hands has occasioned
great tumults. County conventions and petitions to the
Legislature of Massachusetts for redress. The People un-
satisfied take to arms, stop the Courts of Law, and under
several leaders, the chief of which is Daniel Shays of Pel-
ham, greatly alarm Government, which send out a party of
horsemen; and after a skirmish take Job Shattuck, who is
said to be mortally wounded, and two others, who are now
prisoners in Boston Gaol, which more exasperates a large
proportion of the people, especially in the Western parts of
the State, where they have formed into regular squadrons
under General Shays and disregard the Act of Pardon to all
that return to their allegiance and take the oath before the
1 day of 1787. Wherefore, the Governor, J. Bowdoin, collected an army of 7,000 men, volunteers and drafted from
the Militia, under the command of Gen'l. Lincoln, who
march, about the 20 January, 1787, for Worcester, to suppress the Rebellion that was dying away of itself. . . .
Shays' party daily fell off, and all of them publickly declared they are for Government. If the Courts could be suspended till the new election of Representatives, as they
had requested to chuse last election, they would sit down
peaceable, subjects of the whole Legislature, whose wisdom
they would rely on for redress of their grievances, and which
would save the enormous expense with which the people
must be saddled for their expedition, and prevent the disaffection of many good citizens, much irritated at the precipitancy of Government for staining their hands with
human blood, needlessly as they say.
Jan. 30. News that Shays' men are dispersed.

It is evident that Dr. Ames — a man of liberal and
democratic views — was one of the "good citizens" who
partially sympathized with the grievances, especially since

the chief of these grievances was the oppression which the rebels claimed arose from activities of the lawyers as a class — a sentiment which Dr. Ames in many later entries in his Diary thoroughly shared. The only other political event which he recorded was, on September 30, 1787: "New Constitution of Government of the United States published and seems agreeable to everybody as yet, for all know we have lost millions for want of an head sole."

Meanwhile, his brother Fisher, the brilliant youth who had graduated from Harvard in 1774 at the age of sixteen, was becoming a leading figure in the field of National politics. Admitted to the bar in Boston in 1781, he had from the first taken an active interest in public affairs. At the time of the Shays Rebellion in 1786 his essays in the daily newspapers had made considerable stir. "In a free government, the reality of grievances is no kind of justification for rebellion," he wrote, and he demanded vigorous suppression of the "traitors" before any attention should be paid to grievances — an attitude far different from his brother's. Like his brother, however, he had been one of the early supporters of a new form of government for the United States. "It is the time to render the federal head supreme in the States," he wrote in March, 1787, over two months before the Federal Convention met in Philadelphia to frame the Constitution.[1] He had been an able member of the Convention called to adopt the Constitution in Massachusetts, and had been elected to the First Congress from the Boston district (which included the town of Dedham), defeating the veteran Samuel Adams.[2] In Congress he had sprung at once into prominence as a skilled debater

---

[1] Letter of "Lucius Junius Brutus" in *Independent Chronicle*, October 12, 1786: letter of "Camillus" in *ibid.*, March 1, 1787.

[2] Fisher Ames practised law in Boston until 1793, when he returned to Dedham for his future permanent residence.

and brilliant orator.[1] An ardent Federalist in his political views, he acquired a strong antipathy to Virginia statesmen, including Jefferson and Madison; he became a devoted admirer of Hamilton, and an adherent of all measures tending to increase the power of the Federal Government. In fact, as he was reëlected in 1790, 1792, and 1794, he grew to represent more and more every political idea which his brother Nathaniel felt to be particularly abhorrent. In person he was a man of slight frame and delicate health, of charming and affable manners, a cheerful neighbor, though inclined to extremes of gayety and depression. "I am habitually a zealot in politics," he wrote. "It is, I fancy, constitutional, and so the cure desperate. I burn and freeze, am lethargic, raving, sanguine, and despondent, as often as the wind shifts." [2] Witty and brilliant in writing and conversation, he had strong passions and a violent temper when aroused.

Into the life of Dr. Nathaniel Ames, and arousing him from his absorption in medicine and farming, there crashed the French Revolution — an event which violently affected the future course of American politics and of American history, and which split the American people into two sharply divided parties.

During the first years of that Revolution, the American people had been almost a unit in exultation over the up-

[1] For laudatory remarks as to Fisher Ames, early after his appearance in Congress, see *New York Daily Gazette*, August 4, 1789 — "shining abilities of Mr. Ames, who, though a very young man is second only to the great Madison; in oratorical powers, he perhaps exceeds him." For adverse criticism, see *Boston Gazette*, September 13, 1789.

[2] *Works of Fisher Ames* (1854), vol. I, sketch by Reverend John T. Kirkland (President of Harvard College); see also Fisher Ames to T. Dwight, December 31, 1792. To Minot, he wrote, May 29, 1789, of "my proneness to represent things too strong."

Jefferson wrote in his *Anas*, March 11, 1800, that Mr. Dowse of Dedham, visiting him, had told him that Fisher Ames "is a man of the most irritable and furious temper in the world."

rising of the French against their king. The taking of the Bastille occurred on July 14, 1789, three months after the inauguration of President Washington. Three years later, in 1792, the reëlection of Washington and John Adams followed only a few months after the attack on the Tuileries on August 10, 1792, and the imprisonment of Louis XVI. Each of these events in France was celebrated throughout the United States by "Civic Feasts," songs, and speeches, and in no place with more enthusiasm than in Massachusetts.[1] Typical of this Gallomania was a festival held in Boston, January 29, 1793, in honor of the victory of the French Republican army under General Dumouriez, and termed "A Peace Offering to Liberty and Equality." As announced in the papers, "a number of citizens anxious to celebrate the success of our Allies, the French, in their present glorious struggles for liberty and equality, and that every member of the community should partake in the general joy, have agreed to provide an ox, with suitable liquors." The advertisement of this festival, inserted in the *Columbian Centinel* by the Committee of Arrangements, set forth: "Nothing shall be wanting in their power to produce that brotherly affection and conviviality which ought ever to operate on the minds of Freemen, while commemorating the glorious struggles of their Fellowmen in the cause of Liberty and Equality." The procession, it was stated, would pass through certain streets, "thence to the dwelling house of Citizen Hancock, thence through Winter Street to the house of Citizen S. Adams. . . . The

[1] As to these "Civic Feasts," see *Columbian Centinel*, January 23, 26, 1793; *Boston Gazette*, January 21, 28, 1793; *Independent Chronicle*, February 14, 1793; and satirical poem and articles in *Connecticut Journal*, April 1, June 22, August 19, 1793. See also *Life, Journals and Correspondence of Manasseh Cutler* (1888), vol. I, p. 489; *The Federalist Party in Massachusetts to the Year 1800* (1909), by Anson Ely Morse; *Contemporary Opinion of the French Revolution* (1897), by Charles Downer Hazen; *Jeffersonian Democracy in New England* (1916), by William A. Robinson.

Committee anticipates the utmost convenience to the citizens, and the prevalence of order and fraternal affection." The procession thus referred to was formed to escort to the barbecue on Copp's Hill a great ox, mounted on a cart, its horns gilded, and bearing the flags of the two republics. Following the ox came carts bearing 1800 loaves of bread and a hogshead of punch, all drawn by six horses. When the procession arrived at the place known as Oliver's Dock it halted, and a ceremony was gone through rechristening that spot Liberty Square.[1] Finally, State Street was reached, where tables had been placed from the Old State House to Kilby Street. Here the bread and punch were distributed, although, as the *Centinel's* account said, "from the immense number of citizens assembled on State Street, the refreshments provided could not be so equally distributed as was wished; but notwithstanding the circumstances, the highest degree of goodwill and cheerfulness prevailed; and the sacrifice being speedily demolished, the citizens retired in good order." In the afternoon a banquet was served in Faneuil Hall, decorated for the occasion with flags, figures of Liberty, and mottoes of Liberty and Equality, at which "Citizen" Governor Samuel Adams and the French consul presided. Many toasts were drunk to France, accompanied by discharges of artillery. In the evening there were fireworks and illuminations. Even the children participated, as described in the *Centinel*: "Pleasing scene. To impress the tender minds of the rising generations with the precepts of equal liberty, at 11 o'clock all the youths of this town were paraded in State Street in ranks; between which a cart was driven from whence each was presented with a civic cake impressed with the words 'Liberty and Equality.'"

---

[1] Oliver's Dock extended on Kilby Street from Central Street to Water Street.

The recognition by President Washington of the new government in France and the arrival of the new French Minister, Genet, increased the enthusiasm for the French cause. French tricolor cockades and liberty caps were everywhere worn. "*Ça ira*," the song of the French Republicans (the refrain of which originated with Benjamin Franklin), became the popular tune.[1] The French sympathizers even addressed each other as "Citizen," and adopted for themselves the name of "Sons of Liberty." No one was more enthusiastic for the French cause than the Governor of Massachusetts himself — that old Revolutionist, Samuel Adams.

On the other hand, ever since the news of the beheading of Louis XVI in France had become known in this country, about the time of the arrival of Minister Genet, a considerable portion of the community had become horrified at the excesses of the Revolution and seriously alarmed at the possibility of the spread of its spirit to the United States.[2] Gradually, this faction became as extravagant as were the partisans of the Revolutionary cause; moreover, as their anti-French mania increased, their pro-British attitude became more and more marked. By the end of 1793 the country was divided sharply on French and British lines. It must be noted, however, that this division was not the mere product of sentiment and sympathies. Many

[1] See letter of "North-End" in *Independent Chronicle*, April 25, 1792: "Those upstart young *Aristocrats* who attempt to show their dislike of the glorious Revolution of our beloved friends, the French, by *hissing* when the modern Liberty Song, *Ça ira*, is called for or played at the Theatre, are seriously advised to desist from such obnoxious behaviour, and no longer provoke the Sons of Liberty, with which this part of the town abounds, lest punishment little expected overtake them and they be turned out of the Theatre with disgrace."

[2] Jeremy Belknap wrote from Boston to Ebenezer Belknap, March 23, 1793: "We are still uncertain whether Louis XVI is Louis Capet or Louis sine capite; but I hope, if he is yet living, he will not be put to death by the sanguinary faction." "Belknap Papers," *Massachusetts Historical Society Collections, 5th Series* (1877), vol. III.

other factors contributed to create it. The geographical
and economic distribution of the pro-French partisans in
Massachusetts was highly significant. They were strong
in the farming districts in the middle and western counties
— localities in which the American revolutionists had been
active and in which centred the radical sympathizers with
the Shays Rebellion of 1787. They were strong among the
older patriots of the American Revolution, whose hostility
to England was of long standing and deeply embedded;
they were strong in Boston among the devoted adherents
of Samuel Adams and among those who shared his apprehensions of an American National Government with too
greatly centralized power; they were strong among the
Irish and the Scotch-Irish. On the other hand, the anti-
French or pro-British faction flourished among those who
had taken the lead in favoring the Constitution without
need of amendment — that is, the leaders of the Federalist
party; it flourished also among the merchants, factors,
shipowners, and importers, whose trade would be seriously
impaired by a war, military or economic, with England,
and especially among the clergy, the lawyers, and other
professional men, many of whom had been Tories in the
Revolution or were affiliated with Tories, and all of whom
had fears of the attitude of the French Revolution towards
the rights of property. But while such a classification
might be made, in general, it could not be applied too dog-
matically, for there were cross currents and varying sentiments even in the same section of the community, so that
persons of the same class often reacted differently towards
the course of events in France. As complication followed
complication in the foreign relations of Washington's administration, each party assumed towards the members of
the other a more and more intolerant attitude. The pro-

French called their opponents "aristocrats and monocrats"; the anti-French termed the others "Jacobins." [1]

The political contest was particularly aggravated by the
assumption by the Federalist or anti-French party of an
attitude of superiority towards their opponents which was
galling in the extreme. They affected to comprise all the
wisdom and virtue of the country — "all the wise, the
good, and the rich," as Fisher Ames was fond of saying.
And as Elbridge Gerry of Cambridge, a leading Antifederalist, wrote, five years earlier: "There seems to be a
disposition in the dominant party to establish a nobility of
opinion under whose control will be placed the Government of the Union and of the States, and whose insuffer-
able arrogance marks out for degradation all who will not
submit to their authority. It is beginning to be fashionable
to consider the opponents of the Constitution as embody-
ing themselves with the lower classes of the people, and
that one forfeits all title to the respect of a gentleman unless he is one of the privileged order." In the eyes of the
Federalists of New England, their opponents were wholly
disreputable persons, who were to be treated "almost as
outlaws, with the humiliation which attaches to an inferior
and degraded caste." [2] Sympathy with the French cause

[1] Jefferson assumed to classify the factions in a letter to Madison, May 12,
1793, as follows: "The line is now drawing so clearly as to show on one side (1)
the fashionable Order of Philadelphia, New York, Boston and Charleston
(natural aristocrats); (2) the merchants trading on British capitals; (3) paper
men. All the old Tories are found in some one of three descriptions. On the
other side are (1) merchants trading on their own capitals; (2) Irish merchants;
(3) tradesmen, mechanics, farmers, and every other possible description of our
citizen." In his famous letter to Philip Mazzei, April 24, 1796, he wrote: "Against
us are ... all timid men who prefer the calm of despotism to the boisterous sea of
liberty, British merchants and American trading on British capitals, speculators
and holders in the bank and public funds." *Writings of Thomas Jefferson* (Ford
ed.) (1907), vol. VII.

[2] Elbridge Gerry to General James Warren, *Life of Elbridge Gerry* (1828), by
James T. Austin, vol. II, p. 89. As described later in *Independent Chronicle*, May
22, 1806: "Nothing would pass current without being stamped with Federalism.

was sufficient, in Federalist eyes, to class its holder with all that was dangerous and degraded. The Jacobin of that day was the Bolshevik of today as he appears to the ultra-conservative men of property. "We see the facility with which a wicked faction has triumphed over public liberty, by assuming popular names," wrote George Cabot of Beverly to Theophilus Parsons. "We have seen the expression of the general will of a great society silenced, the legal representatives of the people butchered, and a band of murderers ruling in their stead with rods of iron. Will not this, or something like it, be the wretched fate of our country? ... The fact is so alarming that the real friends of liberty and order (in this country) can no longer indulge themselves in that repose with which they are lulled by a confidence in the rectitude of their principle. *The Anarchists are up and doing.*" [1] Stephen Higginson of Boston wrote to Alexander Hamilton: "In this State, there is but one opinion, except in this town. There dwell all the seditious and desperate." Those few who advocated the French cause, he said, "are made up of inveterate Antifederalists and men desperate in their circumstances. The former will join any party and pursue any measures to

A man could hardly sell his bread, his milk, or his meat, without designating it Federal. If he wanted to hire a house, the first question asked would be: 'Are you a Federalist or a Republican?' If a tavern was advertised in the paper to be let, there would be a *nota bene* at the foot of it, 'None but Federalists need apply.'" And an interesting instance of the effect of political beliefs upon business is to be found in an advertisement, a few years later, in a Boston newspaper: "The Subscriber would inform his Friends and the Public, that he will carry on the Sail-Making Business at his Loft on Hancock's Wharf. Being deserted by many of his former Customers, on account of his Republican politics, and having a large family to maintain, he invites those who are disposed to employ him to call at his Loft, where they may depend upon having their work done with fidelity and dispatch." *Independent Chronicle*, April 7, 1803. For an account of the social ostracism of Jacobins, see *Memoirs of Theophilus Parsons* (1859), by Theophilus Parsons.

[1] *Life and Letters of George Cabot* (1877), by Henry Cabot Lodge, Cabot to Parsons, August 12, 1794.

embarass the Union; and among these are our Governor and Lieutenant Governor.[1] . . . Some of them have so conducted from habit and inclination, having been always connected intimately with the disaffected opposers of all Government, whether of the State or the Union." [2] And the Federalist view of these "Jacobins" was well expressed in a pamphlet published in 1795 which had a wide circulation, entitled *The Jacobin Looking Glass, by a Friend to National Liberty*:

I see all the detestable arts, all the machinations of disappointed demogogues, and all the malice of even Hell itself, employed to deceive the people and destroy our government. . .
The sons of faction leaped like Cerberus in the Styx to quench their thirst with blood and charge their tongues with poison. Now, a new chief having appeared to lead them, they enlisted under his banners with avidity. Genet was a member of the Jacobin Club in France, and consequently a connoisseur in the black art. He was an officer on the fast-sailing ship Anarchy. . . . He soon collected round him a horde of malcontents. . . . The democratick dens re-echoed with abuse and high-toned anathema against the Supreme Executive [Washington]. . . . Their object is to overthrow the present Constitution and to establish one upon its ruins more consonant to their depraved appetites. . . . Sowing discontent . . . they effect their diabolical purposes, and could they once attain their object, another machine would soon be erected, called, in the Jacobin language, a guillotine or shaving mill, of which every one, not of their party, would soon feel the effects.

One thing which especially excited Federalist fear and denunciation was the rise of the "Constitutional Societies"

[1] See remarks on Federalist attacks on Samuel Adams in *Independent Chronicle*, January 8, 12, 1795. George Cabot wrote to Rufus King, September 13, 1795, stating that Governor Adams, "this weak old man, is one of the loudest bawlers against the (Jay) Treaty and the boldest in proposing schemes of opposition to the Federal Government."

[2] *Works of Alexander Hamilton* (J. C. Hamilton, ed.), vol. v, Higginson to Hamilton, July 26, August 24, 1793.

or "Democratic Societies," termed by them "Jacobin Clubs." The first of these, modelled after the famous Jacobin Club of Paris, was founded in July, 1793, in Philadelphia, by Peter S. Duponceau, an eminent Antifederalist lawyer; and the reasons for the existence of such clubs, which soon spread over the country, were stated with vigor in an address by the founder, as follows: "Should the glorious efforts of France be eventually defeated, we have reasons to presume that, for the consummation of monarchical ambition and the security of its establishments, this country, the only remaining depository of liberty, will not long be permitted to enjoy in peace the honors of an independent, and the happiness of a republican, government. Nor are the dangers arising from a foreign source the only causes, at this time, of apprehension and solicitude. The seeds of luxury appear to have taken root in our domestic soil; and the jealous eye of patriotism already regards the spirit of freedom and equality as eclipsed by the pride of wealth and the arrogance of power." [1]

---

[1] See *Life of John Jay* (1833), by William Jay, for interesting account of these clubs. See also *Boston Gazette*, January 20, 1794, and *Independent Chronicle*, January 16, 1794, as to the declaration sent out by "The Massachusetts Constitutional Society."

The Reverend Jedidiah Morse, a stiff-necked Federalist of Charlestown, writing to Oliver Wolcott in Connecticut in 1793, thus referred to the Massachusetts club: "We have some grumbletonians among us, who, when the French are victorious, speak loud and saucy, but when they meet a check, sing small. They form a sort of political thermometer by which we can pretty accurately determine what, in their opinion, is the state of French politics. The French cause has no enemies here — their conduct, many. There are some who undistinguishly and undoubtedly approve both, and most bitterly denounce as aristocrats all who do not think as they do. This party, which is not numerous, nor as respectable as it is numerous, are about forming a democratic club, which, I think, they call the 'Massachusetts Constitutional Society' — I don't know their design, but suppose they consider themselves as the guardians of the rights of men, and overseers of the President, Congress, and you gentlemen, the heads of the principal departments of State, to see that you don't infringe on the Constitution." *Memoirs of the Administrations of Washington and Adams* (1846), by George Gibbs, vol. I, p. 124, Morse to Wolcott, December 16, 1793.

The spread of these clubs aroused the Federalist leaders and press to extreme and vituperative anger. Even the calm Washington somewhat lost his poise, and attacked the clubs, in his annual message to Congress in 1793, as "self-created societies" (forgetting that his own famous Society of the Cincinnati, composed of officers of the Continental army and headed by himself, had been decidedly "self-created").[1] At an early date, the *Massachusetts Mercury* averred that "the business of this Nocturnal Club will be to denounce citizens, pack juries, abuse Government, instruct Congress, and, for aught we know, erect guillotines."[1] A satirical pamphlet written by Reverend J. S. J. Gardiner, assistant rector of Trinity Church in Boston, entitled *Remarks on the Jacobiniad* furnished an example of the personal abuse and political venom of this period.[2] In describing a supposititious meeting of the Boston Jacobin Club, and a debate over the admission of a negro as a member, on the grounds of "Equality," this clerical Federalist described the Jacobins as:[3]

> At Pandemonium meets the scoundrel throng,
> Hell in their heart, and faction on their tongue.
> Who are the men these caitiff chiefs command?
> A strange, unlettered, multifarious band —
> Some with weak heads, but well-intentioned hearts,
> Are simple dupes to Anti-Federal arts;
> Who, viewing tyrant acts in useful laws,
> Mistake foul Faction's, for fair Freedom's cause.

[1] *Massachusetts Mercury*, November 29, 1793. See also *Columbian Centinel*, August 7, November 30, 1793, January 1, 1794; attacks by "Manlius" in *ibid.*, September 3, 6, 10, 13, 17, 20, 24, 27, 1794; by "Deodatus" in *ibid.*, October 18, 25, November 1, 1794. See also *Independent Chronicle*, September 18, 1794.

[2] See attacks on the author in *Boston Gazette*, January 5, April 6, 27, May 4, 1795; also attack on the author in *Independent Chronicle*, April 30, May 2, 1795, in which he was termed "The Episcopalian Jack-ass or the Clerical Lampooner."

[3] "Pandemonium" was the name applied to the Green Dragon Tavern, on Union Street, Boston, where the Jacobin Club held its meetings.

The rest are genuine progeny of dirt,
Who, for a pint of rum, would sell their shirt!
With heads of adamant, and hearts of steel,
The worst of passions are the best they feel.
An envious, restless, swearing, drinking crew,
Whom sense ne'er guided, virtue never knew;
Some foreign ruffians, hireling tools no doubt,
French, Irish, Scotch, complete the "rabble rout."

Broad caricatures were drawn, both in word and in picture, of the leading Boston Jacobins, the "motley crew"
who "the baneful arts of anarchy pursue." Benjamin Austin, Jr. (their principal writer, known as "Honestus" and
"Old South"), was described as "lank Honestus with his
lanthorn jaws"; jibes were made at his "withered pair of
Chinese chops" and his "huge proboscis of a nose"; and
his writings were described as "a hodge-podge of lies,
slander and nonsense, cooked by him and served up twice
a week in the lying *Chronicle*." A Boston justice of the
peace, Thomas Crafts, was described as: "Great Justice
Crafts, great Faction's sapient son, Who holds of sense a
gill, of zeal a ton." John Vinal, the town writing-master,
was described: "Who everywhere is seen but in his school,
And passes current for the City fool." Frequent reference
was made to "the ignorance, the weakness of Jacobinical understanding, and the low profligacy of Jacobinical
morals." [1] The natural anger caused by such personal
invective elicited from Fisher Ames the sarcastic remark:
"Is it not possible to pacify the wrath which I hear is
raised by *The Jacobiniad?* The Boston poets are formidable, and would be guillotined if the Robespierres whom

---

[1] All this, however, was mild compared with a brutal libel upon two Boston
Jacobin leaders, Benjamin Austin and Dr. Charles Jarvis, entitled *The Lyars* —
a Political Eclogue, published in the *Federal Orrery*, September 10, 1795, in which
Jarvis and Austin were represented as contesting for the palm in lying, Genet,
the Frenchman, being umpire, the contest ending in a tie and Genet awarding to
one a Revolutionary bonnet, to the other a pike.

they oppose had the power."[1] It was not surprising that
Benjamin Austin should have retorted: "The scurrility
of the whole performance is such that the author must be
considered as the most abandoned wretch in society, after
giving this public specimen of the baseness of his mind and
malignancy of his heart, to attempt to screen himself from
responsibility under a fictitious signature"; or that the
Independent Chronicle should say: "What a continual
yelping and barking are our swindlers, Aristocrats, Refu-
gees, and British Agents making at the Constitutional
Societies! But how gratifying must it be to the friends of
Constitutional Government to observe these Societies proceeding in the paths of patriotic virtue, with a composure
and dignity which become men engaged in such important
and timely service."[2]

The fact is that these clubs were neither so evil nor so
beneficent as the respective parties claimed. Undoubtedly
they led to some excesses in political action and to some
disorderly, even riotous proceedings.[3] Everywhere, they
emphasized the necessity of adherence to the cause of
France and stirred up opposition to any measure, whether
of neutrality or otherwise, tending to interfere with that
cause. Everywhere their efforts were directed towards re-
awakening the hostility of the United States towards
England.

Of all the New England Federalists, no one was more bitter in his attacks upon the Jacobins and their clubs than
Fisher Ames, whom Jefferson termed "the Colossus of

---

[1] Fisher Ames to C. Gore, January 7, 1795. Wherever, in this book, letters of
Fisher Ames are quoted, the reference (unless otherwise stated) is to *Works of
Fisher Ames* (1854).

[2] *Independent Chronicle*, September 14, 1795.

[3] James Sullivan, an ardent Boston Antifederalist, had his name erased from
the books of the Boston Society because of its extreme views and actions; see
Life of James Sullivan (1859), by Thomas C. Amory, vol. I, p. 275.

Monocrats." [1] No one was more bitterly hated by the Jacobins themselves; and in New York and Charleston, they burned together effigies of William Pitt, Benedict Arnold, the Devil, and Fisher Ames. "The French mania here is the bane of our politics," he wrote from his Dedham home in 1794: "Jacobinism and Gallomania are stronger here than anywhere else." [2] And again in the same year: "The Democratic Club met lately in Faneuil Hall. This is bold, and everything shows the fixed purpose of their leaders to go desperate lengths. It is a pleasant thing for the yeomanry to see their own Government taken out of their hands and themselves cipherized by a rabble formed into a Club. Thus Boston may play Paris, and rule the State." And again: "Such strong grounds may be taken against those Clubs that it ought not to be delayed. They were born in sin, the impure offspring of Genet. They are the few against the many, the sons of darkness (for their meetings are secret) against those of the light; and above all, it is a town cabal attempting to rule the *country*. . . . They are rather waning here."

Such were the political opinions of the Federalist party and of his own younger brother when, in 1794, Dr. Nathaniel Ames began to renew his interest in politics and to record once more his views in his Diary. As already stated, Dr. Ames' home town of Dedham was strongly Jacobin in its politics. The doctor himself was then a man of fifty-four years, of powerful prejudices and vigorous passions. He, therefore, embraced the Jacobin cause with all the

---

[1] *Works of Thomas Jefferson* (Ford ed.), vol. VII, Jefferson to Thomas Mann Randolph, November 16, 1792.

[2] Fisher Ames to C. Gore, March 26, 1794; see also Ames to Gore, February 28, 1795; Ames to Theodore Dwight, August, 1793, August 8, September 3, 11, 1794. Writing to Dwight from Congress in Philadelphia, November 29, 1794, Ames said: "The Clubs are everywhere the echoes of the faction in Congress; the Speaker is a member of the Democratic Club. . . . Madison and Parker are honorary members. Oh Shame! Where is thy sting!"

intensity of his nature; and naturally, as a supporter of the French, he hated England and the Federalist party with an extreme bitterness, which he took every occasion to display in his Diary entries.

It was not until the middle of the year 1795, however, that the doctor began to record his opinions in fully characteristic form. In November, 1794, the famous Jay Treaty had been signed at London, although it had not been laid before the Senate until the following June. While the terms were kept secret, the mere fact that any treaty of amity and commerce would have been concluded with "the perfidious nation" was sufficient to arouse to its depths the anti-British faction in the United States; and violent denunciations of both Jay and his treaty appeared in the "Jacobin" newspapers. Notwithstanding the attacks upon it, the Senate ratified the treaty in secret session. When, on June 29, the substance of it suddenly appeared in Bache's *Aurora*, the storm at once broke. In New York and throughout the country the celebration of the Fourth of July was made the occasion to insult Jay in every possible fashion. Derogatory toasts containing all manner of puns on his name were drunk. In many places he was burned in effigy. Meetings were held, begging Washington not to sign the treaty, and denouncing the "perfidious, corrupting and corrupt Nation whom you vanquished with your swords, now endeavoring to vanquish you with their usual, but alas, too successful weapon, British gold."

The following entries by Dr. Ames described in vivid terms the feelings which the treaty provoked:

March 31, 1795. To the glorious success of the French Republic against the British combined Powers, not the justice or moderation of England or the merits of our Envoy, are we indebted for our continuance in peace with the insolent English.

June 6, 1795. Sketch of Treaty with Britain before the President and Senate, and Senate's decision thereon published. Jay, the American Ambassador to Britain, that agreed to the Commercial Treaty, burnt in effigy with his Treaty at Philadelphia and other places. It is the highest insult on the feelings of Americans of anything that has happened this long time.

July 4, 1795. Independence celebrated at Philadelphia by burning Jay in effigy with his Treaty with Britain.

July 13. Boston Town Meeting unanimously condemn it, and it seems strange that a majority and so large a majority of American Senators could be found so tainted with aristocratic notions as to approve it. If they had voted to reproclaim the right of the British Parliament to bind America in all cases whatsoever, I should not have been much more surprised! and the best celebration of the 4th July was to burn Jay's effigy and his Treaty. And perhaps the people now may see the importance of punctually exercising their only act of sovereignty at election of Senators, etc. But this incapacity of change or want of attention to election is the rock on which our Republic will split. It is scarcely possible for the people of a large Republic to attend to politics enough for their own preservation. Discussion in a public town meeting is not the right way to try the merits of a treaty, but in private deliberation.

The meeting of Boston citizens referred to was held in Faneuil Hall, July 10, 1795, Dr. Charles Jarvis, a leading Antifederalist, being the principal speaker.[1] Indignant resolutions of protest were urged and supported by other Antifederalists, like Thomas Dawes, William Eustis, and William Tudor; and at an adjourned meeting of fifteen hundred citizens on July 13 the resolutions were carried unanimously. Boston, however, did not stop with resolu-

[1] See *Independent Chronicle*, October 27, 1794, as to Dr. Charles Jarvis and Ames.

tions. On September 11 and succeeding nights there were mobs and riots in the streets; the windows of treaty sympathizers were broken by shots, and effigies of Jay were carried about, one of the devices being a watermelon shell cut out like a man's face, bearing scurrilous labels. While this was probably the work of boys, the Federalist newspapers became fiercely excited, the *Centinel* saying: "The laws prostrate — the magistrates literally trodden under foot — women and children frightened — bonfires made in the centre of the town — oaths and imprecations united with threats to tear the hearts of magistrates from their breasts and roast them at a fire." Governor Adams was appealed to, but declined to interfere, terming it "a mere watermelon frolic, the harmless amusement of young persons." To this Thomas Paine's *Federal Orrery* made reply: "However harmless and amusing you may view the 'watermelon frolics' — as you have been pleased to term them — they may be death to your fellow-citizens and constituents. Against your apparent connivance, let us not remonstrate in vain. . . . The dwellings of our citizens have been attacked and recourse for self-preservation, 'Nature's first law,' has been had to a measure the most dangerous and fatal. If your supineness is not construed to an approbation of these riots, it is at least suspected to have proceeded from your enmity to the Federal administration." [1] Fisher Ames wrote: "The mobs are quiet in Boston, and Dedham has not the spirit to raise any." [2] His brother Nathaniel did not consider these "mobs" of sufficient importance for mention in his Diary. The Federalist Stephen Higginson, however, became exceedingly excited over the "high doings in this town". "This has been a Jacobin measure, disapproved by all good men, and not countenanced by any mer-

[1] *Columbian Centinel*, September 12, 1795; *Federal Orrery*, September 14, 1795.
[2] Fisher Ames to Dwight, October 3, 1795.

chant of eminence, not by ten in all. . . . Such instances are dangerous, and will or may eventually bring every great national question before the people for decision, to the destruction of our Constitution and Government. . . . I often think that the Jacobin faction will get the administration of our Government into their hands ere long. . . . Foreign intriguers will unite with the disaffected and disappointed, with seekers after places, with ambitious, popular demagogues and the vicious and corrupt of every class." And as to the "mobs" in Boston, Portsmouth, and other places which expressed their disapproval of the Jay Treaty, Higginson wrote that they were "intended only to intimidate and prevent any further exertions in approbation of the Executive. . . . This is a fair example of our Jacobins' regard to equal rights, etc. Every man and every measure is in imitation of Robespierre. They are all Tyrants in their views and feelings." [1] And another extreme Federalist, George Cabot of Beverly, wrote despondingly to Rufus King in New York as rejoiced to find "that the insanity which is epidemic in this quarter is less prevalent with you. . . . It cannot be sufficiently regretted that some of our respectable men have on this occasion joined the Jocobins. . . . After all, where is the boasted advantage of a representative system over the turbulent mobocracy of Athens, if the resort to popular meetings is necessary? Faction, and especially the faction of great towns always the most powerful, will be too strong for our mild and feeble government." [2]

On September 21, 1795, the anniversary of the founding of the French Republic was again celebrated in Boston by

[1] "Letters of Stephen Higginson," *American Historical Association Report* (1896), Higginson to Timothy Pickering, July 14, 1795. See also letters of August 13, 18, 19, September 21, 1795.

[2] *Life and Correspondence of Rufus King* (1894), vol. ii, Cabot to King, July 25. See also letters of July 27, August 14, 1795.

a procession and banquet of "Republican Frenchmen and American Republicans," at which Governor Adams, the French consul, and the selectmen were guests. Although, as the *Centinel* said, "the day ended without the intervention of one disagreeable event," the Federalist newspapers indulged in insulting attacks on the participants. The *Federal Orrery* published a "Song of Liberty and Equality which ought to have been sung," which included the following choice epithets: "An old Baboon" (William Cooper, the town clerk); "A Jacobin whelp" (Samuel Hewes); "Citizen Goose" (John Keebin, a tailor); and these scurrilous stanzas:

> From the State-house in order the Sansculottes move
> Like cattle or swine in a drove — a drove
> Composed of all colors and figures and shapes,
> Two and two as the patriarch Noah of old
> Drove into the Ark, the unclean of the fold,
> Skunks, woodchucks and apes,
> Toads, adders and lizards
> And vultures and buzzards.
> Now striving amain for a fortunate chance
> To taste of the Freedom of France, of France,
> Stealing softly through alleys and winding through lanes,
> Our mob-loving Governor wanders in haste,
> His eyes up to heaven — his heart with the feast;
> In anarchy's strains
> Psalm-singing and praying
> He smiles at man-slaying.
> Farewell, ye Sanculottes, — I leave ye to dine
> With your hoofs in your dishes like swine — like swine.

As the summer of 1795 progressed, the Antifederalists, or Jacobins, enraged at the abuse poured upon them for their attacks upon the treaty, became more and more violent in their opposition. That "wicked instrument," they called the treaty; that "damned arch traitor," they called Jay. They denounced Washington himself as a "political hypocrite" who had negotiated "with a nation that is the abhorrence of our people and treated our remonstrances with pointed contempt," and they termed him "a supercilious tyrant"; "a man in his political dotage"; "a ruler who tramples on the laws and Constitution"; "the American Caesar."

Dr. Ames noted in his Diary: [1]

> *August 14, 1795.* The President Washington ratified the Treaty with Britain, and Hammond, the British Minister here, immediately sailed for England. Washington now defies the whole Sovereign that made him what he is — and can unmake him again. Better his hand had been cut off when his glory was at its height, before he blasted all his Laurels.

Washington having approved the treaty, and the Senate having ratified it, the fight was then transferred to the House of Representatives, which must enact the legislation necessary to put the treaty in force. The far-reaching effect which the issue of foreign affairs was having upon the American Nation was strikingly shown by the fact that in the Congress which met in December, 1795, President Washington was confronted, for the first time in his seven years, with personal opposition. The scene was interestingly portrayed by a contemporary writer. "When the President arrived at the House this day, he found it in that state of composed gravity, of respectful silence, for which the Congress is so remarkable, and which, whatever witlings may say, is the surest mark of sound understanding. The gallery was crowded with anxious spectators, whose orderly behaviour was not the least pleasing part of the

---

[1] Throughout Dr. Ames' Diary the word "Sovereign" with a capital letter expresses his democratic sentiment in describing the people or the popular vote.

scene. The President is a timid speaker; he is a proof, among thousands, that superior genius, wisdom, and courage, are ever accompanied with excessive modesty. His situation was at this time almost entirely new. Never, till a few months preceding this session, had the tongue of the most factious slander dared to make a public attack on his character. This was the first time he had ever entered the walls of Congress, without a full assurance of meeting a welcome from every heart. He now saw, even among those to whom he addressed himself, numbers who, to repay all his labors, his anxious cares for their welfare, were ready to thwart his measures, and present him the cup of humiliation filled to the brim. When he came to that part of his speech, where he mentions the Treaty with his Britannic majesty, he cast his eyes towards the gallery. It was not the look of indignation and reproach but of injured virtue." [1]

Finally, in April, 1796, after a long, hot, and close struggle, the House enacted a law to execute the treaty, largely owing to the remarkable speech in its favor delivered by Fisher Ames — a speech which enrolled his name forever in the list of great American orators. This accomplishment of his brother Fisher was gall and wormwood to Dr. Nathaniel Ames; and throughout his Diary he never hesitated to record his detestation of Fisher's political actions. In this year he commented on his brother's influence over the local Dedham newspaper as follows: "*Oct. 17, 1796.* Wholly dictated by F. A., to smother political inquiry and make public servants, Lords!" The following sarcastic comment on Fisher's speech, written by the Jacobin Benjamin Austin, Jr., which presented the view prevailing

---

[1] *Prospect from the Congress Gallery during the Session begun December 7, 1795* (1796), by W. Cobbett (Peter Porcupine).

among the opponents of the treaty, must have given great satisfaction to the doctor: [1]

The most curious part of the farce was the *sublime* speech of Mr. Ames in Congress. He rose in that august assembly, apparently under all the infirmities of a man in the last stages of dissolution; he introduced his observations as the dying legacy of a departing patriot; fatigued and almost expiring under the weight of his observations, he was obliged to stop at proper periods and renew his strength by the assistance of a smelling-bottle. Under these impressions, he ran through the horrid detail of "Indian scalping-knives." He portrayed with pathetic energy the desolation of our fields, the conflagrated cities, the cries of frantic mothers and helpless orphans. He almost shook the sun in its stationary position, and arrested the moon and stars in their career; after exhausting his poetic fire, he at length vented his pathos on the rainbow whose thousand tints were to expire under the agonizing expulsion of the British Treaty. Such a complication of natural disorders to arise from a political cause were unparalleled in the pages of history. No wonder that the citizens were alarmed; if the British Treaty convulsed the system of nature, we cannot be surprised that the inhabitants of the globe were interested in its adoption.

The following were Dr. Ames' comments on the final success of the treaty and on English aggressions:

> *March, 1796.* On Mr. Livingston's motion in Congress to request the President to lay before them all papers and instructions relating to the Treaty with Britain, which involved the fate of the Treaty, a great majority — the true Patriots — were for it, i. e., the motion, and with the People, reprobating the Treaty!
>
> *April 1.* Strength of parties in Congress tried on Livingston's motion.
>
> *April 6.* President refuses the request of the House for Treaty papers and appoints Commissioners to meet the British for

---

[1] *Constitutional Republicanism* (1803), by Benjamin Austin, being a series of letters published by him in the *Independent Chronicle*, under the signature of "Old South."

Courts unknown to Federal Constitution, and appoints a son of a refugee, a conspirator, one of the High Commission Court.[1]

May 2. Priests made politicians by Boston Torys. The Treaty fish swallowed, tail foremost, by Congress. The President is a rebel against General Washington and United States.

June 9. Federal Government become near as arbitrary as any European; the worst Tories and Conspirators with English, caressed.

July 31. The insults of British commanders of vessels impressing our seamen and flogging some of them to death; and others — as Captain Jessup, flogged on board Pigot's Frigate till he fainted, then vomited blood and just escaped with life — and Capt. Wyat St. Barbe, after saving 300 Britons in a sinking ship, then Potter, the captain of her, making a prize of his saviour as soon as escaped — are so brutally shocking as not hereafter to be credited perhaps, as our Government hugs the British closer for it, while the people are bursting with indignation!!!

As to the lack of support of President Washington given by his Jacobin opponents, Fisher Ames wrote, in description of his home town: [2]

Many of my plain neighbors who read the *Chronicle* will not commend the President. Their reasoning is from what they know and they take facts from that paper. Yet at the same time, I see the men of sense more zealously in the right than ever, yet as the seekers of popularity are corrupters of the multitude, the malady is endemical and indurable. I went to the meeting in this

[1] Christopher Gore, an ardent Massachusetts Federalist, whom the *Boston Gazette*, August 24, 1795, termed "Sly Kit of Waltham a sycophantic British agent, a funding Federalist of passive principles" had been appointed to serve on an arbitral tribunal provided for by the Treaty.

[2] Fisher Ames to Oliver Wolcott, November 14, 1796. As to the President's refusal to submit to the House of Representatives in Congress the papers and instructions relating to the Jay Treaty (referred to in Dr. Ames' Diary), see Fisher Ames to Gore, March 11, 1796; to G. R. Minot, April 2, 1796.

place. Almost every gentleman was there and acted with me; but a word about liberty and putting bridles in the people's mouth routed us all, altho we were very cautious on that tender ground. . . . Here the influence of the *Boston Chronicle* and the orations in the market is most pestiferous . . . All that is folly and passion in man is opposed to all that is virtue or disdain.

To Fisher Ames, the views which his brother, Dr. Nathaniel, and his "plain neighbors" held as to Washington were signs of "folly and passion"; but the Jacobins in Massachusetts did not equal those of Pennsylvania in violence of expression. It was at this time that Benjamin Franklin Bache, editor of the *Aurora* in Philadelphia, was writing as to the President: "If ever a nation was debauched by a man, the American Nation has been debauched by Washington. If ever a nation has suffered from the improper influence of a man, the American Nation has suffered from the influence of Washington. If ever a nation was deceived by a man, the American Nation has been deceived by Washington. Let his conduct then, be an example to future ages. Let it serve to be a warning that no man may be an idol, and that a people may confide in themselves rather than in an individual. Let the history of the Federal Government instruct mankind, that the masque of patriotism may be worn to conceal the foulest designs against the liberties of a people." [1] And in a pamphlet published a few months later, Bache wrote: [2]

His character having been founded upon false appearances can only command respect, we may affirm, while it remains unknown. Without any eminent qualities in war beyond those of many partizans, and many inferior Generals, whose names slip through history, Mr. Washington has crept into fame by means

[1] *Aurora*, December 23, 1796.
[2] *Remarks Occasioned by the Late Conduct of Mr. Washington as President of the United States* (1797), by Benjamin Franklin Bache.

of his office and by the merits and the success of a cause which he has since deserted. As a patriot indeed he will urge loud pretensions; and yet we know that his pride alone was sufficient to prevent his becoming the slave of the English, and that his pride and his vanity together have since led him into measures which tend to enslave his countrymen. His farce of disinterestedness was easily and usefully played; for while his private fortune (and be it observed that he is without children) had leisure to accumulate immensely, when his expenses were by agreement constantly defrayed by the public, his want of talent made the progress of his political fortunes difficult on any other terms.

In view of such indefensible attacks, it is small wonder that Washington alleged as one reason for declining a renomination for the presidency in 1796 his "disinclination to be longer buffeted in the public prints by a set of infamous scribblers" and said that "as every act of the Executive is misrepresented and tortured with a view to make it appear odious, the aid of friends to government is peculiarly necessary, under such circumstances and at such a crisis as the present." [1]

The fact is that a policy of neutrality was as objectionable to both parties in this country and as difficult to maintain at that period as it was one hundred and twenty years later. And John Quincy Adams, writing from Holland,

---

[1] *Writings of George Washington* (Ford ed.), vol. xiii, Washington to Hamilton, June 26, 1796. The newspapers had in previous years been full of defence of Washington against attack. Thus the *Columbian Centinel*, February 16, 1793, said: "The President of the United States has come in for a due share of the dirt thrown from the mudcarts of these traducers of all good men. But his patriotism is proof against every assault, and the confidence and veneration of the friends of virtue will support him to the end of his days, in being the protector and preserver of our free and glorious Constitution." See also *New York Daily Advertiser*, August 6, 1793. The *Connecticut Courant*, November 23, 1795, said: "The President's house, on the days he sees company, is crowded with all descriptions of citizens; and the abuse which flows from that sink of venality, the *Aurora*, serves only to inspire new feelings of gratitude, and if possible cement more closely those attachments which every true American feels for the Father of his country."

December 24, 1795, presented a picture of the situation which was closely similar to that of the later era:[1]

It is not a little remarkable that this is the critical situation of our country at a moment when the national prosperity continues to grow with a luxuriance of which the annals of the world give no example. One would think our people determined to dash the cup of happiness from their own lips, merely because it overflows. To give you an instance of our commercial state, a Boston newspaper of October 14, states that within the month preceding that date, one hundred sail of vessels had entered there from foreign ports. It is said here to be unquestionable that the exports from the United States during the year ending September 30, 1795, amounted to more than thirty-five millions of dollars. When we recollect that at the same date only four years before, one half of this sum was considered as the proof of some extraordinary cause, which would not be supported to an equal extent during the years subsequent, is it possible to avoid the reflection, that the American government, and the President in particular, do not meet with that retribution which has been richly deserved? At the present moment if our neutrality be still preserved, it will be due to the President alone. Nothing but his weight of character and reputation, combined with his firmness and political intrepidity, could have stood against the torrent that is still tumbling with a fury that resounds even across the Atlantic. He

[1] *Writings of John Quincy Adams* (1913), vol. I, p. 466; see also letters to John Adams, which picture a close parallel to events of 1914–1917. Writing, May 22, 1795, as to the French, he said: "They envy us the immense advantage we have derived from our neutrality; they think we have grown rich upon their impoverishment; that we have drained them of their specie and they do not scruple to charge our merchants who have supplied their most urgent necessities, with having taken advantage of their wants to extort extravagant profits upon their commerce. Peace has become an object of extreme necessity to them; their finances, their commerce, their manufactures, their agriculture, their population, all by an inseparable chain are connected in a dependence upon the return of peace. Yet the brilliancy of their victories, and especially the security of the prevailing party, make it indispensably necessary to them to insist upon conditions, to which their enemies in the present state of affairs will certainly not submit. It is for their benefit alone, therefore, that they wish to see us engaged, and should they succeed in this intention the principal, perhaps the only use they will make of their success will be to obtain more glorious terms of peace for themselves."

is now pledged and he is unmoved. If his system of administration now prevails, ten years more will place the United States among the most powerful and opulent nations on earth. If he fails, though the demon of discord may raise a cloud of prejudice and obloquy around the splendor of his fame for the present moment, it will only serve to add a brighter radiance to his future glory. . . . Now, when he does not unite all hearts, when on the contrary a powerful party at home, and a mighty influence from abroad, are joining all their forces to assail his reputation and his character, I think it my duty as an American to avow my sentiments as they concern that man.

III

JOHN ADAMS, COCKADES, AND LIBELS

FROM the date of the election of John Adams as President in the fall of 1796, Dr. Ames' Diary was chiefly devoted to record of his spicy political views. Four entries towards the close of the year 1796 comprehended in a few lines the four bugbears of American politics, his abhorrence of which he never tired of expressing — the Federalist party (which he termed the "prigarchy"), John Adams, the British, and the lawyers:

> *Nov. 4, 1796.* The Prigarchy straining every nerve to carry election.
>
> *Dec. 7.* Election of President through U. S. A.
>
> *Dec. 19.* Aristocrats crowing that Adams will be President of U. S. A.
>
> *Dec. 24.* Our Governor, Samuel Adams, has 15 votes Virginia, for President or Vice President.
>
> *Dec. 31.* At the end of this year, a sharp conflict between the Lawyers or Aristocrats on one side, and the Democrats or '75 men (or Jacobins, as stigmatized) on the other, to get a new President. The first party strive for John Adams, who favors the Britons our enemies; the second party strive for Thomas Jefferson, who is a friend to the French, who are friends to the Human Race, and helped us out of the paws of the British Government. It seems every man must be a lawyer to enjoy the rights of man under our Federal Government! . . . After violent conflict between partisans for French and Britons through United States to get President and Vice-President, it is confidently affirmed that Adams, an aristocratic lawyer, in favor of British dignities, manners and Government, will be President, — and Jefferson, late Governor of Virginia, a firm supporter of the Rights of

Man, and admirer of the French Revolution, will be Vice-President, which I hope will introduce him to be finally President, and prevent a threatened war with France that gave no power to choose President and form of Government!!!

In contrast to these sentiments, Fisher Ames (who had refused to run again for Congress) wrote to Christopher Gore, December 2, 1796: "I was vexed with our Dedham Antis for voting as they did for Governor Adams and J. Bowdoin, yet H. G. Otis is chosen very handsomely and will sustain the cause of order and his fame in Congress [1] . . . Some among us are so wicked as to justify the French; and others so mean, so unspeakably mean, as to say we must choose a President that will conciliate that Nation. . . . To celebrate French victories may be right for Jacobins; but *we* should cease to celebrate the Fourth of July."

The first year of John Adams' administration was comparatively a quiet one; and Dr. Ames had few entries of political interest, although the following show his indignation at the establishment of a British newspaper and the rise of the "Monarchical" party in Massachusetts: [2]

[1] Fisher Ames, and later Otis, were elected to Congress from the district comprised of Suffolk and Norfolk Counties (including Boston and Dedham, the one Federalist in politics, the other Antifederalist). Christopher Gore wrote to Rufus King, November 6, 1794: "Ames will be elected. The town of Boston never looked more joyous than it has since Monday; and there never was an election where our wealthiest merchants and respectable citizens exerted themselves more, or persevered so long. . . . On the whole, the state of our politics is good. Many falsehoods told of Ames have been refuted. His character is deservedly high." Ames' opponents entertained distorted views as to the cause of his election. James Madison wrote to Jefferson, December 21, 1794: "Ames is said to owe his success to the votes of negroes and British sailors smuggled under a very lax mode of conducting the election there"; and the *Independent Chronicle*, November 5, 1798, referred to Ames and Otis as "two lawyers whose election has too much been carried by negroes and foreigners."

[2] Heretofore Samuel Adams, a strong Jacobin, had been Governor. In 1797 Judge Increase Sumner, a Federalist, was chosen Governor by a majority of 3752. The Jacobin or Republican strongholds in the State were Middlesex, Norfolk, and Bristol Counties and the northern parts of Berkshire County.

Oct. 28, 1797. A Royal or Monarchical party of high Federal public servants grow very bold! Here, too!!

Feb. 1798. Having taken the *Dedham Minerva* of Herman Mann . . . from Thursday, 14th December last to Thursday, February 1st, at 7*s*. 6*d*. per annum — but as it is of a base, British, aristocratical complexion and therefore loses its customers, tho' Mann promised to devote half of it to the French side, yet doth not perform but gleans the *Mercury*, *Walpole*, *Porcupine* and *Centinel* papers for lies against the French — I sent his paper back, directing him to send me no more such stuff signifying that I may go and starve in France as I eat the bread of this [that] country and find fault with Jay's Treaty. I sent him word he ought to go to England to print.

It is interesting to note that the editor of the *Minerva* refuted the charge that his paper was a Federal sheet, in a spicy editorial, saying: "The report current among some of the readers of this paper that the printer has actually been bribed by the *lure of money* to make it an *English* — or what is deemed equally as bad, a Federal partisan paper, is as false as it is maliciously cruel." [1]

If ever there was time when an English and anti-French faction was justified in this country, it was between the

---

[1] See *Dedham Minerva*, September 20, 1798. Dr. Nathaniel's action was certainly unjust to the unfortunate editor; for it appears that, five years later, Fisher Ames stopped his subscription because the paper was too Jacobinical; and the editor later wrote that "the political state of the times at different periods were perilous and peculiarly trying to an editor espousing the republican or democratic cause of his country," and that "my publication as well as myself were rendered at times politically obnoxious to that distinguished personage" [Fisher Ames]. See *Columbian Minerva*, March 1, 1803: "The Hon. Fisher Ames, Esq., this day ordered his name to be struck off the *Minerva* list of subscribers. The Editor returns his warmest thanks for his patronage hitherto, sensible he has long patronized the paper by taking it in direct contradiction to his wishes and consequently his interest . . . and from a late (spirited) interview with Rev. S. Palmer and some others, it is feared that all the clerical and civilian warm Federalists will cry 'Away with the Norfolk Republican Printer!' Mr. Palmer has not yet erased his name, and it is devoutly to be hoped we may mutually bear and forbear, that a reconciliation may take place."

months of October, 1797, and June, 1798. This was the
period when the French Directorate were disregarding the
rights of this country on sea and on land, and were declining to receive the American envoys, John Marshall, General Charles Cotesworth Pinckney, and Elbridge Gerry.
The vigorous War Message issued by President Adams in
March, 1798; the enactment of statutes preparing the
country for war; the President's message of June com-
municating the so-called X. Y. Z. despatches from the envoys at Paris — all received very general support, not only
from the Federalists, but from many of their political opponents. So that Fisher Ames wrote exultingly as to the
local Jacobins of Dedham: "The President and his Ministers are decidedly popular, and if a strong impulse should
be given to the people by the measures of Government, the
disorganizers would fall. The late communications have
only smothered their rage; it is now a coal-pit, lately it was
an open fire. Thacher would say, the effect of the despatches is only like a sermon in hell, to awaken conscience
in those whose day of probation is over, to sharpen pangs
which cannot be soothed by hope." And again: "When
the despatches from our Envoys were published here, the
Jacobins were confounded, and the trimmers dropt off from
the party, like windfalls from an apple-tree in September.
. . . Jacobinism in the vicinity of Boston is not yet dead;
it sleepeth." [1]

Dr. Nathaniel Ames, however, was not to be seduced
into any approval of President Adams or of Federalist
acts, and he indited the following pungent attacks: [2]

[1] Fisher Ames to Pickering, June 4, July 10, 1798; see also Fisher Ames to
Otis, April 23, 1798; to Gore, December 18, 1798.

[2] The Federalist party in the spring State elections in Massachusetts showed
rapidly increasing strength, Governor Increase Sumner being reëlected by a vote
of 17,498 to 2167.

March 28, 1798. An infamous Gallomania seized the coca-doodle doo Government.

April 3. Towns in their primary assemblies of the Sovereign People remonstrating to Congress against war with France! While the British Junto are crowing against France, lying, and deluding farmers.

May 10. Adams' Fast, to engage Powers above against the French.

June 7. All connexion with the French forbid by Traitors in Congress who carried a Law.

June 17. Frenchmen abused in Boston, their cockades torn off and trampled.

June 19. Talleyrand, Minister of France, gives complete answer of the Directory to our Envoys who will treat only with Gerry, and convicts our Executive of rash, ungenerous conduct. But still our traitorous servants bellow War against France!

As the summer of 1798 wore on, nevertheless, the country became stirred to a white heat in its support of the administration. The pugnacious sentiment uttered (or alleged to have been uttered) by General Pinckney, "Millions for defence, but not one cent for tribute," which became the Federal slogan, rightly represented American public sentiment. Patriotic demonstrations spread over the country like flame. Private subscriptions to build warships and to raise volunteer companies were made everywhere. Social meetings, business meetings, the gatherings of farmers, of societies, and of charitable organizations, became the occasion for political toasts and addresses. The pulpits resounded with political sermons. Two songs, composed for the purpose of voicing the Federalists' devotion to their country, as opposed to France, were heard from every lip — *Hail Columbia*, written by Joseph Hopkinson, an eminent Philadelphia lawyer, which was sung for the first time on April 24, 1798, to the tune of the *Presi-*

dent's March;[1] and *Adams and Liberty*, written by Thomas Paine, the editor of that rabid Federalist paper, the *Federal Orrery*, and set to the tune of *Anacreon in Heaven* (a tune better known now as *The Star-Spangled Banner*). "After *Adams and Liberty*," wrote the editor of the *Centinel*, "a song must be preëminently good to be relished in the least degree."[2] Even the theatres (which had at that time existed in Boston for only two years) became the arena for partisan propaganda. The introduction of politics into contemporary drama was interestingly shown by an advertisement in the *Centinel* of the opening of the Haymarket Theatre in Boston, July 23, 1798, in which it is stated that, after the production of *The Dramatist*, "at the end of the play, Mr. Hodgkinson will sing 'Adams and Liberty,' after which all Federal Americans are invited to a patriotic effusion in 2 parts called *The Federal Oath — Death or Liberty*." Apparently, however, politics and the drama were not a popular mixture, for the *Centinel's* dramatic critic wrote, two days later: "The Haymarket Theatre opened on Monday evening with *The Dramatist* and *Federal Oath*, a new piece by Anthony Pasquin, Esq. The principal characters in each were well cast and ably supported. The song of *Adams and Liberty* was sung in the

[1] The *Independent Chronicle*, May 21, 1798, said: "Hopkinson, the author of the late Federal song to the tune of the President's March which was published in a late *Centinel*, has been nominated a Commissioner to transact some business with some Indians. He has written this song to some *tune* and the *right* tune — that's clear. Humphries, who attempted to assassinate Mr. Bache [the Antifederalist editor in Philadelphia] of which he was convicted and fined fifty dollars, on going to pay his penalty received notice it had been paid already, and he has since been selected by Mr. Adams to carry despatches to our envoys at Paris. ... If the writing of adulatory songs to the President, and the assassinating of men who have firmness to expose the improper measures of our Government are to recommend men to Executive appointments, to what an alarming pass has our Government arrived!"

[2] See *Columbian Centinel*, August 4, 1798. Thomas Paine changed his name to Robert Treat Paine, Jr, in order to escape the odium of bearing the name of the famous Jacobin writer of *The Age of Reason*.

best style, the whole house accompanying the chorus. If, as at Cambridge, the audience at the line 'And swear by the God of the Ocean and Land' had elevated their hands, the spectacle would have been more impressive, and sincerity more apparent. The house was thinner than it ought to have been. The *Federal Oath* is full of the pith and marrow of the times." American politics were even discovered in Shakespeare; for the *Mercury*, a Boston Federalist newspaper, said about this time: "The lovers of Shakespeare are this evening offered a classic treat in the representation of *King John*, one of the best acting plays of that inimitable author. . . . Many of its political sentiments with respect to the French Nation are not inapplicable to the Gallic character at the present day; some references have peculiar point, and will undoubtedly be strongly noted by the popular praise. The stage is an 'engine of the public weal'; as such it should be supported. We may therefore venture to assert that at the presentation of *King John* politicians will applaud as well as criticize." [1]

The most prevalent mode of expressing their patriotism adopted by the Federalists was the framing of formal addresses to the President in support of his war policy. These were sent to him by legislatures, societies, colleges, towns, and individuals throughout the country; and most of them elicited a personal reply from Adams. Dr. Ames commented in his Diary on the address from the Massachusetts legislature, against which thirty votes were cast, as follows: "Names of the faithful minority in the Gen'l. Court, June 7, on the question of addressing J. Adams, Pres. U. S. A. for committing us to the Lyon's paws." And his irate scorn of the address from the town of Dedham was deepened by the fact that the undertaking was inspired and fostered by his brother Fisher:

[1] *Massachusetts Mercury*, November 6, 1798.

June 30. A subscription paper presented me for a dinner at Gay's 4th July, in a mixed medley of British and Americans but as Government has defeated the best objects of Independence, I told them I chose to consider yet [to see] if the Gag bill, etc., is crammed down our jaws, as well as Stamp Act, etc., direct taxes, etc.

War against France in effect, contrary to wish of Landlords.

July 4th. In face and eyes, when half seas over, an Address obtained to President, but the great mass of People said "Alliance with France, defiance to Britain."

July 5. Tools of F. A. work hard to get signers to an Address.

July 6. The Freeholders of this town grumbling at the High Federalist frolic, and make great stir for counter address, but stop short.

July 11. J. Varnum in Congress a turncoat and is for War against France.

July 13. American, Capt. Smith, 12 guns, 12th, taken by French Privateer of 4 guns. War begun.

July 14. Dedham Address occasions much quarreling and caricature pictures . . . and produces counter address from most of the Landholders in Dedham.

The dinner referred to was held on the Fourth of July at Gay's Tavern and the address was issued. The *Columbian Centinel* of July 11, noticed it as follows: "An Address has been presented for the town of Dedham. We mention this circumstance with pleasure, for the representative of that town voted against the Legislative Address." In contrast to Dr. Ames' sarcastic and bitter thrusts at the success of the occasion, the *Centinel* rejoiced over the fact that the good people of Jacobin Dedham were beginning to see the light, as follows: "At Dedham, John Lothrop, Junior, Esq., pronounced in the midst of boundless applause a truly federal, patriotic, elegant and spirited oration. The toasts were verve itself. . . . They form the condensation of genius, fire and federalism. Truth is indeed a slow traveller, but let the Jacobin deceivers of the people remember

she is very long-winded. The people of the county of Norfolk hear her voice at last, and they receive her with the
cordiality of an old acquaintance." The general tone of
the address, which had been penned by Fisher Ames himself, was shown by the following: "Having been led by the
occasion to consider the insults, perfidy, and hostile aggression of France . . . now will we disgrace ourselves by hesi-
tating a moment between war and submission to the exactions of France?" An interesting account of the dinner
was also written by Fisher Ames to Timothy Pickering
which presented quite another view from that of his
brother Nathaniel:

Finding the minds of our people in Dedham and its vicinity
unexpectedly well prepared, I recommended to some very capable young men an oration, dinner, patriotic song, etc., etc. A
week only remained for preparation before the 4th instant; but,
anti-Federal and Gallic as our people have been, the proposition
took exceedingly well. I am happy to announce to you that it
has succeeded; and, inconsiderable as the politics of a village may
be, yet, as an indication of the progress of right opinions, and as
a proof of the rapid decline of Gallicism where it was lately
strongest, and is still perhaps the most malevolent spirit that
exists, it will not be deemed quite unimportant. The company
at dinner was about sixty. The number of men of education was
unusually great. Five clergymen attended, whose hearts are
with us. Three signed the Address, two others retired before it
was proposed, a sixth was invited, and like the rest of his valuable order, was Federal but could not attend. Among the signers
are magistrates, men of influence in their several circles, enlightened farmers and mechanics. On the whole, I may say with
truth, no meeting has been held in this part of the country,
within my memory, equally respectable. . . . I am persuaded the
effect of the meeting will be salutary and will rally the friends of
Government to their posts.

President Adams, on July 14, sent a reply to this address, and a meeting was held in Dedham, August 2, to

receive it, described by the local newspaper as follows: "On Thursday last, a number of signers of the Address to the President and others collected in the afternoon at the Episcopal Church to receive the President's answer. Although the notice was so short that many were prevented from attending, yet the occasion was honored by the company of a very considerable number of ladies. The astonishing and unrivalled powers of Mr. Williamson in vocal music (accompanied by an excellent band) were happily displayed in *Adams and Liberty* and other patriotic songs. The musical performances were received with admiration, and no doubt contributed to impress the patriotic sentiments of the President's answer, sentiments which he had conceived with a noble energy and expressed with a plainness and sincerity worthy the uprightness of his character and the dignity of his station." [1] Of President Adams' attitude toward the numerous addresses which were sent to him from every State a picturesque though partisanly exaggerated view was given by an Antifederalist writer in a somewhat scurrilous history written in 1802: [2] "The childish vanity Mr. Adams displayed upon receiving these addresses gave surprise even to those who had the best opportunity of being acquainted with his weaknesses. They usually formed part of his table equipage, as regularly as a newspaper or a dish of coffee. A file of five hundred of them suspended in front of his library served as a political dictionary for civil, naval, and military appointments on all occasions. None whose name was not found entered upon this sacred register, could claim any pretension to the favor of Mr. Adams. The magistrate, the soldier and the sailor, equally owed their birth to this bundle of federal

---

[1] See the *Minerva*, August 9, 1798.
[2] *The Suppressed History of the Administration of John Adams*, by John Wood (written in 1802, suppressed at that time, but published in 1846).

parchment, which is now preserved in the palace of Braintree. Those addresses which were not couched in the most submissive terms were treated with the greatest contempt."

Display of patriotism by the Federalists, however, was not confined to the framing of addresses to the President, the composition of songs, and scurrilous newspaper abuse of their opponents. Their enthusiasm demanded further outward symbolism; and, consequently, another vent for it was found in the adoption of a distinctive emblem to be worn by all "good patriots," in the form of a black cockade — a counter to the French tricolor cockade sometimes worn by the Jacobins. Such a cockade of black ribbon, four inches in diameter and borne on the hat, had been formerly worn by soldiers in the Revolution; and its renewed use had been suggested by William Cobbett in May, 1798. On the Fourth of July, Benjamin Russell in the *Columbian Centinel* earnestly urged its adoption: "It has been repeatedly recommended that our citizens wear in their hats on the Day of Independence the American cockade, which is a rose composed of black ribbon with a white button or fastening, this symbol of their attachment to the Government which cherishes and protects them. The measure is innocent; but the effect will be highly important. It will add cement to the Union, which so generally and so happily exists. Every cockade will be another edition of the Declaration of Independence, and the demonstration of it by this national emblem will be as highly laudable as the display of the immortal instrument of 1776 was then. Those who signed the Address to the President are pledged to display this evidence of it to the world; and they may be assured that the influence of their example in this measure will be productive of as great good as the influence of their names on the paper. . . . The ladies, we understand, are universally in favour of the measure; and if they lead, who will not follow?" The next issue of the *Centinel* said: "The Jacobins have the impudence to say that the people of Boston were really divided; and they give as a proof that not more than half of them wear the American cockade. This being the case, let every Bostonian attached to the Constitution and Government of the United States immediately mount the cockade and swear that he will not relinquish it until the infamous projects of the external and internal enemies of our country shall be destroyed." And on July 28 Russell wrote: "The black cockade is now universally worn in town and country. It is considered as the open and visible sign of Federalism, and an immutable determination in the wearers to support the Constitution, Government, Independence and Happiness of their Country. Those who do not wear it are . . . men who bellow for their country but who wish to betray. All the members of Congress we have seen have worn the American Cockade. Major General Hull in division orders has recommended the wearing of the American cockade every day, and uniform on Sunday and other public days." On July 10 the *Mercury* indulged in a characteristic onslaught on the Jacobins, and supported the cockade idea: "The cockade is a pledge of friendship among Federalists and of attachment to our Constitution and Government, while at the same time it proves an eyesore to Jacobins. Let it then be worn by all Federalists and the lye will at once be given to those lying dogs, the Jacobins, who have dared to assert that we are a divided people!" [1]

[1] In a debate in the House of Representatives, February 28, 1828, John C. Wright of Ohio said: "I remember well the time when party spirit in this country ran so high that even ladies wore different cockades as badges of party attachment, and to have seen them meet at the church door and violently pluck the badges from one another's bosoms." *Congressional Debates, 20th Congress, 1st Session*, p. 1447.

The Antifederalists in Dedham and other towns near Boston, however, made much fun of this black cockade, and parodied it in every possible way. Dr. Ames in his Diary said with sarcasm: "*July 31, 1798.* Judge Metcalf, with his cockade on, came down to see General Washington, expecting to get a commission to fight the French, being enraged against the French and infatuated at the slanders of the Progress of the Cannibals that the French skin Americans to make boots for their Army." And as Benjamin Austin, Jr., wrote (under the pseudonym of "Old South") in the *Independent Chronicle*: "Every wheel is set in motion, and even the insignificant, childish bauble of a cockade is exhibited as a token of servile submission to all the dogmatical mandates and gross impositions which the supercilious Junto are pleased to enjoin." "The Tory Junto, being baffled in their projects, had recourse at last to the despicable insignia of a cockade," wrote Austin. "In this part of the farce they appeared more ridiculous then ever. To see a group of old men swaggering through the streets, *en militaire*, and a cluster of boys interspersed with a few straggling negroes, with a huge throng (to fill up the chasm) of sycophants who were courting public favor, exhibited a scene which naturally excited the laughter and pity of every considerate citizen. This cockade influenza was rather harmless, as folly was the only conspicuous trait which marked its progress." [1]

In the town of Roxbury, the Fourth of July celebration of 1798 was enlivened by the appearance of a leading Jacobin politician wearing a cockade made, with a certain crude, vulgar humor, of a material unflattering to his Federalist opponents. Reference to this appeared in the *Centinel*: "A certain Jacobin Quack Doctor, not five miles

[1] *Constitutional Republicanism* (1803), by Benjamin Austin, Jr., pp. 57, 71.

off, actually assumed an appropriate cockade on the 4th;
— it was a piece of dried cow-dung, four inches diameter.
There is so much congeniality between this cockade and
the Jacobins that we expect the whole party will follow the
example of this illustrious ringleader." [1] The next week the
Centinel indulged in the following coarse but humorous
attack on the meeting in Dedham on July 14 (described
above by Dr. Ames), when the Jacobins concocted a
counter address to the President:

A Jaco in a village not five miles off did, it seems, on the 4th of
July, wear a cockade after his own heart. Nothing is so catching
as example; accordingly, we hear that a gang of four — some say
only three — assembled at Dedham on the 14th instant — the
anniversary of the French Confederation — to confer together
on the gratitude we ought to show by words and deeds to our beloved France, provided our oppressive Government should go to
war with that happy and free nation. . . . This gang is to meet
again the 10th August and 3d September, anniversaries famous
for insurrection and assassination. They are to wear cockades of
cowdung. A flag is to be displayed with the words "We are but
dross and dung," — and, in order to denote the humbleness of
souls that will befit the expected and desired downfall of our
"aristocratic government," the members are to assume the name
of "The Cowdung Club." The denomination of "muck worms"
was not approved, though proposed — although it was insisted
that the insect grows so fat in cowdung that when trod upon by a
French foot he is crushed to death, without turning, which is
more than can be said of other worms. Therefore it was a proper
emblem of American Jacobinism. This, however plausible, was
overruled, the Quack Doctor having actually mounted his cockade and begun to distinguish Jacobins by a proper badge from
Federal Americans. It is a good beginning, said they, let us
stick to it.

Even such coarse abuse as the above was exceeded by
articles in other newspapers directed at the "traitors" who

[1] *Columbian Centinel,* July 14, 21, 1798.

refused to wear the black cockade; and the following letter, which appeared in another Federalist newspaper, is an example of the torridity of political attack:[1]

As it has been suggested that some traitors in one or two neighboring towns have had the audacity to appear with the French cockades (that emblem of treason) in their hats, I would request of all good Federalists who know the caitiffs to communicate to some editor of a newspaper their names, that they may be exposed to public notice. It is expected that every miscreant will be avoided by all Federalists as if infected with the leprosy or plague, that they will neither buy, sell, or have any dealings whatever with them; but will treat them with utmost abhorrence as wretches unfit for society — as Arnolds or Randolphs who would sell their country for gold — or bloody heroes who would rip up its very vitals. (Signed) *A Hater of Treason.*

These Antifederalist "traitors" who were bold enough to mount the French cockade were not only verbally assailed, but were treated with actual violence. Nor did Federalist political passion stop even at the threshold of the church, as is seen from the following extraordinary episode, described in the *Centinel*. It appears that in the town of Raynham, after morning communion, at afternoon service, an Antifederalist took his seat in the front of the gallery wearing a French cockade in his hat. At the end of the service, "to the consternation of the pastor before he was able to leave the pulpit, the hat fell from the gallery and the Federalists over benches, pews, etc., ran and caught it, from which they dismounted the 'ade. This was followed by clinching, swearing, and even by blows. The screechings of old women heightened the scene. Here were in view justices, lawyers, and even grand juries, all clinched by collars, hair, and cheeks, until at last the Jacobins were thrust out of the house, some with no hats, others with

[1] *The Mercury*, July 13, 1798.

bloody cheeks, and nearly all with dishevelled polls. After a short debate, all retired. By this, we learn that justice and right will be promoted without reluctance." Political mania certainly could go no further — and a political row in a church building after divine service is a curious example of the promotion of "justice and right." It was even more picturesquely described in the *Mercury*, August 10: "Some who infamously exult in a foreign attachment appeared with the French cockade. The Americans, from their devotional spirit, remained quiet till the religious services were ended, when, unable longer to contain their indignation, before the Doctor had left his desk, they flew at the enemies of their country and after a short struggle divested them of the badge of slavery and treason." The meetinghouse, indeed, seems to have been a favorite scene for the display of cockades by political antagonists; for the *Mercury*, September 25, described another episode of this kind, and indulged in bitter sarcasm on the participants: "On Sunday last, in the forenoon, at Quincy Meeting House, three particles of Jacobin dirt were discovered with tri-colored tints. The deleterious infection of the air from this circumstance so deeply affected the Quincy assembly that they were not brushed off as they ought to have been. These atoms in the afternoon rolled to the Milton Meeting House, where the patriotic auditory were not quite so drowsy; and instantly after divine service, the besom of vengeance was exercised till the grains were almost annihilated. These *things* are numbered and marked by a correspondent thus: 'Atom No. 1 Elisha Gould; No. 2 Joe Phinny; No. 3 Pitcher.'"[1]

That the people in general should go to such extremes in political action is not to be wondered at when one realizes

[1] *Columbian Centinel*, August 14, 1798; *Massachusetts Mercury*, August 10, September 25, 1798.

the extent of vituperation in which their party leaders indulged in public and private utterances against their political opponents. The utter detestation of the Federalists for the Jacobins, as shown in their statements regarding them, accounts largely for the course of history in the administrations of Washington and Adams. It could not be expected that that history would be free from personal violence, when a chief justice of Massachusetts could, in an address to the grand jury, term the French faction and the Vice President and minority in Congress "apostles of atheism, and anarchy, bloodshed, and plunder"; when Fisher Ames could write of the Jacobins as "men equally destitute of private virtue and of public spirit"; when Noah Webster could write: "I believe such a pack of scoundrels as our Opposition and their creatures was never before collected into one country — indeed they are the refuse, the sweepings of the most depraved part of mankind"; when George Cabot could refer to them as "demons", and allege that: "Men of lost character and broken fortunes, disappointed seekers of office, rapacious men, idle profligates, and desperadoes of all descriptions, were the natural members of their body. . . . Successful Jacobinism is the consummation of vice and tryanny, and therefore to be viewed as the greatest possible political evil; and it is justly to be feared, because it is propagated by eloquence and sophistry, and is exhibited in the garb of virtue and of liberty, whose sacred names it profanely usurps." [1] The following letter, which appeared in the *Centinel* of August

[1] *Works of Fisher Ames* (1854), Essay No. 2, by "Laocoön"; Fisher Ames to Christopher Gore, November 10, 1799; Cabot in *Massachusetts Mercury*, January 15, 1798; "Pickering Papers," *Mass. Hist. Soc. Coll.*, vol. xxi, Webster to Pickering, July 7, 1797; Cabot to Alexander Hamilton, October 11, 1800. The *Columbian Centinel*, November 3, 1798, termed General William Heath (whom H. G. Otis defeated for Congress) "a ridiculous, despicable, weak-minded, weak-hearted Jacobin."

14, 1798 (probably written by Fisher Ames), expressed the views of his party associates: "In some of the towns near Boston, they [Jacobins] are working day and night to keep up the passions of those whom they have misled, and to persuade them that the whole blame of bringing on our public troubles lies upon the Government. Unless our farmers are blinder than the moles in the ground, you will say, they will not believe the *Chronicle* lies because the truth has been published. The justification of our Government is as complete as the proof of French wickedness, and a great proportion of the French party have renounced their cause and declare they hold them in abhorrence. All this is very true. A man must be either a knave or a fool to be a Jacobin now. There is, however, no lack of such characters. . . . These Jacobins are much despised; but, say men of candor, are they despised too much?" The bench, the bar, and the clergy were especially vigorous in denunciation. Thus, the Reverend Jedidiah Morse of Charlestown, in a Fast Day sermon, May 9, 1798, referred to those men who dared object to President Adams' anti-France policy, as follows: "That we should have men among us so lost to every principle of religion, morality, and even common decency, as to reprobate the measure, as to condemn the authority who recommended it, and to denounce it as hypocritical and designed to effect sinister purposes, is indeed alarming. That such vile sentiments should find their way into a newspaper and be read and tolerated by a people who profess Christianity, indicates a degree of corruption and depravity in the public mind more truly threatening to our dearest rights and interests than the hostile attitude and movements of foreign matters." Jeremiah Smith, Chief Justice of New Hampshire, wrote to Oliver Wolcott, June 14, 1798: "I have never yet known a real, thorough Jacobin converted by light or knowledge.

The defect lies in the heart. They hate the light because it reproves their deeds which are evil." [1]

The New England Federalists were, in fact, obsessed by the view that all who differed from them were little less than criminals and traitors. And this arrogant Federalist confidence in their own infallibility was accurately depicted by a contemporary writer, as follows: [2]

Every man who opposed the measures of the Administration, of what kind so ever they were, or from whatever motives, was stigmatized as a disorganizer and a Jacobin, which last term involved the utmost extent of human atrocity; a Jacobin was, in fact, an enemy to social order — to the rights of property — to religion — to morals — and ripe for rapine and spoil. . . . In pursuit of this object, their own partisans are all angels of light, whose sublime and magnificent plans of policy are calculated to produce a political millenium; and their opponents demons incarnate, intent on the destruction of the best interests of the country. These portraits are equally unjust and incorrect. Among the frightful consequences resulting from this odious practice, a plain and palpable one presents itself. These horrible portraits engender a satanical spirit of hatred, malice and abhorrence in the parties towards each other. Men on both sides, whose views are perfectly pure and public spirited, are to each other objects of distrust and jealousy. We attach all possible guilt and wickedness — political at least — to our opponents and then detest the hobgoblins which we have ourselves created.

And as the *Independent Chronicle* said: [3]

What is a Jacobin? That it is a party nick-name is sufficiently notorious; that it has been constantly used both in England and America as a term of reproach, is equally well known; — but whether the citizens of this country are to be imposed on by the arts of a desperate faction remains to be proved by time, which

---

[1] *Office Seeking during the Administration of John Adams*, by Gaillard Hunt, *American Historical Review* (1897), vol. II, p. 241.

[2] *Olive Branch or Faults on Both Sides* (1814), by Mathew Carey.

[3] *Independent Chronicle*, April 4, 1799.

in its progress cannot fail to develop the dark designs of the enemies of Liberty in both countries. One of these arts, and not the least considerable, has been the perpetual use of this mystical word; a word forever to be found in their writings and speeches, but never explained — a word, in short, the true meaning of which they have industriously overwhelmed in torrents of abuse. Let any candid man, attached to no party, read the productions of the Federal presses, and judge if Jacobinism and Republicans are not synonymous terms, if they are not equally the abhorrence of the British Federalist, the Aristocratic and Monarchical Federalist, whose voices are all in perfect unison for war and whose system is diametrically opposed to Peace, Liberty and the equal Rights of Man.

The Antifederalist political leaders maintained an equally violent attitude towards their Federalist opponents, but their attacks were directed in terms more of political and less of personal denunciation.

It was with the newspaper editors, however, on both sides that a climax of rancorous and venomous abuse was reached. Of the Federalist editors, the most voluminous masters of scurrility were William Cobbett of *Porcupine's Gazette* and John Ward Fenno of the *United States Gazette*, at Philadelphia; Noah Webster of the *American Minerva*, at New York; and at Boston, Benjamin Russell of the *Columbian Centinel*, Thomas Paine of the *Federal Orrery*, and John Russell of the *Boston Gazette*. Chief of these was Cobbett, whose control of abusive epithet and invective may be judged from the following terms applied by him to his political foes, the Jacobins: "refuse of nations"; "yelper of the Democratic kennels"; "vile old wretch"; "tool of a baboon"; "frog-eating, man-eating, blood-drinking cannibals"; "I say, beware, ye under-strapping cut-throats who walk in rags and sleep amidst filth and vermin; for if once the halter gets round your flea-bitten necks, howling and confessing will come too late." He

wrote of the "base and hellish calumnies" propagated by
the Jacobins, and of "tearing the mask from the artful and
ferocious villains who, owing to the infatuation of the
poor, and the supineness of the rich, have made such fear-
ful progress in the destruction of all that is amiable and
good and sacred among men." [1] Among the milder examples of his description of Jacobins was the following: [2]

> Where the voice of the people has the most weight in public
> affairs, there it is most easy to introduce novel and subversive
> doctrines. In such States too, there generally, not to say always,
> exists a party who, from the long habit of hating those who ad-
> minister the Government, become the enemies of the Govern-
> ment itself, and are ready to sell their treacherous services to
> the first bidder. To these descriptions of men, the sect of the
> Jacobins have attached themselves in every country they have
> been suffered to enter. They are a sort of flies, that naturally
> settle on the excremental and corrupted parts of the body politic.
> . . . The persons who composed this opposition, and who thence
> took the name of Anti-Federalists, were not equal to the Fed-
> eralists, either in point of riches or respectability. They were in
> general, men of bad moral characters embarrassed in their pri-
> vate affairs, or the tools of such as were. Men of this caste
> naturally feared the operation of a Government embued with
> sufficient strength to make itself respected, and with sufficient
> wisdom to exclude the ignorant and wicked from a share in its
> administration.

A close rival to Cobbett in the wealth of his venomous
vocabulary was Benjamin Russell, who was accustomed to
apply the following epithets to the Antifederalists: "galli-

[1] For examples of Cobbett's scurrilous abuse of his opponents, see *Porcupine's
Gazette*, October 24, 1797, September 7, November 28, 1798, January 21, 1799;
The Porcupiniad (1799), by Mathew Carey; *A Plumb Pudding for the Humane,
Chaste, Valiant, Enlightened Porcupine* (1799), by Mathew Carey.

[2] See chapter on "The American Jacobins" by William Cobbett in *The History of Jacobinism, its Crimes, Cruelties and Perfidies — Comprising an Inquiry
into the Manner of Disseminating, under the Appearance of Philosophy and Virtue,
Principles which are Equally Subversive of Order, Virtue, Religion, Liberty and
Happiness* (London, 1796), by William Playfair.

can traitors"; "gallic Jackals"; "filthy Jacobins"; "demons of sedition"; "malignant knaves"; "despicable mobocracy." He described a convention to nominate a Republican candidate for Congress as "a convention of Parisian cut-throats assembled in solemn divan, for the purpose of selecting some devotee of republicanized France as a candidate." He termed his newspaper rivals of the other party "Jacobin foxes, skunks and serpents," and "vermin," and spoke of their papers "through which they ejected their mud, filth and venom."[1] Two choice phrases applied to his Antifederalist opponents by the editor of the *Massachusetts Mercury*[2] may be added: "Lying Jacobin miscreants"; "Monsters of sedition." And with reference to the Antifederalists' leading paper, the *Aurora*, an opponent, the *Portfolio*, printed the following: "Wanted for the *Aurora* service, three fellows without ears, two with backs flagrant from the beadle, one traitor, and a couple of Deists, none need apply but who can come well recommended from Newgate, or their last place. N. B. Any young imp of sedition who would make a tolerable devil may have everything found him except his washing."[3]

---

[1] The following is an example of Russell's skill in scurrility regarding his personal newspaper opponents: "Who and what is Cobbett? He is known to the people of the United States as a vagrant alien, and a hectoring blackguard. His threats to pursue us with his vile calumnies excite nothing but contempt; they will recoil on himself — they will twine round his black heart, and a life of infamy will end, as it ought to, in agony and torture." And again: "We feel that an apology is due to our respectable readers for having called their attention to so disgusting a subject as William Cobbett, editor of *Porcupine's Gazette*. His smuttery can never excite anything but contempt; for, strip his compositions of the slime that envelopes them, and his most hardened advocates will admit they contain nothing to please, instruct or inform. Necessity obliged those whose duty it was to check him, to tolerate his gallimaufry; and while he confined himself to ejecting his filth on Jacobins as filthy as himself, it was well enough." See *Columbian Centinel*, April 24, 1799, and May 8, 1799. These editorials were called forth as a rejoinder to a reply made by Cobbett to the *Centinel's* previous attack of April 10, 1799.

[2] *Massachusetts Mercury*, August 17, 1799.

[3] *Portfolio*, June 5, 1804.

Another Federalist paper described the gazettes of the opposite party as "absolutely the most stupid, lifeless, and vapid diaries that ever abused the public ear.":[1]

They do not possess wit enough to divest their malice of any of its odium; base and groundless, it strikes one like the dull monotonous prowlings of an hungry wolf. Divested of all the common qualities of a newspaper and passing over news, domestic intelligence and the acts and doings of government, their sheets subserve the sole purpose of pampering the depraved appetites of a set of villains to whom long familiarity with vice and crime has rendered their abominable contents congenial and delightsome; wretches who like some odious beast shun all wholesome aliment and ravenously prey upon the most loathsome garbage to be found.

The Antifederalist editors, in general, however, quite equalled their opponents in virulence.[2] Their chief mudslingers were Mathew Carey, a bookseller and pamphleteer of Boston, James Cheetham, a New York editor, who referred to Noah Webster's Federalist paper as "a polluted vehicle for a great portion of the filth produced by antigovernment allies,"[3] and the Philadelphia editors of

[1] *Oracle of the Day*, December 29, 1798.

[2] See "Transition Period of the American Press," *Magazine of American History* (1887), vol. xvii; *Journalism in the United States* (1873), by Frederic Hudson. For rancorous vilification, see especially *A Plumb Pudding for the Humane, Chaste, Valiant, Enlightened Porcupine* (1799), by M. Carey, in which Cobbett is described as "a wretch so far sunk in infamy, so detested, despised and abhorred by all those whose good opinion can reflect honour, that it is madness and folly to enter the lists with him. What is to be gained in a controversy with a scoundrel whom no lie, ever so barefaced, can shame; who has taken out his diploma by the unanimous vote of the college of blackguards . . . a low-bred, cowardly alien, an unprincipled ruffian who hardly prints a single paper void of the vilest abuse and scurrility . . . a disgrace to human nature . . . the most nefarious blackguard newspaper that ever disgraced a civilized country. . . . Wretch as you are accursed by God and hated by man, the most tremendous scourge that hell ever vomited forth to curse a people. . . . Callous and casehardened, you draw subsistence from your infamy and notoriety . . . a blasted, hated, loathsome coward."

[3] *American Citizen*, May 4, 1801.

the *Aurora*, Benjamin Franklin Bache whom his opponents described as "the greatest fool and the most stubborn sansculotte in the United States," and William Duane (Bache's successor) whose bitterness towards President Adams was such that the latter wrote to Timothy Pickering, "Is there anything evil in the regions of actuality or possibility that the *Aurora* has not suggested of me?" The ablest and most caustic pen, though not the most venomous, among the Antifederalists was wielded by Benjamin Austin, Jr. of Boston, in the *Independent Chronicle*, of whom the *Centinel* said: [1]

If the writer of this thing of shreds and patches, which appears in the *Chronicle* over the signature of "Old South," be the contemptible biped to whom it is generally attributed, we shall not insult our readers by condescending to notice a fellow whose heart is a libel on everything benevolent or generous; whose hand has ever been employed in defaming everything wise, patriotic and virtuous; and who is sunk so deep in the sewer of public contempt that, if he moves at all, he must of necessity ascend. Deeper he cannot be sunk.

Another Antifederalist master of the art of libellous writing, though of a lower order than Austin, was John Williams in Boston who wrote under the name of "Anthony Pasquin," and of whose work the following dedication of his *Hamiltoniad* is a sample: "To perpetuate the brutal infamy of John Park, M.D., a Galenical excrescence,[2] who is the vile and crawling minion of the Essex

[1] *Columbian Centinel*, December 9, 1801. The following is a mild example of scurrilous retort by a Boston Antifederalist newspaper on a rival Federalist editor: "Ben Russell's remarks . . . issuing from a polluted fountain which is continually casting up mire and dirt, would, of course, have been unworthy our attention did we not conceive it a duty to expose to the view of our republican fellow-citizens this paragon of Billingsgate." *Constitutional Telegraphe*, February 8, 1800.

[2] Dr. John Park was the editor of the *Repertory*, the most violent and foulmouthed of all the Federalist press after 1802.

Junto that has been laboring to destroy the Federal fabric of our Republican Constitution and introduce a monarchical depotism upon its ruins — who has desolated the fair regions of Truth and Taste and Science by a torrent of venal barbarism, which is only congenial with the mind and temperament of a low ruffian — who is ignorant of the responsibility of a gentleman to his own honour — who is maintaining a dirty existence at the expense of human esteem. He is the pensioned scavenger and servile dog of the Royal Faction of New England, who are now gasping on their death-bed. To hold this miscreant up to endless contempt, this work is published by the Author." [1]

Such unbridled license as is shown in the foregoing, chosen at random from thousands of instances, amply justified the language used by Thomas McKean, Chief Justice of the Supreme Court of Pennsylvania in his charge to the Grand Jury at the trial of William Cobbett, for libel, November 27, 1797: "Every one who has in him the sentiments of either a Christian or a gentleman cannot but be highly offended at the envenomed scurrility that has raged in pamphlets and newspapers printed in Philadelphia for several years past, inasmuch that libelling has become a kind of national crime. . . . Our satire has been nothing but ribaldry and Billingsgate; the contest has been who could call names in the greatest variety of phrases; who could mangle the greatest number of characters; or who could excel in the magnitude and virulence of their lies. . . . This evil, so scandalous to our government and detestable in the eyes of all good men, calls aloud for redress. To censure the licentiousness is to maintain the liberty of the press." [2] That the leaders of both

---

[1] For a merciless attack on "Antony Pasquin," see *The Baviad* (1798), by William Gifford.

[2] See *Federal Gazette and Baltimore Advertiser*, February 6, 1798.

political parties suffered equally from the scandalous license indulged in by pamphleteers and newspaper writers, they themselves have testified. George Washington wrote to a friend: "If you read the *Aurora* of this city or those gazettes which are under the same influence, you cannot but have perceived with what malignant industry and persevering falsehoods I am assailed, in order to weaken if not destroy the confidence of the public." [1] John Adams wrote of the "narrow bigotry, the most envious malignity, the most base, vulgar, sordid, fish-woman scurrility, and the most palpable lies" against him in the press.[2] And Jefferson wrote in 1798: "I have been for some time used as the property of the newspapers, a fair mark for every man's dirt." [3]

[1] *Writings of George Washington* (Ford Ed.), vol. XIII, letter to Benjamin Walke, January 12, 1797.

[2] *Works of John Adams*, vol. X, letter to James Lloyd, February 11, 1815; see *ibid.*, vol. IX, letter to Dr. Benjamin Rush, August 28, 1811, saying: "If I am to judge by the newspapers and pamphlets that have been printed in America for twenty years, I should think that both parties believed me the meanest villain in the world."

[3] *Writings of Thomas Jefferson* (Ford Ed.), vol. VII, letter to P. Fitzhugh; see *ibid.*, vol. IX, letter to Dr. Walter Jones in 1814, saying: "I deplore with you the putrid state into which our newspapers have passed, and the malignity, vulgarity, and the mendacious spirit of those who write for them."

IV

THE GAG LAW, LIBERTY POLES, AND TAXES

THE proper remedy for all the flood of scurrility and calumny, which swelled each succeeding year of the Adams administration, was a more rigid enforcement of the law of criminal libel by State officials and courts. A criminal libel proceeding, however, was a weapon which could be employed by both parties; and the Federalists wished absolution for their own words, and punishment only for their opponents. Moreover, some of these political attacks were not indictable as libels, but consisted of mere criticism of governmental action; and the Federalists wished to stop forcibly the mouth of every man who would not admit the Adams government and the Adams policies to be perfect. In their opinion, failure to support Adams constituted treason, in fact. To make it such in law was now their determination. Accordingly, on June 26, 1798, James Lloyd introduced in the United States Senate the notorious bill, which, in amended form, was enacted and signed by the President on July 14, and which became known as the "Sedition Act" or "Gag Law." The extremities to which the Federalists were willing to go are well illustrated by the provisions of this Act. They made it a criminal offence to write, print, utter, publish, or cause, procure, or willingly and knowingly help anyone to write, print, or publish, any false, scandalous, and malicious writing against the Government or against the Senate or the House or the President, with intent to defame or to bring them into contempt or disrepute, or to excite against them the hatred of the good people of the United States, or to stir up sedition or to excite any unlawful combination to resist, oppose, or defeat any statute of the United States or act of the President. The punishment to be inflicted was a fine of two thousand dollars and imprisonment for not more than two years.[1] As has been well said: "Had the Federalist Congressmen assembled in caucus and debated by what means they could make themselves more hated than they had ever been before — by what means they could destroy their present power, they could not by any possibility have found a means so efficient as the law against libellous and seditious writing. From the day the bill became law, the Federal party went steadily down to ruin. . . . What, asked the Republican newspapers, is a libel? A libel is whatever a Federal President, Marshal, Judge and Grand Jury choose to make it. The President orders the prosecution. The process goes out in his name. He appoints the Marshal. The Federal Judges are named by the President. Does any man hope for an impartial trial before such a tribunal as this?"[2] Moreover, in many of the States jurors were not drawn by lot, but were selected by the Marshal. Under such a system there was nothing to prevent political trials and political proscription under judicial forms — the worst type of tyranny.

[1] The bill as it passed the Senate was even more extreme in its provisions, as follows: "If any person shall by any libellous or scandalous writing, printing, publishing, or speaking, traduce or defame the Legislature of the United States, by seditious or inflammatory declarations or expressions, with intent to create a belief in the citizens thereof that the said Legislature in enacting any law was induced thereto by motives hostile to the Constitution or liberties and happiness of the people thereof; or shall, in manner aforesaid, traduce or defame the President of the United States or any Court or Judge thereof, by declarations tending to criminate their motives in any official transaction."

[2] *History of the People of the United States*, by John Bach McMaster, vol. II.

Naturally, Dr. Ames was hotly opposed to this Gag Act, and he recorded in his Diary his opinion of the Member of Congress from his district who voted for it, Joseph B. Varnum:

> *June 26.* Gen. Lloyd brought in a bill defining treason and for publishing sedition, etc., the boldest traitor of any! Who is he? . . . The greatest crime a public agent for a district of the sovereign people can commit is to abuse the confidence reposed in him, by acting directly contrary to the Constitution and combining to bind the speech and presses of his constituents against complaining of that very *abuse* of trust — to gag them by a pretended law, made by a wicked, self-created junto of conspirators, in that instance, as soon as they broke over the law sanctioned above all other laws — the very foundation on which common laws are built — the very frame of the whole building of the Government, which must fall in confused ruins when the corner posts or main beams, free speech and press, are so violently burst out.
>
> *July 11.* J. Varnum in Congress a turncoat, and is for war vs. France.

And at the end of his 1798 Diary, Ames, referring to a letter from Timothy Pickering, one of the most objectionable and hated of all Massachusetts Federalists, answered his arguments in behalf of the Gag Law thus: [1]

> I am every day more amazed at the growing insolence of our public Servants; they now make it a crime to address Government against gross violation of the supreme law of the land and other grievances! Had I not seen T. Pickering's letter to P. Johnston, Esq., of Prince Edward County, Virginia, in answer and refusal to present the address of the freeholders thereof to the President of the U. S., I should not have believed him so base, weak and insolent. This letter must fix him a base tool of the war faction in every impartial mind — an advocate for consolidation, for the voracious

[1] See letter of Timothy Pickering to P. Johnston, September 29, 1798, published in full in *Columbian Centinel*, October 17.

jaws of the barking Order to gulph down States and Sovereign at a swallow. He says: "They who complain of legal provisions for punishment of intentional defamation and lies, as bridling liberty of speech and of the press, may with equal propriety complain against laws made to punish assault and murder as restraints upon the freedom of men's action."

Why Timothy — nobody complains of such laws made by the proper legislators, our own State Assemblies; but we will always complain of usurpation, arrogance and treason, of pretended, self-created legislators and makers of such pretended laws, only to fence themselves against that responsibility to which we will hold our public servants attempting thus to gag us or to leap over the limits we have set them. The matter of legislation of our General Department is totally distinct from the matter of legislation of our divisional departments, and we mean still to keep it so, and both subjects to Ourself, and responsible through speech and press, uncontrollable otherwise than by laws made by the proper department!

The Antifederalists, as soon as the Gag Law passed, flamed forth in attacks upon it. Some of the Antifederalist editors were, however, inclined to treat the new law with flippancy; and a Norfolk County paper with mock solemnity stated: "The people of New England are so strenuously desirous of putting the Sedition Bill into operaton that an honest magistrate in the vicinity of Quincy has committed a man to prison for saying John Adams was born with a shirt!!! Another man was apprehended for calling the President's dog a son of a b——h; but for want of sufficient proof was discharged!!!" This called forth a reply from the *Massachusetts Mercury*, entitled "Jacobinic Meanness," and referring to the "contemptible paragraph — published for the purpose of deceiving and irritating the simple, unsuspecting tillers of the earth who are remotely situated from the focus of intelligence. Who is there who will side with those who are capable of such dirty tricks?" Of another Jacobin opponent who attacked the Sedition Law in the *Chronicle*, the *Mercury* wrote demanding the indictment of "the seditious wretch whose vile declamation is addressed merely to the passions of the uninformed — the tocsin of treason." [1]

No case shows more clearly the wide scope of the Gag Law and the perils to free speech which that law constituted than the first prosecution begun under it. Of all the Jacobin politicians, perhaps no one was more detested by Federalists than Mathew Lyon, a Congressman from Vermont, a man of rough manners and scathing tongue — the "Vermont beast," as the *Centinel* ungracefully called him. Although many of his speeches had been undoubtedly libellous, and well warranted indictment even under the Common Law, he had hitherto escaped punishment. In July, 1798, however, the United States Government obtained an indictment against him under the new Gag Law in the Federal Circuit Court in Vermont, based largely on the following comparatively mild criticism of John Adams — a criticism which was mellifluous praise compared to many of the Federalist attacks on his "Jacobin" opponents:

As to the Executive, when I shall see the efforts of that power bent on the promotion of the comfort, the happiness, and accommodation of the people, that Executive shall have my zealous and uniform support; but whenever I shall, on the part of the Executive, see every consideration of the public welfare swallowed up in a continual grasp for power, in an unbounded thirst for ridiculous pomp, foolish adulation, and selfish avarice; when I shall behold men of real merit daily turned out of office, for no other cause than independency of sentiment; when I shall see

[1] See *Independent Chronicle*, July 19, 1798, commented sarcastically on in *Columbian Centinel*, July 24, 1798; *Massachusetts Mercury*, September 25, November 1, 1798.

men of firmness, years, abilities and experience discarded in their applications for office, for fear they possess that independence, and men of meanness preferred for the ease with which they take up and advocate opinions, the consequence of which they know but little of; when I shall see the sacred name of religion employed as a state engine to make mankind hate and persecute one another, I shall not be their humble advocate. . . . When we found him borrowing the language of Edmund Burke, and telling the world that, although he should succeed in treating with the French, there was no dependence to be placed on any of their engagements, that their religion and morality were at an end, that they would turn pirates and plunderers, and it would be necessary to be perpetually armed against them, though you were at peace — we wondered that the answer of both Houses had not been an order to send him to a madhouse. Instead of this, the Senate have echoed the speech with more servility than ever George III experienced from either House of Parliament.

For these and similar comments Lyon was convicted and sentenced to a fine of fifteen hundred dollars and four months' imprisonment. How simple and broad was the question left to the jury to decide under this extraordinary law is shown by the fact that the presiding Judge — William Paterson, a Justice of the Supreme Court of the United States — instructed the jury that all they had to find was the fact of the publication, and whether it was published "with intent of making odious and contemptible the President and Government, and bringing them both into disrepute." The Federalist newspapers throughout the country exulted over this conviction, the *Centinel* saying: "Justice, though late, is sure. May the good God grant that this may be the fate of every Jacobin — to use the words of the hero of Mount Independence — 'from the St. Croix to the St. Mary's and from the Atlantic Ocean to the Lake of the Woods.'" [1] Later the *Centinel* printed

[1] See *Columbian Centinel,* October 17, November 3, 1798.

a full report of the trial with this preface: "We feel confident our readers will wish to amuse themselves with the perusal of the particulars of the trial of a man whose name is companion with reproach, whose fate excites no pity, and his confinement no exultation." [1]

It was not to be expected that Dr. Ames would remain silent at this new display of "tyranny" from the "monarchic faction"; hence he is found, four days after the passage of the Gag Law, recording in his Diary:

> *July 20, 1798.* Because I decently exercise the right of speech and press, like an independent Republican, my friends fear for me, while I am in no danger of being hanged for treason!

While he was not likely to be "hanged for treason," the peppery Doctor soon found himself involved in one of the earliest criminal proceedings begun in the Federal Court in Massachusetts under the new statute.[2] This was the trial for sedition of one of Dr. Ames' own townsmen and associates, and arising from a very characteristic episode of the times. A favorite and harmless method of showing their antagonism to the obnoxious measures of the Adams administration was the erection by the Antifederalists of so-called "liberty poles" bearing denunciatory placards. An early instance was thus described in a Federalist paper: [3]

> Symptom of insurgency cured. A few days since in expectation of the immediate operation of the law for laying stamp duties, a number of Vermonters met at Wallingford, erecting a liberty pole, and used abusive language against Congress, the president, etc. A number of true republican federalists as-

[1] See *Columbian Centinel*, October 17, November 3, 1798.

[2] The first indictment found in Massachusetts under the Sedition Law was against Thomas Adams, publisher of the *Independent Chronicle*, in October, 1798.

[3] *Federal Gazette and Baltimore Advertiser*, January 31, 1799.

sembled soon after — a contest ensued; and the pole was cut down, burnt to ashes and scattered in the wind. A Bennington paper mentions that a spirit of insurgency similar to the above was rising in the back part of New York State.

These harmless liberty pole ebullitions aroused the Federalists to quite unwarranted fury and almost laughable apprehension; and the *Centinel* referred to them in the following extreme language: "We hear that on the road to Providence there are several poles hoisted, with the American cockade, and tar and feathers below. The men (brutes, rather) who could do this were certainly born to be slaves or to be hanged. An Eastern correspondent informs us that a gang of insurgents have erected a sedition pole at Vassalboro, and burnt the Alien and Sedition Laws. . . . The arm of Government ought to punish these Jacobins immediately to prevent the baneful consequences of civil commotion. The erection of these poles and the burning of the laws is an open insult to the Government of the people." [1] In Pennsylvania, the Federalists formed associations "to destroy the sedition poles" and cut down these "emblems of sedition." [2]   And as an incredible illustration of the superheated politics of this era, the mere erection of one of these poles in Dedham was magnified by the Government officials into a grave outbreak of "sedition and insurrection." Dr. Ames' native town was at this time strongly Antifederal by a majority of three to one. The Third Parish, in the west end of the town, quaintly known as Clapboardtree's Parish, was a

[1] *Columbian Centinel*, August 19, 1798. The *Alexandria Advertiser* (Va.), Dec. 21, 1798, printed a despatch from Augusta, Maine, saying: "The Sedition pole around the foot of which was burnt the alien and sedition acts recently erected in Vassalborough . . . by ignorant and misguided followers, disorganizers and revilers of our virtuous administration, on Thursday last met its merited fate . . . cut down, hewn in pieces, while the ringleader of the party stood trembling with fear."

[2] *Federal Gazette and Baltimore Daily Advertiser*, February 6, 1799.

hotbed of politics; its minister, Reverend Thomas Thacher, was addicted to introducing partisan topics into his sermons; and it is related that, on one occasion, a sermon of this nature having caused certain parishioners to rise and leave the church, "I see," said Thacher, "I have at least one apostolic gift — the powers to cast out devils." Of this Parish Fisher Ames wrote, December 7, 1798: "Dedham thrives in house and business, and our tradesmen are growing richer. I do not think we grow worse in sin and Jacobinism. Thacher's Parish is confessedly the worst. The south (Chickering's) is decidedly Federal; and the old Parish where I live is divided — the old are all Demos., the young chiefly Feds." In this Clapboardtree's Parish some of the young men became so stirred by the eloquence of one Brown, a travelling Antifederalist agitator, that they erected on one of the main roads a pole topped by a liberty cap, and containing the following inscription: "Liberty and Equality — No Stamp Act — No Sedition — No Alien Bills — No Land Tax — Downfall to the Tyrants of America — Peace and Retirement to the President — Long Live the Vice-President and the Minority — May Moral Virtue be the basis of Civil Government." These sentiments would seem to have been harmless, and certainly very far from constituting treason. The Federalist newspapers and the Government authorities, however, became much excited over this "outbreak of sedition." One paper called the liberty pole itself a "rallying point for the enemies of a Free Government;" another paper called it, even more emphatically, "a rallying point of insurrection and civil war;" the *Independent Chronicle*, for approving the liberty pole, was termed "a sink of sedition and infamy." After allowing the liberty pole to stand for a week, the Federal Government was stirred to take decided action, the United States Marshal being authorized by Dis-

trict Judge John Lowell "to demolish the above mentioned
Symbol of Sedition"; but "the honest zeal of the well-
disposed people of the neighborhood prompted them to
effect its destruction before the Marshal's arrival." The
Government did not stop with demolition of the pole; it
demanded a victim on whom to experiment with the new
Sedition Law. Accordingly, arrest was made of one of the
leading citizens, and a former selectman of the Town,
Benjamin Fairbanks, "a deluded ringleader, charged with
being an accessory in erecting this rallying point of insurrection and civil war;" and, as stated by the *Centinel*, this
"Dedham insurgent, such is the leniency of the Federal
Administration, was admitted to bail. In 1786, he would
have been committed to close goal." [1] At such an outrage
committed by Federalist "tyranny" Dr. Ames was, of
course, stirred to the bottom of his soul, and his Diary
thus voiced his indignation:

> *November 6, 1798.* Ben Fairbanks and others before Fed.
> Court. Benjamin Fairbanks, one of the richest farmers in
> Dedham, taken by S. Bradford, the Marshal of the High
> Fed. Court, with Gen. Eliot and a number of coadjutors, in
> pompous array of tyrant power, seized on suspicion and
> carried out of his own County to answer to charges solely
> within the jurisdiction of his own State laws and in courts
> of his own County — and held to the excessive bail of
> 4,000 dollars to answer to a tyrannic usurpation on our
> own Sovereign State!

The affair was regarded as of so much consequence that
Fisher Ames described it in great detail in letters to his
political friends. [2] To Christopher Gore, he wrote:

[1] *Columbian Centinel*, November 7, 10, 1798. See in general the Boston
papers of the day, and particularly *Massachusetts Mercury*, November 7, 9,
1798; and see also *Courier of New Hampshire*, November 10, 1798.

[2] See Fisher Ames to Christopher Gore, December 18, 1798; to Jeremiah
Smith, November 22, 1798; to Timothy Pickering, November 22, 1798.

One, David Brown, a vagabond ragged fellow, has lurked about in Dedham, telling everybody the sins and enormities of the Government. He had been, he said, in all the offices in all the States, and knew my speculating connection with you, and how I made my immense wealth. I was not in this part of the country, otherwise I should have noticed his lies — not to preserve my reputation, but to disarm his wickedness. Before I returned from my trip to the westward, he had fled, and a warrant to apprehend him for sedition was not served. He had, however, poisoned Mr. Thacher's Parish, and got them ready to set up a liberty pole, which was soon after actually done. The insult on the law was the cause of sending out the marshal with his warrant; but the Feds of Mr. Chickering's Parish had previously cut down the pole. . . . There is at least the appearance of tardiness and apathy on the part of Government, in avenging this insult on law. . . . The Government must display its power *in terrorem*, or if that be neglected or delayed, in earnest. So much irritable folly and credulity, managed by so much villainy, will explode at last, and the issue will be tried, like the ancient suits, by wager of battle.

To Jeremiah Smith, he wrote that Democrats "abound in Dedham, though the liberty pole is down. . . . The devil of sedition is immortal; and we, the saints, have an endless struggle to maintain with him." And to Timothy Pickering, he wrote that "the liberty pole in this town was cut down by some Federal young men of Dedham, who were attacked by the seditious. . . . One of the persons concerned in raising the pole, an opulent farmer, has been arrested and bound over. The deluded are awed by this measure, but the effect is not so great as their intemperance and folly merit. The powers of the law must be used moderately but with spirit and decision; otherwise great risk of disorders will be incurred."

Benjamin Fairbanks was bound over to the grand jury in June, 1799, and meanwhile David Brown, the instigator of the affair, was arrested in Andover in March, 1799, held in $4000 bail, and unable to furnish bail was taken to jail in Salem.[1] Indictments were found against both Fairbanks and Brown at the June session of the United States Circuit Court, and the cases came on for trial before Judge Samuel Chase, an Associate Justice of the United States Supreme Court. At first, both men determined to stand trial, but later changed their minds and pleaded guilty. "Fairbanks presented a paper to the Court in which he freely confessed his fault, stated that he had been present at the erection of the pole, but had been misled and had not known 'how serious an offence it was.' He protested that he was now fully sensible of his offence and in the future would try to conduct himself as a good citizen." As Fairbanks had been a former selectman and was a man of reputation and means, Fisher Ames himself, though declining to act as his counsel, made a plea to the Court for clemency. Dr. Ames recorded the result as follows:

> *June 7, 1799.* Ben Fairbanks retracts, pleads guilty; fine 5*s.* cost 10*s*, 5, & 6 hours prisonment.
> *June 8.* David Brown pleads guilty. Received two illegal summons to the High Fed. Circuit Court.
> *June 9.* In at High Fed. Court.

David Brown did not get off with so light a sentence. It appeared that he was a man under fifty years of age, a native of Connecticut, a laboring man, and a former Revolutionary soldier, who had wandered about over most of the States of the Union, in the last few years, engaged in preaching and writing politics. It appeared also that he had considerable information about Massachusetts towns; but Judge Chase sought, without avail, to elicit from him the names of persons who aided or prompted him or who

---

[1] See long despatch from Salem as to "Brown, the Jacobin," in *Oracle of the Day*, April 6, 1799; and in *Federal Gazette and Baltimore Daily Advertiser*, April 9, 1799.

intended to subscribe to his writings. The heavy sentence imposed by the Judge was thus described in the *Centinel*: "Brown, the insurgent, who was lately checked in sowing sedition in the interior country, having plead guilty at his indictment before the Circuit Court, was yesterday sentenced to 18 months' imprisonment, and a fine of 480 dollars." And, as stated in the *Independent Chronicle*: "Judge Chase, previous to declaring the sentence of the Court, made some very impressive observations to Brown on the nature, malignity and magnitude of his offenses; on the vicious industry with which he had circulated and inculcated his disorganizing doctrines and impudent falsehoods, and the very alarming and dangerous excesses to which he attempted to incite the uninformed part of the community." [1] To the reader of today who examines Brown's pamphlets and his remarks when the indictments were found, the allegedly seditious language used seems little more than ordinary partisan political talk. Brown, in fact, was hardly more than an illiterate political crank.

To the panic-stricken Government authorities, however, Brown's manuscripts were "replete with the most malig-

---

[1] For full accounts of the trial, see *Virginia Argus* July 2, 1799, and *Independent Chronicle*, June 13, 17, 20, 1799.

The sentence imposed on Brown was the heaviest ever imposed under the Sedition Law. In July, 1800, after having been in jail 16 months, including the period while awaiting trial, he addressed a petition to President Adams, who was then at Quincy, asking for a pardon but it was refused. The term for which he was sentenced was up in December, 1800, but he was not released as he could not pay the fine and the costs. On February 5, 1801, he addressed a second and very pathetic petition to Adams, setting forth the long period he had been in jail, and that on account of his poverty there was no prospect that he would ever be released, unless the fine should be remitted. Shortly after Jefferson became President, a third petition was sent. That petition was not necessary for Jefferson had already granted a full pardon, March 12, 1801. Brown thus actually remained in prison fully two years, and was altogether the most grievous sufferer from the penalties of the Sedition Law. See "The Enforcement of the Alien and Sedition Laws," by Frank M. Anderson, *Amer. Hist. Ass. Report* (1912), pp. 122–125.

nant and perverse misrepresentations of the views and measures of the Government of the United States. . . . All the means which a vicious ingenuity could suggest appear to have been used by him to create discontent and to excite among the people hatred and opposition to their Government." [1] The extravagant fears aroused by Brown may be seen in a letter published at this time in a Salem Federalist paper: [2]

There is now on foot a plan of the Jacobins, which they are pursuing everywhere with the most indefatigable industry, to have a majority in our next Legislature, who will favour the views of France, and the Virginia and Kentucky Resolutions calculated to that object. Already one, Brown, is now in our jail committed for seditious conduct to accomplish such purposes; and from most respectable authority I am assured the plan is assiduously pursuing by the disorganizing agents in every county in the Commonwealth, and there is much fear they will in many instances accomplish their ends.

It would have been surprising if, in the midst of all these exciting events affecting his native town, Dr. Ames had been a mere spectator. Nor was he. His Diary is silent as to his own participation in the affair; nevertheless, as a staunch Jacobin, not only was he in touch with Brown's actions in the Third Parish, and with the erection of the liberty pole, but it is probable that he himself was the author of the "seditious" inscription on the pole. [3] He was one of the witnesses summoned to testify in the Circuit Court at Brown's trial in June; but he failed to attend, on the ground that the summons was insufficiently served. For this alleged contempt he was arrested in October and

---

[1] See *Independent Chronicle*, January 13. See also January 20, 1799.

[2] *Salem Gazette*, March 29, 1799.

[3] This fact did not appear until thirteen years later, apparently — see *Columbian Centinel*, August 3, 1811.

taken before the Court; his own account is graphic and indignant:[1]

> *Oct. 22.* Carried to Circuit Court, prisoner, and fined 8 for contempt pretended by J. Davis. I was not legally summoned and had not time to attend. I am, by Homans, by special warrant from Fed. Court, carried without warning to Boston before Circuit Court, delivered to Sam Bradford, the Marshal, like a felon, for pretended contempt of its process that I am not guilty of; and am, by instigation of John Davis fined by Court, Cushing and Lowell, 8 dollars, then the Marshal, taking me off to gaol. I obtain liberty to address a request to Court for copies of any papers out of the Clerk's office, which they refuse me, altho' I offer to pay the price of copies. Davis said he was afraid I should make a bad use of them. I have more reason to suppose that Tiptoe novel Courts will become like the Inquisition by secreting their process and dark arbitrary vexations — the citizens ought to know how they proceed, but they yet fear the public eye. I was set among pickpocks at the Bar and was spunged of 8 dollars.
>
> *Nov. 13, 1799.* Judge Cushing here, refuses redress for gross injury and adds insult by referring me to F. A.

Three years later Dr. Ames was still hot with ire at his treatment by the "High Fed. Court," and recorded in his Diary at the end of the year 1802:

> It was on 21st, 22d October, 1799, I was seized by the Marshal of High. Fed. Court, carried prisoner to Boston for contempt. W. Cushing, J. Lowell, on bench, and pert, sputtering John Davis, Attorney, charged me with intended contempt, for court to fine at discretion, for that I did not obey illegal summons to give evidence as to David Brown according to process.

This whole episode throws a curious light upon the extreme sensitiveness of the Federalists, and the panic-

[1] John Davis (later United States District Judge) was United States District Attorney and a Federalist in politics. The Judges were William Cushing, one of the Justices of the Supreme Court of the United States, and District Judge John Lowell, both Federalists.

stricken condition of the officials of the Adams administration.

While the good doctor and his Jacobin associates in Dedham were experiencing personally the rigors of the Federal Gag Law, criminal prosecutions for seditious libel were being initiated under this statute throughout the country for the erection of both liberty poles and liberty trees, as well as for newspaper publications and private utterances of attack upon Government measures. "How changeable are the opinions of men," wrote the *Independent Chronicle*. "Some twenty years ago, a flagstaff surmounted with the American standard was called a Liberty Pole and was approved and cherished by Government. Now they are called Sedition Poles and discountenanced and suppressed by Government. It is true, in '75, the British Government destroyed the poles as the rallying posts of sedition and rebellion; but they were tyrants for so doing. And it is true that in '98, the American Federal Government did the same; but they were not tyrants for doing it, for the Sedition Law forbids our calling them so." On the other hand, a Federalist correspondent in the same paper wrote that: "Liberty Poles were raised by a shallow, deluded set whom artful rogues had set on and then left in the lurch. Every reflecting person will be sorry that except in the case of David Brown and Matthew Lyon, the law has not dragged these plotters of mischief out of their hiding places." [1] The actual number of persons arrested under the Gag Law was about twenty-five, of whom eleven were actually brought to trial and convicted. Among them were Anthony Haswell of the *Vermont Gazette*, Thomas Adams of the *Independent*

---

[1] *Independent Chronicle*, January 17, 1799, giving an account of the planting of a liberty tree with a motto on it at Bridgehampton, N. Y. See *Ibid.*, February 28, July 22, August 19, 1799.

Chronicle, Benjamin F. Bache of the *Aurora*, Charles Holt
of the *New London Bee*, William Duane of the *Aurora*, and
James T. Callender of the *Richmond Examiner*.[1] Most of
the publications (with the exception of those by Callender)
for which these convictions were obtained could be termed
seditious only by the broadest possible construction of
that word. Every political campaign in this country, and
especially in modern times, has furnished examples of far
more extreme attacks upon existing administrations. The
Federalists, however, were determined to stop every form
of criticism of the Government; and they found in this
statute a ready instrument. It is interesting to recall that
when members of the Federalist party in New England
during the War of 1812 were indulging in seditious (if not
treasonable) attacks upon President Madison, their opponents lamented the lack of a Federal statute under
which prosecutions might be brought and pointed out the
fact that the Sedition Act of 1798 was not so much objectionable as a law as in the manner in which it was applied by too facile juries.[2]

[1] See articles on these prosecutions, in *Virginia Argus*, May 9, 13, June 10,
13, 1800; and see also accounts of arrests of New York editors in *Guardian of
Freedom* (Frankfort, Ky.) July 31, September 4, 1798.

[2] Matthew Carey, an Antifederalist, writing in *The Olive Branch* in November, 1814, while admitting that he had been among the opponents of the Sedition
Act, stated that it was, in fact, "a measure not merely defensible, but absolutely
necessary and indispensable towards the support of the Government"; and that
"as it requires an extraordinary degree of corporeal sanity to resist the effects of
a violent epidemical disorder; so it requires great strength of mind to keep out of
the vortex of factious contagion when prevalent with those whose opinions are
generally congenial with our own; of this strength of mind the writer was destitute, in common with a large portion of his fellow citizens." "It would be un-
candid not to state," he wrote, "that the trials under this Act. . . . were managed with very considerable rigour, and from the abuse of the law tended to give
an appearance of propriety and justice to the clamour against it. The cases of
Thomas Cooper and Matthew Lyon were both treated with remarkable severity
and excited a high degree of sympathy in the public mind. . . . But the censure
did not attach to the law. It lay at the door of the juries."

Dr. Ames' comments on some of these criminal prosecutions and intervening events were characteristic:

Oct. 14, 1798. Lyon of Vermont prosecuted on Sedition Act, fined 1500 dollars and 4 months' imprisonment.

Oct. 24. T. Adams, printer of the *Chronicle*, indicted in High Federalist Court, William Patterson, judge.

Nov. 7. Devil reigns in Vermont. Judges and Justices all turned out office for not returning back to Britain.[1]

Nov. 10. Buonaparte and French fleet again taken by Ben Russell's beloved Britons.

Nov. 30. Hand bills again killing, for 4th or 5th time, Tyger Buonaparte, 9 times not yet.

Feb. 4, 1799. Lyon free from Bastile.

Feb. 21. Lyon's imprisonment ended, takes seat in Congress.

Feb. 23. Lyon and Logan are feasted at Philadelphia and endeared to all the People of the United States, tho' abused in Congress.

Feb. 28. More sedition. Editor of *Chronicle's* bookkeeper indicted on Judge Dana's charge in State Court and tried March 1st, continued to 4th, while editor himself is indicted in Federal Court for same crime of sedition. Two Sovereigns hold of *Chronicle* printer, and now Abijah, said bookkeeper, is found guilty of publishing only.[2]

March 7. Two Sovereigns gripe the *Chronicle* at once for warning us to watch our public servants.

Sept. 30, 1799. Charles Holt, editor of the *Bee* at New London, about last of this month seized, carried to Hartford out of his own County before a strange tribunal to answer to charge solely within jurisdiction of his own County Court. He had finely suggested how apropos for the adulterous Commander to allure giddy youth to the new levies by telling them that "they would have nothing to do but to eat,

[1] See *Jeffersonian Democracy in New England* (1916) by William A. Robinson, for account of this action in Vermont.

[2] Abijah Adams was indicted for publishing an article in the *Chronicle* charging the Legislature of Massachusetts with having violated their oaths. The indictment was based on the Common Law, and not on the Federal Statute, and was found in the Massachusetts Supreme Court — see interesting reviews of the trial in the *Independent Chronicle*, from April 8 to April 29, 1799.

drink and play with the girls!" Treason now triumphant
here! ! ! Liberty of speech and of press are both abridged.
April 9, 1800. Thomas Cooper, an attorney and man of curious learning who hath published in England five tracts
ethical, political, etc., before High Federalist Court at
Philadelphia for a true and important address to his fellow
citizens of Northampton County, is fined 400 dollars and 6
months prison. Sundry other prosecutions! Sedition and
Treason against Usurpers! ! !

Meanwhile, the opposition to the Sedition Act was not
confined to individuals. Some States began to feel that
not only was this Act unjust and tyrannical, but that it was
absolutely beyond the power of Congress to enact and
therefore unconstitutional, as not being within the authority delegated by the States to the Federal Government.[1]
Although the defence of unconstitutionality whenever set
up in the various criminal cases had been uniformly overruled by Federal Judges, a movement was now set on
foot to obtain the opinion of the State Legislatures on the
point. Thomas Jefferson suggested to George Nicholas
of Kentucky that that State should join with Virginia in a
formal protest against these most obnoxious laws, the
Alien and Sedition Acts. Accordingly, a set of resolutions
was passed in Kentucky, November 14, 1798, and in Virginia, December 24, largely inspired by Jefferson. These
resolutions set forth in the boldest and most unmitigated
language the unconstitutionality of the Alien and Sedition

[1] The *Gazette of the United States*, February 8, 1799, published an advertisement in which the alien and sedition laws were warmly defended as follows:
"This Day Published and For Sale at this Office The Essays under the signature
of Virginiensis on the Alien and Sedition Laws (price 25 cents 12 mo.). It is perhaps futile to expect to work conviction in the minds of so inveterate and vicious
a class of men as the Democrats of America, by any arguments, however favorable, or any display of truth, however irresistible: these writings are, however,
calculated to produce a more important and useful effect, by placing the subject
in its true light, before honest men, who are uninformed, or have been misin-
formed as to the nature and objects of those bills."

Laws, and the right of a State to nullify any law passed by Congress in abuse of its delegated powers. These resolutions Dr. Ames, as might be expected, highly applauded in his Diary:

> *December 27, 1798.* Gov. James Garrard's speech and Resolves of Kentucky Legislature in *Chronicle* this day, masterly, sovereign, and pertinent lashing of Tiptoe Traitors in Congress.
>
> George F. Hopkins, printer of the *Spectator* at New York, Dec. 15, calls the Governor of the State of Kentucky "one Garrard" to black him for his excellent remarks on the Acts of the last session of Congress in his speech to the Legislature. I hope they will be published thro' the whole States. ... This editor's servility to the Federal Government is so mean and abusive of State authority as sinks him below public animadversion. Now all foreign disputes are absorbed by internal aggressions, usurpations, treasons! ! ! The free-spirited resolves of Kentucky and Virginia, with truth flashing thro' clouds of aristocrat delusion, have begun to stagger the people at the Westward, who have been made to foam with rage against the French, their benefactors. It is amazing to see the apathy of the people under worse usurpation that that which once excited them to war. Now they can patiently see the omnipotence of the British Parliament transferred to Congress, usurping all State jurisdiction retained by the Sovereign People in State Government.

When the Kentucky and Virginia resolutions were forwarded to the legislatures of the other States in the Union for their concurrence, the Federalist newspaper press at once began to volley against them. The *Columbian Centinel* wrote of them as the work of "Gallic jackals who have contemplated in the ancient Dominion a servile colony of the faithless Republic, France," and said that "the Virginia Resolutions in conjunction with several late measures leave no doubt but the object of the Virginia demagogues is to bring on a quarrel between the ancient

Dominion and the Union — and it must come to an issue
whether the Union or Virginia shall govern." [1] Fear of the
dominance of Virginia had always absorbed the mind of
Fisher Ames; and he now wrote: "Virginia, excited by
crazy John Taylor, is fulminating its manifests against the
Federal Government. . . . The General Court [of Massa-
chusetts] is convened and are not in the humour of falling
in with the rage of Virginia." [2] As to the Alien and Sedition Acts themselves, he wrote: [3]

When the despatches from our Envoys were published here,
the Jacobins were confounded, and the trimmers dropt off from
the party, like windfalls from an apple-tree in September. . . .
The wretches looked round, like Milton's devils when first re-
covering from their too stunning fall from Heaven to see what
new ground they could take. The alien and sedition bills and the
land tax were chosen as affording topics of discontent, and, of
course, a reviewal of the popularity of the party. The meditated
vengeance and the wrongs of France done by our treaty were
less spouted upon. And the implacable foes of the Constitution
— foes before it was made, while it was making and since — became full of tender fears lest it should be violated by the alien
and sedition laws. . . . The *Salus Reipublicae* so plainly requires
the power of expelling or refusing admission to aliens, and the
rebel Irish and negroes of the West Indies so much augment the
danger, that reason, one would think, was disregarded by the
Jacobins too much to be perverted. Kentucky is all alien; and
we learn that Governor Garrard has made a most intemperate
address to the Legislature of that State, little short of a mani-
festo. This is said to be echoed by the Legislature. . . . John
Marshall, with all his honors in blossom and bearing fruit,
answers some newspaper queries unfavorably to these laws.
George Cabot says that [Harrison Gray] Otis, our Representative, condemns him *ore rotundo*, yet, inconsistently enough,
sedulously declares his dislike of those laws. G. C. vindicates

[1] See *Columbian Centinel*, January 23, 30, 1799.
[2] Ames to Gore, December 18, 1798.
[3] Ames to Gore, January 11, 1799.

J. M. and stoutly asserts his soundness of Federalism. I deny
it. No correct man — no incorrect man even — would give his
name to the base opposers of laws, as a means for its annoyance.
This he has done. Excuses may palliate — future zeal in the
cause may partially atone — but his character is done for. . . .
False Federalists, or such as act wrong from false fears, should be
dealt hardly by, if I were Jupiter Tonans.

The doctrines of the Virginia-Kentucky resolutions were
vigorously rejected by the Federalist-controlled legislature
of Massachusetts, the Senate voting against them with
only one dissenting vote (John Bacon of Berkshire) — "a
proceeding," said the *Centinel*, "which will exist an ever-
lasting record of the wisdom, patriotism and enlightened
policy of the present times. . . . Indeed, he who doubts
the rectitude of such principles must be worse than an
infidel." [1] The opposite view, however, was presented
with amusing force in Dr. Ames' Diary:

> *Feb. 8, 1799.* Massachusetts Senate, except Bacon, basely
> yield our most important rights to High Fed. Gov't. and
> degrade the State, stript of its glory by approving of the
> Alien & Sedition Law of Congress, so as really to have no
> recognizance as Legislators but of swine and alewives!
> And on 9th February '99, in Massachusetts Senate on Vir-
> ginia Resolves, Hon. John Bacon of Stockbridge's sole Nay
> on question for rejecting them, makes a most excellent
> speech against said Sedition Bills, etc., and all arbitrary,
> unconstitutional acts of Congress, whereupon I with thou-
> sands congratulate him; and on 20th received his polite
> answer to my letter by the hand of Rev. Mr. Sanford. . . .
> Although ever since our ancestors at Plymouth ceased to
> be their own Legislators and we are forced to confide our
> dearest rights to public trustees, we daily see or shut our
> eyes and won't see that confidence abused or shamefully
> forfeited; and among the black list of abuses of public trust
> is that of Massachusetts on the 12th.

[1] See *Columbian Centinel*, February 16, 1799; see also February 20, 1799.
See also *American Historical Review*, vol. v, pp. 58, 225.

April 7. I am astonished to find that I am probably elected
Senator, when my business will so little bear it; it is so announced in the *Gazette.* The seat must be *cleaned* or I cannot sit there, after the foul 12th February last.

The rejection of the resolutions, and also of a resolve requesting the repeal of the Alien and Sedition Laws by the
House of Representatives in Maryland, called forth the
following from Dr. Ames: "Is their House made of Lawyers also? Fatal change or delusion of America from 1775
time. These Kentucky Resolutions are grand! and must
prevail when the people come to their senses again!"

The rejection by Congress of a bill to repeal the Sedition
Act aroused Dr. Ames to the following dire predictions of
civil war:

It is enough to make old Patriots sick of life to see with what
high hand the new riders brandish their whips and fetters
over their dozy Sovereign! See Congressional proceedings
of the House, 17 Jan. 1799. While whole States remonstrate against their acts — the People amazed, aghast, some
petrified with fear — others suffering in gaol or under excessive bonds to answer unto charges in strange tribunals
out of their own counties — Civil War threatening all over
U. S. drown foreign disputes. But the people must wake at
last. Such reiterated insolence of the British Junto cannot
long be borne. Asses would resist such jibes and goads. Our
quondam servants of the Sovereign States, by gagging our
mouths and licensing our presses, strive to prevent that
scrutiny into their usurpations and treason that must sink
them, unless screened from responsibility by such terrific
Acts.

The fiery doctor was so indignant at "the wretches who
would gag us" that he took the pains, "in order to stigmatize the traitors," to mark the names in the printed list of
Congressmen appearing in the current almanac, as follows: "Thinking it important to perpetuate the stigma of

the Traitors in Congress Feb. 25, 1799, on the myriads of
petitions for repeal of Sedition, Alien, and other unconstitutional acts, those against repeal are marked T in this
Register List, and those for repeal P as good patriots."
And he recorded with enthusiasm the discovery of the
printed report of a trial and acquittal, in old Colonial
days, of a newspaper editor for seditious libel — the famous Zenger trial in New York in 1735, in which the
liberty of the press was so valiantly and successfully defended against the contentions of the royal Governor and
Attorney-General:

> A narrative of the trial of John Peter Zenger, a Printer of the
> *Weekly Journal* at New York in 1734 or 5 for sedition,
> printed by Thomas Fleet at Boston in   being found
> among the lumber of Joseph Metcalf, deceased of Dedham,
> being seen and read by the people of Dedham, they are so
> smitten with the true picture of present proceedings under
> the Sedition Bill of the Junto of public conspirators, when
> sundry good and peaceable citizens in various parts of U. S.
> are prosecuted before strange tribunals out of their own
> county, in many instances for charges solely within juris-
> diction of their own County Courts, and with the glorious
> defence of old Andrew Hamilton, a volunteer gentleman of
> the law from Philadelphia refusing any fee, that now in
> February '99, they subscribe lavishly to have it printed —
> and Deacon Bullard telling of two men who would subscribe
> for 100 each, if they on sight find it worthy, I carried it to
> them. They like it much, but fail of their promises, as I
> foretold they would.

One of the other laws of the Adams administration extremely objectionable to all good Antifederalists was the
famous Logan Act, occasioned by the visit which Dr.
George Logan of Philadelphia had paid to Paris in the
summer of 1798, in an effort to enlighten the French officials as to the attitude of the United States and to convince

them that there was no political party which would give aid and assistance to France in case of the opening of hostilities between the two nations. The Logan Act made criminal any interposition of private individuals in any controversy between the United States and a foreign country. Dr. Ames' sympathies with Logan were shown in the following entry:

> *Dec. 21, 1798.* . . . It is astonishing to consider the mean servility to which a war party in this country can stoop in favor of Britain against our benefactors the French. Now, because Dr. Logan has lately been to France, and has done more than the President with all his tiptoe envoys to avert war with sister Republic — and it is suspected that Jefferson privately sent him — it inexpressibly mortifies Administration and the war party to lose the honor heaped on Jefferson and Logan for their adroitness in extricating the country from such expense of blood and treasure. While the people bless them, the Lawyers and seekers of offices are trying to blast them; but now the people of Philadelphia have completed Logan's triumph by electing him into the House of Representatives of Pennsylvania — and ere long I expect he will be raised higher, if civil war don't take place.

> *January 1, 1799.* Griswold's motion to extend Sedition Act beyond this country. Nicholas, Gallatin, etc., as if divinely inspired, thunder against it with irresistible argument and reason, justify Logan's services, etc.; but argument is lost on Harper, Rutledge and other tyrants or tools of tyrant power! But, at same time, Southern States will not concur in Massachusetts' amendment to exclude Gallatin, etc., from seats in Congress as foreigners.

> *January 2.* Aristocrats in Congress trying to extend Sedition Act to other countries, tho' Nicholas for its total repeal — 58 for, 37 against.

In contrast, Fisher Ames wrote to Gore, January 11, 1799: "By looking at Congress, you will see that the French faction there is no better than formerly. Gallatin and Nicholas vindicate Logan's mission very boldly. The country where such abominations as they utter can be even tolerated is to be tried and purified in the furnace of affliction."

The proclamation issued by President Adams on March 6, 1799, recommending the observance of April 25, "as a day of solemn humiliation, fasting and prayer," and that "the citizens on that day abstain as far as may be from their secular occupations," elicited much Jacobin criticism; and Dr. Ames recorded:

> *April 10, 1799.* Proclamation for political Fast thro' U. S. Many people provoked thereat. People of Dorchester, it is said, intend to work on highways that day, 25th inst. Others say they'll take no notice of it. But curiosity to hear the political drum draws people against their intentions — but at Dover one, Bacon, was ploughing near the Meeting house, while others heard the drum at Charlestown half the people left meeting, one telling the minister [Jedidiah] Morse there was no truth in what he said.

Still another measure of the Adams administration met with violent and active opposition from Dr. Ames. Before the passage of the Alien and Sedition Acts, the Federal Congress had enacted several laws equally obnoxious to the people. The Act providing for the raising of an army of fifteen thousand men, to be placed under command of General Washington to repel French attack, was an especial object of attack by Antifederalists, who declaimed against "the pernicious tendency of mercenary troops," and held that "a militia may justly be called the Pillars of a Republic, while a standing army is properly called the 'caterpillars.'" [1] To this Act Dr. Ames referred on June 3, 1798: "Standard, and beating for army in peace. Capt. Tolman and Lieut. Gardner here on recruiting service in

[1] See *Independent Chronicle*, October 31, 1798.

time of peace." Still more objectionable were the statutes imposing new taxes. As to the tax on notes, bonds, certificates, etc., Dr. Ames wrote, July 1, 1798: "Stamp Act crammed down by imps of Britain." As to the assessment of the Federal tax on houses, which, though comparatively light in amount, was regarded as especially oppressive because of its method of imposition, the tax being in part calculated according to the amount of window glass in each house, Dr. Ames' Diary recorded his stiff-necked views, as follows: [1]

> *December 2, 1798.* New occasions to pity the weakness of human nature. Seeing N. Kingsberry, etc., accept assessment foreign tax! ! ! In Milton, December, I am informed they have begun to take the valuation of houses and land under Act of Congress, and Col. Jon. Vose refused them admittance to his house, for that Congress have no authority to take a Valuation, but only to lay direct taxes according to numbers, which implies such tax shall be assessed and collected under State Authority and town privileges of choosing our own Assessors and Collectors without consolidation by having them fixed perpetual and inexorable over us to increase Executive influence by infinite multiplication of officers — but Might will overcome Right.
>
> *January, 1799.* House and land tax of Congress goes on heavily, causing great uneasiness. Some refuse and then to avoid the penalty have to conform. No assessor in Dedham will yet take office but N. Kingsberry, Esq. Silent indignation hath not yet exploded — tho' hard threatened. I fear civil war must be the result of Government measures. But now, January 20, I hear that Nehemiah Fales and Oliver

---

[1] That the tax did not in fact fall with any hardship on Massachusetts may be seen from the following figures. In that State, in December, 1799, there were 50,449 dwelling houses, of which 18,733 were appraised for taxing as of a value of not over $100; 38,771 from $100 to $500; 7409 from $500 to $1000; 3378 from $1000 to $3000; about 900 from $3000 to $30,000; and only one over $30,000. The tax on these was as follows: for a house valued at $500, $1; at $1,000 $3; at $2000, $8; at $4000, $20. As to opposition to these taxes, see *Independent Chronicle*, January 10, 14, 17, 21, 28, March 29, August 23, 1799.

Guild of Dedham have taken and begun to officiate as understrappers tools to the Perpetual Assessors to number and measure houses for High Fed. Government. Their names ought to be execrated by all Posterity.

But possibly, seeing many will accept, and do, in other towns that have been most bitter against the arbitrary British influence, for the sake of the pay accept, it may be an easement not to be assessed by strangers, if any of our own people will submit to the infamy of the office.

January 23, 1799. Called on by Nehemiah Fales for dimensions of my house and windows, and list of land for direct tax of High Federalist tyrant Government. I introduce it thus:

"Nat. Ames (regretting the short dawn of rational liberty under the Confederation — deploring the blindness and apathy of that People who once dared to defy and trample on the minions of foreign tyrants, only to be trampled on by domestic traitors, in impudent junto, breaking the limits of their Sovereign — greeted with the tyrant songs of 'Energy of the Government' — 'Tighten the Reins of Government,' only to stifle the cheering sound of the great Sovereign's voice — forced to yield, instead of to Law, to the mighty powers that be), exhibits this list and description of his house and land on the first day of October, 1798:

" 1 Dwelling House 40 feet long — two stories high — 30 feet wide — glass, etc. — 198 feet glass — 453 squares.

" 1 Barn, 24 × 35. 7¾ acres Lot and Bog Meadow. Woodland, 10 acres Rocks and Bushes. 1 corn house 10 feet square."

January 29. The great Sovereign grumbles at unconstitutional tax.

June 1, 1800. My direct High Fed. tax — House $5.60; other estate $1.43– $7.03.

In other parts of the country, the opposition to these taxes was not confined to the filing of written objections. In Pennsylvania, the collection of the tax led to an armed resistance known as the Fries Insurrection. One of the active participants, John Fries, an ignorant countryman, was arrested by the Federal troops and was tried in the United States Circuit Court. A verdict of guilty was set aside owing to proof of prejudice in a juryman, and a new trial was held before Justice Samuel Chase of the United States Supreme Court. Fries was again found guilty, and was sentenced to death, but was pardoned by President Adams on the day before the date set for his execution. The generally oppressive nature of the proceedings stirred the Antifederalists, all over the United States, to a high pitch of indignation. It seemed to them simply another example of the tyranny of Adams and his "myrmidons." Dr. Ames made these characteristically vigorous entries:

April 30, 1799. Expressing my regret at the Northampton pretended insurrection, as giving a pretext for a standing army of mercenaries, who at command of their leader will shed brothers' blood — "I am glad of it," says a Dedham High Fed., "and now McPherson's Blues will soon dish them up!" And now we see the effects of a standing army in time of peace.

May 10, 1799. Fries, after nine days' trial before the Federal Court, found guilty of treason, only for joining the old woman in Northampton County who poured hot water on the base assessor attacking her windows. Because Philadelphia is a great way off, we seem little affected at his condemnation. If opposing unconstitutional laws is worthy of death, what are those worthy of who break down the great paramount law, the Constitution itself? Why, a standing army is provided to guard great traitors against the just rage of an insulted Sovereign! What pity we are not provided with a great National Court and perpetual National jury from all the States to sit at this time a hundred leagues from Philadelphia, and McPherson's Blues, to make great traitors tremble! And I have applied for the names of the jurors on Lyon's and the two Adams' trials under the Gag bill; and wish to record the names of all jurors that can consider the Gag bill a law of the land!

May 25. It is amazing to see with what patience the people swallow every trick of the tyrant — Harper's justification of McPherson's troops on the hot water expedition. Harper confirms the account of the outrage.

May 23, 1800. Hot water insurrection ends today by death of Fries. Hainan and Getman to be hanged — but, since, they are pardoned. Good deed of Adams, to pardon resisters of unconstitutional acts!

V

JAIL BREAKERS AND JACOBINS

THE preceding chapters have shown to how great an extent the newspapers were responsible for the embittered political dissensions which rent this country in the later years of the eighteenth century. Their continuous outpourings of political venom heightened and emphasized party differences, blackened the character, and aspersed the intents, of the purest citizens, and even promoted deeds of violence. Editors and newspaper correspondents alike attributed the basest of motives to all party opponents and invented political bases for events far removed from politics. A singular and extreme instance of this practice by the press occurred in 1801, in connection with the noted Fairbanks murder case in Dedham — a case with which Dr. Ames was connected both as a witness at the trial and as a physician attendant on the murderer, and which he noted in his Diary as follows: [1]

> *May 18, 1801.* Betsy F——s found horribly wounded in 11 places, lived half an hour. Jason Fairbanks with throat cut and other wounds lives.
>
> *May 20.* Betsy F——s buried, greatest funeral procession I ever saw.
>
> *May 21.* Jason Fairbanks imprisoned for murder of Betsy F——s, carried in litter.
>
> *Aug. 4.* S. J. C. Went before Grand Jury in case of murder of Betsy F——s.
>
> *Aug. 6.* Jason Fairbanks trial for murder begun this morning when he receives sentence, death! All eyes running but his

[1] The name of the murdered girl has been abbreviated in this transcript.

own. He appears stoical in firmness — his legs fettered according to custom as is said for condemned criminals.

Aug. 8. Jason Fairbanks receives sentence from Chief Justice Dana to be taken to prison from whence he came and from thence to the place of execution and there to be hanged by the neck until dead — "and may Almighty God have mercy on your soul," said the Judge in a sobbing voice. Vast concourse at trial, three days.

Aug. 17. Called at Gaol on Jason Fairbanks convict of murder.

As murder cases in 1801 were not as common as today, and as this murder of Miss Betsy F——s by Jason Fairbanks was attended by romantic circumstances which excited the sympathies of sentimentalists, the story of the girl's unhappy fate was spread over the country in broadsides, pamphlets, poems, and stories. Its impression on contemporary writers may be seen from the advertisements of the pamphlet entitled *The Trial of Jason Fairbanks*, issued in Boston in 1801, which stated it to be "without exaggeration, without the aid of fancy, one of the most awful catastrophies ever exhibited in real life in any age or country or sketched by the most excentric imagination of the most melancholy poet." The parties to this local tragedy were both of well-known old Dedham families. Fairbanks was a youth of about twenty-one, weak, sickly, with a stiff right arm, and the parents of Miss F——s had objected to his attentions to their daughter, a girl of finest character, described in a broadside issued at the time in the following flowery language: "In person, Miss F——s was a model which the pencil of Raphael might in vain endeavor to imitate. Elegance and symmetry in her form were blended: her luxuriant auburn hair flowed in graceful ringlets around her well turned shoulders: her neck and bosom might with alabaster vie: her taper waist, her glowing cheek, ring'd with the crimson blush of virgin modesty, displayed the most happy assemblage of the carnation and lilly that ever graced a mortal form."

The manner in which the newspapers then reported crimes is strikingly illustrated by the quaint language of the correspondent of the *Independent Chronicle* of May 21:[1]

Melancholy Catastrophe. Dedham, May 19. Yesterday about three o'clock in the afternoon, I was called with a great number of others to behold the most tragic, the most melancholy and heart-rending scene . . . perhaps that this historic page ever recorded, as a lesson of the mutability, the frailty and final dissolution of human nature. And though painful the task which devolves on me first to record, it is hoped it will not be received with any disrespect but a sympathetic effusion, with the parents and others more deeply interested in the melancholy transaction. A Mr. Jason Fairbanks, whose age is about 21 years and a Miss Elisabeth F——s, of respectable families both born and had lived near the center of this town, had for a considerable time entertained an attachment towards each other — But it seems some obstacles had been in their way either to an union in marriage or to a tranquil enjoyment of their courtship. They had this day met, it seems, by appointment in a thicket of bushes about 100 rods from her father's house where they had frequently met before, to come (as he says) to a final determination. What particulars here passed between them previous to the comission of the tragic acts are uncertain — but to the horror and consternation of her parents and to the sympathizing grief of every one susceptible to the passions of humanity, about the time of day above mentioned, he came to their house all reeking with blood and holding out at the same time a knife yet warm with the crimson, to some one of the family! — With which, he said, Eliza had killed herself, and that she then lay dead in the birches (pointing to the spot) and that he had attempted to do the same thing with himself but was unable! The amazement, the heart-

---

[1] The *Boston Gazette* published the same account on May 21, and the *New England Palladium* on May 22. The *Columbian Centinel* printed no account until five days after the murder, on May 23, when it presented about a quarter of a column, beginning: "A melancholy event occurred at Dedham on Monday last."

distracting anguish which seized on the parents, brothers, and sisters of the hapless victim, at such a sight and relation, can better be conceived than described. Her companion, though he had walked to the house, had his own throat cut with various stabs with the same knife in his breast, bowels, etc., yet this morning 8 o'clock (May 19) we hear he is still alive but in a most deplorable situation.

The Grand Jury heard the case on Tuesday, August 4, and presented an indictment on the next day, setting forth the crime in the curious and precise legal phraseology of the times: "The Jurors for the Commonwealth of Massachusetts on their oath present; that Jason Fairbanks of Dedham in the County of Norfolk, yeoman, not having the fear of God before his eyes but being moved and seduced by the instigations of the devil — with a certain knife of the value of ten cents, which he the said Jason Fairbanks in his right hand then and there had and held, the said Elizabeth F——s in and upon the fore part of the neck and in the throat of her the said Elizabeth F——s feloniously, wilfully and of his malice aforethought did strike, stab and thrust." At the request of the prisoner, two of the most eminent lawyers of the Massachusetts bar were assigned as his counsel — Harrison Gray Otis and John Lowell; Attorney-General James Sullivan appeared for the Commonwealth; and the case was tried before the highest court, the Supreme Judicial Court sitting in banc — Chief Justice Francis Dana, Robert Treat Paine, Thomas Dawes, and Simeon Strong. "This trial," said the *Centinel*, "has excited a great degree of interest and was attended at the opening by so numerous a concourse of people of both sexes that the Court found it necessary to adjourn from the Court to the Meeting House." [1]

[1] The *Boston Gazete* said, August 13: "The Court was accordingly opened in the Meeting-house, amidst a throng of anxious spectators never before witnessed in this place or perhaps on a like occasion in any other." The building in

As a contrast to modern murder cases, the case began on Thursday morning, August 6, at eight o'clock; the evidence was all in by Friday morning; counsel for the prisoner argued six hours; and the Attorney-General argued two hours, until nine o'clock at night; the judges instructed the jury until half past ten; the next morning, Saturday, the jury returned a verdict of guilty; and sentence of death was at once imposed upon the prisoner by the Chief Justice — the whole case thus occupying a little over forty-eight hours! The witnesses for the government numbered between thirty and forty, Dr. Nathaniel Ames being the first to be examined, and testifying to having been called to examine the corpse and the wounds upon it, as well as to having attended the prisoner, who had inflicted a number of serious wounds on himself. Others testified to the relations between the prisoner and the murdered girl, to threats made at various times by Fairbanks against the girl and her parents, to the borrowing by him of the penknife with which the act was done, and to the impossibility of the infliction by the girl herself of the wounds on her back, throat, and thumbs. Very little evidence was put in for the defendant, except to show his weak condition, and to discredit the sanity of the government's witnesses who testified as to threats. In their arguments, Fairbanks' counsel, Otis and Lowell, made elaborate appeals to sentiment, in order to raise a reasonable doubt in the jury's mind on the line of suicide instead of murder, described by the *Centinel* as follows: "His counsel defended him on the supposition that he and she were fond of each other — that they were both afflicted with adverse circumstances, and agreed severally to kill themselves —

which the trial was conducted was the present Unitarian church, situated on a small common adjoining the Courthouse, and not far from the houses of Nathaniel Ames and Fisher Ames.

that he lent her the knife for that purpose; but that when she had effectually used it, he was not so successful as she was." The *Boston Gazette* described the pleas of Otis and Lowell in most exaggerated language as "managed in a torrent of eloquence with all that ingenuity, sagacity and learning which the genius and wisdom of man could invent and perhaps unequalled, as is the crime, by anything of the kind in this or any other country." The Attorney-General then "closed with a masterly and pathetic plea," in which he pointed out at great length the evils of disobedience of their parents by the youth of the period, and the terrible results of a career of vice once entered upon. The jury having found the prisoner guilty, Chief Justice Dana then passed sentence of death upon him, addressing the prisoner, said the *Centinel*, "in terms spreading the heinousness of his crime before him and exhorting him to repentance; but he, as he always had been, apparently insensible — the only person in the whole assembly who was not affected at the ceremony of the scene. The judgment of the Court and the final verdict of the jury have received universal approbation." The *Gazette* moralized on the end of the trial, in this quaint fashion: "During this solemn, this painful and lengthy process, the aspect of the prisoner was observed to be remarkably uniform. Tears a number of times started into his eyes. Before his sentence, he wished to tell his story and to make remarks on the deposition of two of the witnesses against him. But after having been indulged with every other toleration and privilege which the law and the cause would possibly admit, he received his sentence with that stolid uniformity, both in action and countenance, which one would think must have produced a visible shock in the best or worst of dispositions. But he seemed the only one amidst a crowded assembly who remained insensible and unmoved at the solemnity of the scene. It is hoped this event, unprecedented in the annals of history or perhaps in the ages of the world, will have a suitable impression on the public, on the vast multitude who attended the trial, and especially that salutary effect on the minds of those youth whose dissoluteness of manners have so often led them astray."

If the case had stopped here, it would not have differed from many other very commonplace murder trials. Ten days later, however, events happened which enwrapped the case in a cloud of political passions, and made it famous throughout the country. The following entries in Dr. Ames' Diary narrated in brief a story which warrants more detailed description:

Aug. 17. Gaol broke by mob. Jason Fairbanks and others escaped.

Aug. 18. Bridges watched to catch Jason. Great rewards advertised.

Aug. 20. Bartholomew retaken. A thousand dollars advertised for Jason Fairbanks.

Aug. 21. Norfolk and Dedham doomed to destruction for escape of Jason Fairbanks.

T. Gay turned out from being Gaoler tho' now not faulty. All attention to J. Fairbanks.

Aug. 25. Examination of sundry gaol breakers held in Ct. House.

Aug. 28. Jason Fairbanks bro't back, retaken at Lake Champlain with Dukeham.

Aug. 29. Almost every man in Dedham sign an agreement to keep night watch at Gaol. Country kept in alarm by Jason Fairbanks' conduct and vast expense incurred.

Nat Davis, taken at Hartford, bro't to Dedham, charged with rescuing Jason Fairbanks in letter from Gov. Strong to Gov. Trumbull. Nat could have escaped but voluntarily surrendered.

Sept. 1. On night guard at Gaol, act by substitute.

Sept. 4. Nat Davis taken from Hartford on Governor Trumbull's warrant pursuant of request from Gov. Strong of

Massachusetts. And great parade making for Jason Fairbanks' execution by troops ordered to attend as not willing
to trust Dedham. People wrongly represented mobbish.

Sept. 10. Jason Fairbanks hanged. Great Common held more
people than ever were in Dedham before at once. He died
game i. e., unaffected. But I could not comply to see his
execution, though requested.

Sept. 11. Sudden alteration to cold. Supposed to be 10,000
people at execution.

Sept. 11. Chief Justice bails several rescuers of Jason Fairbanks. Some yet pretend to think Jason innocent.

This rescue of Fairbanks from the jail caused immense
excitement in the town. Active efforts to discover the jail-
breakers were at once taken, and the following curious
paper drafted by Fisher Ames was circulated, and signed
by most of the leading citizens:

The stain of blood is on the land. Jason Fairbanks the murderer has escaped. We cannot tell where to look for him. We must
look everywhere. Therefore we agree and submit to three things:

1. That our houses and premises shall be searched.

2. That we will give an account of ourselves and our inmates
during the night before and the day.

3. That we will exert ourselves in every manner to apprehend
the culprit and his accomplices.

No honest man's eyes must sleep in Dedham this night.

Dedham, Tuesday, 18th Aug., 1801.

A reward of $500 (afterwards increased to $1000) was
offered for the capture of Fairbanks;[1] and the Boston

[1] The advertisement of this reward read as follows:

"Broke open by the violence of a number of evil minded persons from without, on the night of the 17th inst., the Commonwealth gaol in Dedham and
escaped therefrom Jason Fairbanks, 20 years old, a Prisoner under sentence of
Death for murder. Said Fairbanks is rather of a light complexion, marked a little
with the small pox, near six feet high, slender made, dark hair, a stiff right arm
scarred near the elbow, downcast eyes, had on a dark blue coat and overhalls.

"$500 reward for Fairbanks.

"$50 for Andrew Bartholomew a Frenchman under sentence for house-
breaking, 37 years old."

papers, as well as papers all over the United States, flamed with headlines of "Stop the Murderer" over vigorous articles appealing to all citizens to aid in his detection, the following from the *Gazette* of August 20 being a sample:

Stop the Murderer
1000 Dollars Reward

The absconding of Jason Fairbanks from the jail of Dedham has excited much interest in the breasts of every one who regard the peace of society and the security of life; it will be the duty of the citizens of the United States to exert themselves in securing the condemned criminal without pecuniary reward, but as that may be the means of stimulating many who would otherwise be inactive, a large gratuity is now offered. Every newspaper printed in the U. S. it is hoped will publish the advertisement of the Sheriff (on the next page) and by other means extend the hue and cry against him."

The *Centinel*, in its bitter Federalism, had never been able to forget the fact that Dedham had been, three years before, in 1798, the seat of sedition and the spot where the Jacobin liberty pole had been erected. Accordingly, it seized the present opportunity to make another political attack on that town, by professing to see, in this Fairbanks rescue, evidences of another Jacobin outrage and violation of law. In its issue of August 19 it published an article which aroused the utmost indignation in the Republican Antifederalists of the town and of the State. "We learn that Jason Fairbanks, under sentence of death for murder and confined in Dedham jail, was liberated therefrom on Monday night last by a banditti of the liberty-pole gentry of that part of the country. The daring and infamous act, we are told, was threatened before and since the trial in their circles. Every good man in the community is called upon to raise a hue and cry to detect the fugitive criminal that he may suffer the punishment denounced by the

law for one of the most atrocious crimes ever committed."
The *Independent Chronicle*, the next day, August 20, replied to this attack on the fame of Dedham: "Despicable
indeed will be considered the idea illiberally hinted in the
Centinel of yesterday, attributing so flagrant an act in preventing the execution of justice for so heinous a crime to
any party political motives whatever; and it is seriously
hoped that a sense of duty together with a marked dis-
approbation of so atrocious a violation of the laws of God
and society will be manifested among all classes of citizens,
by a vigilant search not only for the perpetrator of so horrid a murder but also for the discovery and detection of the
audacious accomplices in his escape." The *Centinel*, although having absolutely no proof of its partisan assertions, returned to the attack, August 22:

The affair of the liberty pole was certainly no credit to the
town of Dedham or to the county of Norfolk. It was a gross insult to the laws and which was suffered to remain for several
days; and there was said to be a great backwardness among the
people to giving evidence against the offenders. When, therefore, a new outrage on law was perpetrated, and Jason Fairbanks
the murderer was violently set at liberty, the information that a
mob had broken the jail in the same town was credible. Such
information was received and did gain credit. We are now told,
however, that probably not more than five or six persons assisted
at the breach of the prison — and that the inhabitants were be-
comely zealous and active on the occasion and liberal with their
money and services in favor of the outraged laws. This is good
news, and leads the mind to hope that opposition to law appears
in that quarter to be a worse thing than it did in David Brown's
day. Good men at all times and everywhere will of course take
the side of law and justice. There can be no laws or at least no
good fruit from them unless jails are faithfully and watchfully
kept. If an offender is pretty sure of breaking prison, the law will
be no terror to evil doers, and in such a case as the horrid murder
committed by Jason Fairbanks, the very Hottentots and Guinea

negroes would put the monster to death. When the culprits who broke open the jail and assisted Fairbanks in his escape are detected, we are content it shall be seen whether they were Federalists or liberty-pole democrats. The procedure is of a piece with the misdoings of the Jacobins in Georgia who released from prison the murderer of a Federal marshal; and of the insurgents in the western counties of Pennsylvania. We do not charge all the Democrats as being accessories to or in any wise countenancing the crime — we know many of them detest it; but we have well-grounded assurances that all suspected as the perpetrators are thorough-going Jacobins.

To this reiterated accusation the *Independent Chronicle* retorted, August 24:

We have taken some pains to ascertain with correctness the chief facts that occurred at the breaking of the gaol in Dedham. *There was no mob,* is the opinion of our informants, and we are assured that several of the Magistrates of Norfolk attended at the gaol on Wednesday and were fully of opinion that not more than two or three persons effected this outrage. The marks of feet on the grass and on the board fence round the prison yard and other circumstances convinced them of the truth of this conclusion. The inhabitants of Dedham, so far from deserving the stigma and disgrace of rising mobbishly to set a murderer out of gaol, displayed the zeal and ardor that is becoming good citizens. They cheerfully subscribed between two and three hundred dollars in the course of an hour after the subscription was opened — they came forward as guards at all the bridges and passes and great roads; and as the laboring men had been wearied with haying, this is no trifling proof of their zeal; and they also formed a voluntary committee to make a search in all the houses and buildings and to give account of all persons about from home that night and the following day. This again shows that no mob was collected, as no evidence of the kind was obtained. It is candid and proper to vindicate the reputation of that town and country. It would indeed be a disgrace to the laws of the State, if it were true that a mob had risen within eleven miles of the capital to rescue an atrocious murderer. We are also happy to add with confidence that the business from the first has had nothing to do with politics.[1]

In the same issue of the *Chronicle* there appeared a communication which, though unsigned, bears every earmark, in its use of language, of having been written by Dr. Nathaniel Ames himself:

> The ungenerous and unmanly remarks in the *Centinel* in attempting to introduce a party question between the Republicans and Federalists as it related to the liberation of Fairbanks must be ranked among the foremost deceptions to impose on the public mind. Nothing short of a *Demon* would have been capable of such a reflection. But in this instance as in all others, the Tory Faction are industrious to propagate *Lies* to avail themselves of every circumstance which occasionally takes place. If the Editor had not been callous to every principle of honor or common prudence, he would have omitted such an impolitic remark — for while he holds up the idea that the "Liberty-pole" boys committed the outrage he should have reflected that the Cockade-Boys of Norfolk actually committed *Burglary* in breaking open the house in which were deposited the guns for the celebration of President Jefferson's election. As this party have already been proved guilty of Burglary, it would have been but modest in the Editor to have held his peace about Fairbanks. Those who would break open a *private house* to spike a few guns would not long hesitate to break open a public gaol to liberate a friend.

Another Federalist paper, the *New England Palladium*, while evidently wishing to support the *Centinel*, was forced to admit that there was no evidence to support the theory of a Jacobin plot. After speaking of the rescuers as "per-

[1] Another violent Republican paper in Boston, the *Constitutional Telegraphe*, thus referred to the episode, August 22: "If what the *Centinel* says be true that 'the Liberty-pole gentry liberated Fairbanks' and that 'the daring and infamous act was threatened before and since the trial' the Cockade 'gentry' ought certainly to have watched with greater vigilance and not suffered the prisoner to escape."

sons who, to say the least, have suffered their friendship to triumph over the injunctions of religion, their deference for justice and their respect for the laws of the country — laws which form the palladium of life, liberty and property," it continued:

It has been reported here, and the rumor is already spreading fast throughout the continent, that the late outrage at Dedham, the rescuing of Jason Fairbanks the atrocious murderer, was produced by a fermenting of the popular passions in that town and by an armed mob. These opinions, if true, would show that we are already very corrupt and near being very miserable in consequence of our corruption. The people cannot long be governed by laws, if their passions will not let them take their regular course. The first news was such as to leave no doubt that these opinions, however degrading and alarming, were founded in truth. If there was any error in the information, there seems to be no blame in admitting it to be true; for the error was not known till better examination of the affair has led to sounder and more comfortable results. It is now certain, from the examination of the Dedham gaol by the Justices of Norfolk County, and by other evidence, that not more than two or three were actors in this horrid labor of setting a murderer free. The inhabitants of Dedham were animated by a laudable zeal to detect the murderer and his accomplices. They submitted to search and to the toil of guarding by sentinels the bridges and avenues out of town, and filled up a liberal subscription of more than two hundred dollars in half an hour. We are assured that party principles have not disgraced the trial or any of the proceedings.

The *Centinel*, however, obstinately refused to retract any of its statements, and on August 26 made the following additional fling: "The *Chronicle's* trash — we despise. If the miscreants who liberated him were not of the 'sect' reported, is it probable they would have taken pains to release a French thief also?"

After a long pursuit, Fairbanks was finally captured in Vermont near the Canada line, and was brought back to

Boston, where he was placed in the Suffolk County jail, it being thought best, under all the circumstances, not to test the Dedham jail again. With him there was captured as an accomplice a man named Dukeham.[1] Ten days later, the *Centinel* was so lost to the sense of the ridiculous that it tried to strengthen its proof of a Jacobin conspiracy by a statement that this Dukeham was a newspaper carrier of the *Chronicle* — and therefore *ipso facto* a traitor:

If folly and stupidity were not the principal ingredients in the composition of the *Chronicle* printers, they would have permitted the conduct of their jail-breaking brethren at Dedham to have slept in silence. Being held to answer for their crimes to the laws they have violated, we are unwilling to augment the public indignation towards them. We have abundant proof of the truth of every assertion made by us respecting their political principles. We shall only at present say that Dukeham who accompanied and assisted Fairbanks in his efforts from prison was *one of the carriers of the Chronicle* and the disseminator of its falsehood and scurrility in the county of Norfolk.

Even so petty a charge as this seemed very serious to the *Chronicle* in those days of heated politics, and it replied, September 14:

If more mischievous ingredients than folly and stupidity did not frequently mark the character of the *Centinel's* editor and some of his correspondents, the base insinuation respecting the loyalty of the people of Dedham would never have originated in that vehicle of slander. Whatever may be the political principles of the inhabitants of Dedham in general, or even of those few violators of law in the instance referred to, it is difficult to conceive, and much more to prove, that the transaction was in any respect influenced thereby. But we again observe the same precipitancy, the same want of information, or the same folly and stupidity as before appeared in asserting peremptorily that

---

[1] For a lively account of Fairbanks' adventures, see *Connecticut Courant*, September 7, 1801.

Dukeham was one of the carriers of the *Chronicle*! Waiving the paltry idea of the merits of a paper being judged by the character of the carrier — the fact is this: Dukeham was never known to take a paper directly or indirectly for himself or any other person from the *Chronicle's* office. The bold assertion therefore of the *Centinel* is a downright lie, fabricated to answer some mischievous and malignant design.

While the newspaper attacks on "seditious Dedham" gradually died out, over-excitable citizens of that town and of the county of Norfolk sensed another reflection on their loyalty in the proceedings attendant on the execution of Fairbanks. The *Chronicle* of September 10 contained the following article: "This morning about 8 o'clock the unhappy criminal under sentence of death will leave the Gaol of this Town; from thence he will be conveyed under the care of the Sheriff of this county with a *civil escort* and delivered into the custody of the Sheriff for the county of Norfolk at the Roxbury line, from thence he will be conducted by a *Military Escort* to the place of execution in Dedham and there between the hours of 11 and 3 his untimely fate will close the scene. How far a Military Escort is necessary in the county of Norfolk may be subject for future enquiry." Under some apparent fear of Norfolk County citizens, the Governor and Council actually did order out a corps of cavalry to escort the murderer from the Suffolk County line; and two companies of cavalry and a detachment of volunteer infantry to guard the scaffold at the place of execution — the Great Common — in Dedham.[1] Such an extraordinary measure as this show of military force and disregard of the civil authorities was probably never adopted at any other execution in New

---

[1] The *Connecticut Courant* of September 14, 1801, contained a despatch from Boston saying: "During all the incidents solemn and peculiar to such an awful occasion he appeared as insensible of his situation as he did upon the trial and made the signal for his own execution by dropping his handkerchief"

England, and the legality of the Governor's action was doubtful. It is no wonder that the editor of the *Constitutional Telegraphe* wrote, September 19, that it was "unprecedented if not ridiculous. It is difficult to discern whether this parade was ordered to make the appearance of the military familiar to the eyes of the People, or whether to gratify the vain, ostentatious pride of any particular civil officer. Be this as it may, there appears, we think, something in this business that reflects on the loyalty of the citizens of that large and respectable county, which may require elucidation." [1]

Following the execution, a number of accounts of the whole case were printed — a pamphlet issued by the *Centinel's* publishers and placed on sale in five or six towns in New England; a *Life of Jason Fairbanks, a Novel founded on Fact*, by Henry Hunt; and a broadside issued from the "Pandamonium Press." This latter publication was very characteristic of the period. It was headed with a rough woodcut of the corpse suspended from the gallows, the scaffold surrounded by a line of woodeny soldiers, and flanked with an urnlike monument inscribed "F——s," and a hideous black coffin initialled "J. F." Its description of the execution was as follows:

About half an hour previous to his mounting the scaffold, the sun was obscured from view by watery clouds shedding torrents of tears at the shocking event about to take place on the hapless

---

[1] A correspondent in the *Chronicle* also bitterly inveighed against the imputation on the loyalty of the county: "The history of this country does not furnish so pointed an indignity on a county (while in a state of quietude). If you submit to this pointed odium without some serious investigation by application to the Governor, your reputation must inevitably be greatly injured — as violators of law — and the history of Fairbanks will descend to posterity accompanied with the degrading idea that the yeomen of Norfolk were disposed to arrest a murderer from the hands of justice. The horrid deed of this culprit will live for ages; it will be recorded in the annals of America and Europe, and as long as Fairbanks is mentioned, the odium of a Military Guard in Norfolk to conduct him to execution will remain a mark of reproach."

condemned prisoner. The tempest raged with unabated fury for the space of thirty minutes; the forked lightning from the o'er-charged clouds play'd in the ethereal space 'twixt us and heaven, while the thunder with tremendous claps vibrated o'er the heads of the numerous and astonished multitude. 'Twas at this critical instant that the last moment of his hunted existence was just arrived, and he was launched into eternity in the presence of the most numerous assemblage of spectators of both sexes that we ever recollect to have seen together on any former similar and melancholy occasion. (Note— It is rather remarkable, considering the sensibility of the Fair Sex, that they have, in gratification of their insatiable curiosity, always been forward of attending in crowds these melancholy occasions. The ladies of Boston and the adjacent towns resorted in such numbers that had a foreigner passed transiently by he would have supposed it the celebration of some National Festival. The surmise would have been just. The Court of Comus never exhibited the appearance of more boisterous revelry and mirth.)

Two other quaint and curiously characteristic publications were advertised in the *Columbian Minerva* in Dedham, January 19, 1802, as follows:

Just published at the Minerva Press and for sale by H. Mann at this office. *The Solemn Declaration of The Late Unfortunate Jason Fairbanks*. From the original manuscript, composed and signed by himself, and attested by his counsel a short time before his execution — To which is added some account of his life and character, and a Correction of the Depositions of the Principal Witnesses, from the late publication of his Trial, as they were literally delivered in Court.

> Tell them the lamentable Fall of me,
> And send the bearers weeping to their bed.

> Wailings he disdained,
> As marks of base and abject minds, nor gave
> His griefs a voice.

The only conversation held by the sufferer, at the place of execution, was the following reply to the officer at his last moment. "All that I have to communicate is already written in my Declaration."

The whole collected and published by Ebenezer Fairbanks, Jr., a farmer of Dedham, December 8.

ALSO

This day Published by H. Mann, and for sale as above, *The Danger of Despising the Divine Counsel*. Exhibited in a Discourse. Delivered at Dedham the Lord's Day following the execution of Jason Fairbanks, by the Rev. Thomas Thacher of Dedham. In this excellent and interesting discourse are given some of the most important particulars of the conduct and character of Fairbanks, both during his confinement in prison and at the period of his execution — Mr. Thacher having visited him occasionally from the time of imprisonment to the last moment of his existence; together with some pertinent remarks on the nature and evil tendency of Public Executions; preserving through the whole an excellent moral.

To those who may wish to become purchasers of *Fairbanks' Declaration*, the above discourse will be given gratis. Booksellers and others shall have them at the usual rates.

Subscribers will please to call for their copies January 16, 1802.

Over the first of these pamphlets Dr. Ames grew highly indignant in his Diary:[1]

> *Dec. 17, 1801.* Jason Fairbanks' dying speech out, or Ebenezer's catchpenny, with his life and character and of the family. False, perverted facts. It asserts his innocence!

---

[1] Thomas B. Adams wrote April 11, 1802, as to this alleged confession: "I have read the life of that Monster Fairbanks, and his prison confession, which discloses some facts that explain to my satisfaction the reason why his counsel were so firmly persuaded of his innocence of the murder. Still, I say, he suffered a righteous punishment, and the consciences of both jurors and judges are acquitted in the sight of God and man (or ought to be) of all imputation. He was convicted, by the evidence before the Court; and how could he be acquitted without disclosure of the facts which his narration has since brought to light, and which, if strictly true, rest alone on his own testimony, leaving presumption still as strong as before of his guilt. As to his life, I am no convert to the gorgeous decorations, etc., and the sunset splendor of a personal biography. Hic Jacet Jason, quiescat!" *American Antiquarian Society Proceedings* (1917), vol. XXVII.

Dec. 17, 1801. Published this day from the Dedham Press an extraordinary pamphlet containing Jason Fairbanks dying speech, who was hanged the 10th Sept. for murder of Betsy F——s. It . . . doth not illustrate the manner of her death, nor account for her wounds, especially in her back, — to which is added a long account of his life, sweet temper, and angelic accomplishment and piety, with side lashes upon the Court and Jury. Disgusts almost everybody! It is a gross perversion of the truth! Charges some of the witnesses with perjury by retracting evidence since — makes keen resentments among families in Dedham and out town. People mark the pamphlet with contempt. Yet they of his family think it a master stroke to retrieve both fame and interest in sale of the books, as people are cautious of lacerating them with the truth!

The moral which the publications of that day sought to draw from the murder is amusingly shown in the concluding lines of a broadside, entitled "A Mournful Tragedy":

> O may this then a warning prove
> To all young people that's in love;
> That they may shun such dismal fate,
> And each enjoy their loving mate.
> Now parents all where'er you be,
> Who hear this sad catastrophe;
> Now let you this one caution take,
> Where love is fix'd — don't matches break.

VI

JEFFERSON, THE ESSEX JUNTO, AND THE LAW CRAFT

MEANWHILE, owing to the unpopularity of these army and tax and gag laws, the Antifederalists, or Republicans as they were beginning to be called, were increasing mightily in numbers and power, even in the stronghold of Federalism. Dr. Ames himself failed of election to the State Senate by only six votes, in April, 1799.[1] And, spurred to increased invective, Fisher Ames wrote to the *Boston Gazette*, during the same month, a letter in which he spoke of his opponents as "fanatics," "toads," "serpents," "malignant," "mobocracy," and described their progress as follows: "If the laws they complain of really abridge liberty as they pretend, which however is positively denied, it is their own wickedness that has supplied to Government the pretext, and varnished it over with the appearance of necessity. . . . The Jacobins have at last made their own discipline perfect. . . . Emissaries are sent to every class of men, and even to every individual man that can be gained. Every threshing floor, every husking, every party at work on a house frame, or raising a building — the very funerals are infected with bawlers or

[1] Dedham, in the election for Governor in 1799, cast 122 votes for the Antifederalist, General Heath, and 75 for his opponent, Increase Sumner. In Boston, the vote was 1904 to 546 in favor of Sumner.

The *Columbian Centinel* had said, March 18: "The country Jacos, at the late March meetings, put all their tricks in requisition to introduce into every town office creatures of their kidney. At Dedham, they manœuvred with such secrecy and cunning as actually to oust a worthy man from the town clerkship, before the good sense of the town rallied and prevented any further innovation."

whisperers against Government. For talents as statesmen, the New England Jacobin leaders are despicable; their ignorance of commerce, of finance, and of the 'diplomatic skill of France' is not only obvious, but they are concerned to urge the last as an excuse, for if they are not ignorant they are wicked. As to talents in the field, on which side do they appear? The reader may be left to look up Jacobin generals and heroes." And, in a letter of November 10, 1799, Fisher Ames gave a vivid presentation of the spread of the "Jacobinic rabies": "The town of Boston has been so decidedly anti-French that the Sullivans and the Winthrops and the Master Vinals, the leaders of fifties and hundreds, joined the *vox populi*, as it was natural they should; but the captains of thousands, the Honesti, Jarvis, and old S. Adams remain unchanged. If any point is really conceded by that party, it is that of a navy which they admit to be wise and right, perhaps with the sole view of insisting the more on the uselessness and danger of armies which, besides, can go after rebels by *land* which ships cannot. In the heart of even the proselytes, the same rancor still lurks. The Mission is the darling measure of them all. The Jacobins in the vicinity of Boston are as openly bitter as ever, though rather less clamorous; and, on the whole, the *rabies canina* of Jacobinism has gradually spread, of late years, from the cities, where it was confined to docks and mob, to the country. I think it is still spreading silently — and why should it not? All that is base is, of course, Jacobin, and all that is prejudice and jealousy and rancor in good hearts (and even they have a taint of every evil propensity), is susceptible of their impressions."

Notwithstanding the plain signs on the political horizon of its approaching downfall, the Federalist party, as a whole, continued, in 1799, its course of opposition to France. An illustration of the sentiments popular among

them throughout the country is to be found in the following account of the toasts at a dinner given in the town of
Dedham at the Fourth of July celebration, as described in
the local *Minerva*: "In this town, a correct, spirited, and
patriotic oration was delivered by Samuel Haven, Esq. A
company of about sixty gentlemen of the town and vicinity
then assembled at the Court House and partook of an elegant dinner, after which the following toasts were drunk:
'Our Country — John Adams — Washington — The Federal Government, No delaying counsels, No delusive negotiations — The Federal Executive, in its strength may
faction prove impotent and liberty stable — The New
Congress, with more Federalists, more energy —The Army
and Militia — Our Navy — Truxton — General Pinckney
— John Marshall; may the spirit he carried to Paris never
flag in Congress — Rufus King and the Diplomatic Corps
— The American Clergy — The Powers of Europe, spirit
to resist and success in resisting — Frenchmen, as much
government as they need, as much liberty as they can bear
— New England — Law.'" In view of the above sentiments, it is not surprising that all the Antifederalists of
Dedham refrained from attending the dinner, and Dr.
Ames made these entries in his Diary:

> *July 4.* The corpse of our Independence, gained sword in
> hand, still worshipped, in comic form.
> *July 17.* Complete burlesque on Federalism. Pollard's ora-
> tion, ranting nonsense from an infamous character.

A serious split, however, was now taking place in the
Federalist party. President Adams, against the violent
opposition of Alexander Hamilton and his followers, determined to avert war with France, and reopened negotiations
with that country by sending new envoys. For this action
he was assailed by many of his former adherents, including

Fisher Ames, who wrote to Pickering (the Secretary of State whom Adams was about to dismiss) that Adams had caused the Jacobins "to raise their disgraced heads from the mire of contempt." To Rufus King he wrote that, though it was getting to be the fashion to call the Federalists the British faction, "nothing can be more false, for though such men respect the laws and Courts and Government of Britain and detest the arbitrary tyrants of France, yet they allow no country any kind of competition in point of respect with our own." He laid the responsibility for these attacks on Federalism to John Adams (sarcastically "the great man"), who, he said, inveighed "against the British faction and the Essex Junto like one possessed. . . . When a man thinks no cause good or safe *without him,* he may possibly act with as much blindness as extravagance when he resolves to hazard the ship than his captaincy." Adams is "too much the creature of impulse or freakish humor," wrote his former supporter. "He is a revolutionist from temperament, habit, and, lately, what he thinks policy. He is too much irritated against many, if not most, of the principal sound men of the country even to bestow on them his confidence or retrieve them. In particular, he is implacable against a certain great little man whom we mutually respect" (Hamilton).[1] Moreover, Fisher Ames made bitter complaint over the fact that "the Adams writers offer to "fraternize with Jacobins, whom they denominate old friends, and openly rail against the 'exclusive Federalists,' 'Hamiltonians,' 'Essex Junto,' 'Royalists,' 'British Partizans,' as they affect to call the men who stick to the good old principles and old cause."

---

[1] Fisher Ames to Timothy Pickering, October 19, 1799; See also *Life and Correspondence of Rufus King*, vol. III, F. Ames to King, July 15, August 25, September 24, 1800; in the latter letter he wrote of Mrs. John Adams: "The good Lady, his ux., has been often talkative in a similar strain, and she is as complete a politician as any Lady in the old French Court."

Dr. Nathaniel Ames, on the other hand, wrote:

May 16, 1799. J. Adams striving to retrieve popularity by disbanding army, etc. As election approaches, Adams turns out Tim Pickering from Secretary of State's office, disbands in concurrence with Congress the standing army, and seems awhile to retract from high-handed explosions against France and Democracy.

Nov. 6. J. Adams charged with turning Jacobin for resisting Pinckney, Hamilton and British faction, in sending envoys to France to treat of peace.

Nov. 11. Jay's cursed treaty broke by Commissioners seceding, to the joy of true Americans.

Two entries made about this time by Dr. Ames in his most excited manner recall an event which greatly stirred the country against President Adams, and to which, more than any other cause, the country owed the later nomination of John Marshall as Chief Justice of the Supreme Court. A request was received by the President from the British Government for the extradition, under Jay's treaty, of a certain sailor named Thomas Nash, otherwise called Jonathan Robbins. Nash was accused of piracy and murder on board a British vessel on the high sea. He claimed, however, to be an American citizen. Proof of his guilt and of his British citizenship was produced before Judge Bee of the United States District Court in South Carolina; and, with the consent of the President, Nash was surrendered to Great Britain, and was afterwards executed. Because of this action of the President, resolutions of censure were introduced in Congress by Edward Livingston, in February, 1800; and in the debate which ensued, John Marshall, then a member of Congress, made so able and convincing a speech as to earn him the undying gratitude of Adams, made evident a year later by the tender of the Chief-Justiceship. Dr. Ames noted as follows:

Nov. 21, 1799. Infamy of Judge Bee, South Carolina, causing murder of Jonathan Robbins by delivery to British under Jay's Treaty. . . . Why is not Judge Bee denounced to the President as alien to be banished?

Dec. 27. It now comes out by British account of Jonathan Robbins' trial and execution that he never confessed himself an Irishman — but true American. And Judge Bee of South Carolina is guilty of his murder by delivery up to British trial! Thomas Bee, a District Judge, South Carolina, by his single decree without jury causes murder of Jonathan Robbins, an American citizen enslaved in British warship, by delivery to British who hang and gibbet him. Why don't some other citizen denounce Bee to the President to be banished under the Alien Act? How can J. Adams leave such a wretch as Bee in office? Fine times when murderers and adulterers [1] are best candidates for high offices! !

Even the death of Washington could not divert Dr. Ames' mind from the enormity of Federalist deeds, nor could the good Jacobin refrain from sarcasm at the Federalist mourning:

Dec. 24, 1799. Washington died, 14th, of croupe or quincy.

Dec. 27. In all the funeral pomp at Washington's death, it is hoped a thought will be bestowed on poor Jonathan Robbins.

Jan. 2, 1800. All the Gazettes still crowded with accounts of the Parade and Pomp of Woe at Washington's Death and celebrating his Apotheosis! In preference of that of Christ in N. Jersey! ! !

Feb. 22. Bell and Cannon; W's apotheosis, Dedham, etc. Standing army paraded.

Although there were signs in the country at large that the Federalist party was doomed to defeat in the presidential campaign of 1800, the State of Massachusetts still clung to its idols; and in the spring election the Federalist

---

[1] The latter reference is to Alexander Hamilton.

candidate for Governor, Caleb Strong, was elected, on his characteristically arrogant Federalist appeal for "united action by the friends of society, religion, and good order." "The demon of Jacobinism has been effectually laid, for this year at least," exclaimed the *Centinel*.[1]

Throughout the year 1800, the Alien and Sedition Acts continued to occupy much of the doctor's attention:

> *Jan. 31, 1800.* The letter from George Nicholas of Kentucky [as to these Acts] to his friend in Virginia ought to be read like the Bible in every family, sent to selectmen in every town in the Eastern States, and forced on jurymen to be considered!
>
> *Feb. 6.* N. Kingsberry borrowed G. Nicholas' letter on Alien and Sedition.
>
> *March 10.* Charles Pinckney's speech in U. S. Senate, partly given in *Chronicle* this day, excellent, against Non-Intercourse Law and other arbitrary Acts.
>
> *March 26.* Joel Barlow's Letter to Citizens of U. S. strikes the tyrant's power.
>
> *Oct. 31.* The essays signed A Republican [ascribed to Charles Pinckney] especially No. 5, exceed anything I have seen against the Sedition Act! And ought to be put in every man's hands.
>
> *Dec. 31.* Let us ever remember to detest the name of Sedgwick, Speaker, and Morris, Chairman on Committee of House, 23 Jan. 1801, who on question of revival of the Gag Act, 48 to 48, turned the vote for a revival of the traitorous Act.

By the autumn of 1800 it was apparent that the Federalist party was doomed. The unpopularity of the Internal Tax Law, the Army Law, the Alien and Sedition Laws, the

[1] *Columbian Centinel*, February 12; see *ibid.*, June 14, 1800. The Antifederalists in Massachusetts had been growing steadily stronger. In 1799, General William Heath, their candidate for Governor, had carried Middlesex and Norfolk Counties, polling over 8000 votes; in 1800, their candidate, Elbridge Gerry, polled more than 17,000 votes, carrying six counties, including Norfolk. Gerry carried Dedham, by a vote of 156 to 42 for Strong, and also Boston, by a vote of 1555 to 1531.

general belief that its leaders were devoted to British, monarchic, or aristocratic ideals, all combined to weaken the ranks of that party. Moreover, the party had been split into two factions by the antagonism of Hamilton to President Adams. Dr. Ames wrote of the election returns in general, August 31, 1800: "A general grumbling of the Great Sovereign against its Agents attempting to veil, stupify and then bleed to fainting, instead of helping to feed, arm and invigorate and enlighten it! ! !" The views of a large proportion of the voters were fairly expressed in the following attack on the administration by a contemporary writer: "That Administration copied implicitly the acts of the English Government, even in the worst and most vitiated period of its history. We had alien and sedition laws, spies and informers. Our dungeons were converted into habitations for patriots. The will of the Executive became the animating principle of our Federal Legislature, and that will was palpably in favor of Monarchy. The press was arrested, and the tongue stood still. Riot succeeded riot, and he who would not bow obsequious assent to the maniacal deeds of the day, was every moment in personal danger. War with France was courted with all the eagerness and alacrity of self-defence." [1]

The election of Jefferson put the Antifederalists into a better humor; and the decease of the Adams administration was amusingly depicted by one of their newspapers as follows: [2]

50,000,000 Dollars Reward.

RAN away from the subscriber, at 12 o'clock of the night following the 3rd of March, 1801, One Standing Army — One Navy — One Sedition Act — One Stamp Act — One Land Tax

[1] *A Narrative of the Suppression by Colonel Burr of the History of The Administration of John Adams, by John Wood*, by a Citizen of New York (James Cheetham), (1802).

[2] See *Independent Chronicle*, October 30, 1806.

— with a great number of other taxes, too numerous to be mentioned in an advertisement. Also sixteen newly constructed Patent Judges, one eight per cent Loan — and one "stupendous fabric of human invention" — newly built upon an improved model, with improvements.

All of which domestics, together with a great number of an inferior rank, were dressed in uniform, and had on, when they went away, home-made piety cloth outside coats, British-manufactured close-bodied ditto, with vest and pantaloons of the same; British hats decorated with American Eagles for Cockades, and Suwarrow boots, completely finished from the original model. Took with them, when they went away, 2000 Bales of British systems of Taxation — 2000 Superfine Royal Expectations — one partly finished King's Crown — a large number of unfinished Mitres, copied from approved Models by the hand of a consummate artist, together with a large number of Titles of Honor such as Lords, Dukes, Marquises, Viscounts, etc., etc., and an almost innumerable quantity of Coronets, Stars and Garters, all finished by the hand of a master. Whoever will return said deserters and the before mentioned articles to ourself, shall receive the above reward, in approved Bills of Exchange upon the State of Connecticut in America, and John Bull & Co. in Europe.

Given under our own hand at . . . . . ., this Ninth Year of our intended Reign, and first day of the Month Shebeth.

JOHN.

On the other hand, the Federalist *Columbian Centinel* recorded eulogistically the passing of the Adams administration in the following column-long epitaph:

Monumental Inscription
That life is long which answers Life's great end.
Yesterday expired
Deeply regretted by millions of grateful Americans
and by all good men
The Federal Administration
of the
Government of the United States
animated by

a Washington, an Adams, a Hamilton, Knox, Pickering, Wool-
cott, McHenry, Marshall, Stoddart, and Dexter
At 12 years.
Its death was occasioned by the
Secret Arts and Open Violence
of Foreign and Domestic Demagogues
[Here followed a long list of the Federalist good deeds]
And yet — Notwithstanding all these services and blessings —
there are found
Many, very many, weak degenerate Sons
Who, lost to virtue, to gratitude
and Patriotism
Openly exult that this Administration
is no more
and that
The "Sun of Federalism is set forever"
Oh shame — where is thy blush?

The newspapers of the times, however, contain few
articles in as playful a vein as those just quoted. For, with
the inauguration of President Jefferson, there began an era
of mud-slinging on the part of Federalist writers which
exceeded — although such a thing might seem impossible
— the rancorous contest in epithet and vilification between
Federalist and Jacobin newspaper editors and politicians
in the years between 1793 and 1799. As Lodge wrote in his
Life and Letters of George Cabot: "The Federalists hated
Jefferson with no common hatred, but rather with the
vindictiveness of men towards a deadly foe, who, as they
firmly believed, sought the ruin of all they most prized
and cherished. They sincerely believed Jefferson to be in
reality, as he was in seeming, the embodiment of French
democracy, and advocate and promoter of principles which
menaced with destruction all the rights and customs which
alone made life worth living." Vile epithets and charges
against Jefferson's personal character and habits flowed
from the lips of his opponents day in and day out. He was

accused of being an atheist, a "mammoth infidel," a drunkard, an anarchist, and a libertine.[1] Fisher Ames wrote, in mild tones, of Jefferson's "irreligion, wild philosophy and gimcrackery in politics." But Timothy Pickering wrote more vituperatively, a few years later: "I am disgusted with the men who now rule and with their measures. At some manifestations of their malignancy, I am shocked. The cowardly wretch at their head, while, like a Parisian revolutionary monster prating about humanity, would feel an infernal pleasure in the utter destruction of his opponents. We have too long witnessed his general turpitude, his cruel removals of faithful officers, and the substitution of corruption and looseness for integrity and worth."[2] In fact, the Federalists now laid themselves open to the same bitter denunciations for libelling the Government which they had launched against the Antifederalists three years before. As Benjamin Austin, Jr., complaining of their "indecency and virulence," wrote: "Two years since, with Federalists, it was sedition to impeach the wisdom of executive measures. Now calumny and obscenity, too gross for the ear of delicacy, are the evidences of patriotism that vaunts its own praises, and of talent that boasts its own lustre."[3] And the situation was further picturesquely described without exaggeration by

---

[1] This last slander was frequently uttered in the baldest terms; but the following verses are an amusing example of a mild statement of it:

> The ardent, impartial and tender affection
> He feels for the ladies of every complexion
> In our age of reason, are tokens enough
> To prove him not made of corruptible stuff.
> — And, as we conceive from his proneness to love,
> The real descendant of Venus and Jove.

See *A Poetical Dictionary of Popular Terms Illustrated in Rhyme — for the Use of Society in General and Politicians in Particular* (1808), by David Hitchcock.

[2] Fisher Ames to King, September 24, 1800; Pickering to King, March 4, 1804. See especially *Democracy Unveiled* (1805), by Thomas G. Fessenden.

[3] *Independent Chronicle*, March 13, 1803.

Austin: "The history of the world cannot produce a parallel wherein the grossness of abuse and the malignity of temper have been carried to such an unbounded excess. The present Administrations have been attacked with a virulence which has nearly exceeded the ingenuity of grammarians to coin words adequate to its import. The whole vocabulary of the English language, expressive of the malignant passions, has within a few years been exhausted to defame the reputation of almost every Republican in the government. The greatest culprit within Newgate, the most abandoned miscreant that ever made his exit from Tyburn, has been more favored by his opponents than the President of the United States and those who adhere to his Administration. Decency has been sacrificed at the shrine of Federalism; and oftentimes have the libellous paragraphs been so basely defamatory, that a virtuous man felt a conscious guilt in admitting such obscenities within his family. Every epithet of slander was admitted. Our national character has been sported with by men who pretend to respect the honor of their country, with a wantonness which would disgrace a tribe of savages or a horde of Hottentots. Fellow-citizens, it is unnecessary to recapitulate in detail the falsehoods, scurrility, and malicious defamation which have been propagated through these prostituted vehicles, arrogantly styled Federal presses." [1] As if to justify to the fullest the above description, the following characterization of the Antifederalist editor appeared, in 1804, in a rival newspaper, the *Repertory*: "The *Chronicle* is a paper in which the abuse of a free press is arrived to an extent disgraceful to the Commonwealth and injurious to our interests; it has long been a sewer of the vilest slanders and greatest falsehoods and at this day is undoubtedly a rival in infamy to the most detestable publica-

[1] *Constitutional Republicanism* (1803), by Benjamin Austin, Jr.

tions in circulation. When it is known by whose labors this public nuisance is produced, the character of the agents will, we trust, induce many an implicit believer in the *Chronicle* to awake from his delusion and regard it with horror and spurn it from him with virtuous indignation, did he know the depravity of its conductors." [1] In view, therefore, of the abusive language used by Jefferson's opponents, it is not surprising that his adherents should have retaliated by exaggerating his virtues as highly as his enemies misrepresented his vices. Republican newspapers and Republican political pamphlets, which were issued from small presses everywhere to repel the Federalist attacks, contained countless interesting examples of the extremities of partisan diatribe. Nothing, however, in the literature of the times gives a more picturesque view of the attitude of the Republicans towards their idol, Jefferson, or towards their bane and abhorrence, the set of men known as the "Essex Junto," than the following extracts from Dr. Ames' Diary. The election of Jefferson as President and the close of the year 1800 were thus enthusiastically recorded:

> Now in December, 1800, it is ascertained that the old Patriots, Jefferson and Burr, are to be Presidents next four years; it is hoped treason will not be so triumphant as in the last, that the reign of terror is over, and that free discussion will cause terror only to traitors.
>
> *Dec. 31, 1800.* Here ends the 18th Century. The 19th begins with a fine clear morning wind at S. W.; and the political horizon affords as fine a prospect under Jefferson's administration, with returning harmony with France—with the irresistible propagation of the Rights of Man, the eradication of hierarchy, oppression, superstition and tyranny over the world, by means of that soul-improving genius-polisher — that palladium of all our National joys—the printing press

---

[1] Quoted in *Independent Chronicle*, August 30, 1804.

— whose value tho' unknown by the vulgar savage slave, cannot be sufficiently appreciated by those who would disdain to fetter the image of God.

Jan. 16. War Office burnt.

Jan. 17. Treasury Office since burnt, to screen Federal defaulters.

Feb. 20, 1801. News of 11th and 12th, trying at Washington for President all night arrives Boston. Some have their beds and provisions in the Capitol; — had balloted 21 times: Jefferson 8, Burr 6, Divided 2.

Feb. 28. Tim Pickering came home with F. A. The people much gratified in choice of a President, more especially as the Aristocrats opposed by 34 ballots in Congress their will! — intending by holding out to 4th March to stop the wheels of government, to have no President if they could not have a Monarchist — a case unprovided for by the Constitution.

March 4. Bonfires, etc., begin Jefferson's reign.

March 15. New President's speech pleases all parties, yet some try to carp at it.

March 29. On the morning of the 4th March, when John Adams stepped down again to equality with his fellow citizens, Matthew Lyon, a Member of House of Congress, who had been cruelly, unmercifully punished under Gag Act, 4 months' imprisonment in north of Vermont in the severest winter for many years, — 1000 dollars fine for a crime too before any Act made it so, only publishing Barlow's letter from France — then justly and properly for him takes benefit of returning Freedom of Press to address Adams with a true picture of his 4 years' administration.

On the other hand, the election of Jefferson so depressed Fisher Ames that he wrote: "All fears now will be for the safety of all that Government has yet erected. Stocks have fallen, and rich men have begun to find out that they ought to bestir themselves." The *Columbian Centinel* ("Ben Russell's vile sheet," as the Doctor termed it) attempted to minimize the whole Inauguration, by devoting only three lines to the tremendous celebration which had been taking place in Boston. "There were some gun-firing, bell-ringing, faggot-burning, and civic feasting on Wednesday last, but nothing worthy remark or observation." Fisher Ames expressed his belief that Jefferson's victory had been due to the newspapers: "Is it not practicable," he wrote to Dwight, "to rouse a part of the good men, and to stay the contagion of Jacobinism within at least its present ample limits?" [1]

It would be wrong to assail the new Administration with invective. Even when bad measures occur, much temperance will be requisite. To encourage Mr. Jefferson to act right, and to aid him against his violent Jacobin adherents, we must make it manifest that we act on principle, and that we are deeply alarmed for the public good; that we are identified with the public. We must speak in the name and with the voice of the good and the wise, the lovers of liberty and the owners of property. ... The newspapers are an overmatch for any Government. They will first overawe and then usurp it. This has been done; and the Jacobins owe their triumph to the unceasing use of this engine; not so much to skill in the use of it as by repetition. ... We must use, but honestly and without lying, an engine that wit and good sense would make powerful and safe. ... An active spirit must be roused in every town to check the incessant proselytizing arts of the Jacobins.

His belief that the Federalist party contained all that was good in the country remained unmitigated. "The next thing will be, as in France, anarchy: then Jacobinism, organized with energy enough to plunder and shed blood," he wrote in 1802. "The only chance of safety lies in the revival of the energy of the Federalists *who alone will or can preserve liberty, property, or Constitution.*" Again, "The Federalists must entrench themselves in the State Governments and endeavour to make State justice and State

[1] Ames to Dwight, March 19, 1801; see also Ames to J. Smith, December 14, 1802.

power a *shelter of the wise, and good, and rich*, from the wild destroying rage of the Southern Jacobins." Again, "The extinction of Federalism would be followed by the *ruin of the wise, rich, and good*." [1]

In contrast to such ideas, the characteristically exaggerated views which Dr. Nathaniel Ames held as to Jefferson are amusingly shown in the following entry at the close of the first year of his administration:

> *Dec. 7, 1801.* Seventh Congress begin their session under a propitious prospect for the People, a complete contrast to the last, in President and both Houses. Never before, since the children of Israel, conducted by God's prophets, did any Monarch, King, or Ruler of a nation address a people or their Senate in the disinterested, concentrated, pertinent manner of Jefferson, without the usual expensive frippery, parade, and pomp on such occasions. He addresses the people not as slaves or subjects, but as citizens, as Republicans, with the same interest as before his exaltation, without manifesting the cloven foot of power — the same principles, but more energetic, on his change from being ruled, to Ruler and the head of the Nation.

Throughout the two administrations of Jefferson, Dr. Ames wrote in similar exultant and ecstatic vein regarding all of Jefferson's policies. In 1802, when Congress repealed the Internal Tax Law, he marked in his Almanac a "P." for Patriot against the names of Congressmen voting for the repeal, and an "A." for Aristocrat against those voting for rejection of the repeal. The repeal of the bill constituting the new Circuit Courts of the United States, which had been passed in the closing hour of President Adams' administration, was thus referred to:

[1] Fisher Ames to Dwight, April 16, 1802; to Gore, December 13, 1802; to J. Smith, December 14, 1802. See also *Life and Correspondence of Rufus King*, vol. IV, F. Ames to King, October 27, 1801, February 23, April 13, 1802.

Dr. Eustis whom Mrs. — said was an Aristocrat proved so,
3rd March 1802, voting with Connecticut Lawyers against
repeal of midnight Judiciary."

The purchase of Louisiana by Jefferson and the Federalist opposition in New England were thus commented upon
in the Diary:

> *July, 1803.* F. A. under sign of Fabricius in *Centinel*, Ben
> Russell's, tries to black the brightest traits in Jefferson's
> Administration — the purchase of Louisiana for reasonable
> sum of money instead of war, blood, and wealth of all the
> States; but Plain Truth in the *Chronicle* beats him down,
> and still he goes on barking, after beat, like other Lawyers.
> *Jan. 31, 1804.* It is amazing to consider the delusion under
> which the people about Connecticut River remain as to
> politics, by means of aristocratic papers and preaching.
> Mrs. Weatherby, returned from Northampton, says they
> still curse Jefferson; tho' he has denied himself the powers
> put in his hands, to ease the people of burdens — and ac-
> quired at the cheapest rate, without expense of blood of
> good citizens, an immense territory in addition to our do-
> main — removed frontier enemies beyond the power of
> annoyance, and opened immense source of wealth and
> magnificence to the U. S. But the people and Bar will yet
> keep up the delusion.

"Louisiana, in open and avowed defiance of the Constitution, is to be added to the Union," Fisher Ames had
written; and, like his Federalist associates, he regarded
Louisiana as a wilderness, destitute of value, and Jefferson's purchase of it as a "mean and despicable" yielding
to Napoleon. "As to the territory, the less of it the better.
But the abject spirit of our Administration is below all
scorn. . . . Who is to govern this empire?" he asked —
"the Gallo-Hispano, Indian omnium gatherum of savages
and adventurers?" It is probable that part of Fisher Ames'
pessimism in politics was due to his poor health; but he

could still jest on the latter subject, for he wrote at this time: "I am still puny and tender . . . my constitution is like that of Federalism, too feeble for a full allowance even of water gruel, and like that, all the doctor I have is a Jacobin. The Lord, you say, have mercy on me a sinner!"[1] His Jacobin doctor, — his brother Nathaniel, — on the other hand, was robust in his enthusiasm and optimism over the political situation. On March 4, 1805, he thus noted Jefferson's reëlection: "Bright day. Guns and Bells announce regeneration of U. S. in Jefferson's re-election"; and in a letter to the local newspaper he "presents his sincere contempt" to a Philadelphia editor "for the latter's profound queries against the Saviour of the Commonwealth of this United States, and estimates him a vile tool of Federalism which is the genuine quintessence of Pettyfogism — and it is to be presumed these Federal advocates would lack nothing to snatch at the 30 pieces of silver to betray their Lord and Master."[2] On October 31, 1805, he wrote of a certain Thomas Turner of Wheatland, Virginia, as an "infamous wretch who aimed to slander the Saviour of our Commonwealth — T. Jefferson, President United States."

For that particular set of Federalist leaders and opponents of Jefferson known as the "Essex Junto" Dr. Ames, in common with all the Republican writers of the period, had the most bitter contempt. This political coterie, frequently termed by him the "British Junto," had been the reigning power in Massachusetts politics for many years.[3] Because of the cold, bitter, and rancorous

[1] See Fisher Ames to Dwight, October 31, 1803, June 15, 1804; to Gore, October 31, 1803; and in "The Republican No. 2" in *Repertory*, July, 1804.

[2] *Dedham Minerva*, September 10, 1805.

[3] In his *Life and Times of Stephen Higginson* (1907) Thomas Wentworth Higginson wrote that the Essex Junto was headed by "two ex-sea-captains and the chief maritime lawyer of his time [Cabot, Higginson, and Parsons]. . . . The

character, as well as supreme ability, of the men who composed the Junto, it was more cordially detested by its opponents than any other set of politicians in the country. The name had been early applied by John Hancock, in the years prior to the adoption of the Constitution, to a group of Essex County men — Theophilus Parsons, John Lowell, and Jonathan Jackson of Newburyport, George Cabot and Nathan Dane of Beverly, and Timothy Pickering and Benjamin Goodhue of Salem. Later, it was used by John Adams in reference to the group of Federalists who supported Alexander Hamilton against him; and by Jefferson as applied to the most virulent of his antagonists in Massachusetts. In this broader sense it included, besides those above mentioned, Fisher Ames, Theodore Sedgwick, Tristram Dalton, John Lowell, Jr., Stephen Higginson, Josiah Quincy, Caleb Strong, Harrison Gray Otis, Francis Dana, and Robert Treat Paine. The general Republican view of the Junto was expressed by Benjamin Austin thus: "In the first place, I believe it can be clearly proved that every embarassment under which the country labors arises from them, that all the virulence of parties originated through this pestiferous medium, that all the deception which has been practiced, originated from this artful, aggrandizing faction. This Junto have, from the first establishment of the Constitution, been active to effect their plans and for this purpose have inlisted into their service a few time-serving clergymen, aided by a phalanx of sycophants, office seekers, and war contractors, and thus embodied, have watched every favorable opportunity to forward their destructive projects." And "Anthony Pas-

habits of the quarterdeck, in fact, went all through the Federalist party of Massachusetts. The slaveholders themselves did not more firmly believe that they constituted the Nation. To the Essex Junto, Jefferson himself seemed but a mutineering first mate, and his 'rights of man' but the black flag of a rebellious crew. They paid the penalty of their own aristocratic habits."

quin," writing in 1804, said: "From the time that Mr. Jay arrived, after this fatal transaction, we may date a new order of things to have taken place among us. The Essex Junto was formed, and its political relations and ramifications were extended over the United States. These persecutors of human freedom suborned every press that could be corrupted, and established others to confound and destroy the civic privileges of their fellow-citizens. They affected to brand the Patriots of '75 with ignominy, and had the audacity to walk up to the teeth of our best and wisest men and insult them for their constancy to public virtue. A reign of terror was enforced to sustain this woeful delusion, and every man was threatened with the bowstring who would not abandon his regard for his native land and defend this Tory treaty in all its parts and bearings. . . . The Federal Monarchists . . . began that horrid system of proscription, obloquy and violence which has since been properly denominated 'the reign of terror.'" [1]

[1] Perhaps nothing, however, could show more clearly the arrogance and affected superiority of the Federalists and their contempt for their opponents than a "List of Federalists and Anti-Federalists by Professions" published in the *Centinel*, January 14, 1801, which purported to give all the men of distinction in Massachusetts in both political parties, comparing them in number and standing, in order to show the Jacobin inferiority. The list ran as follows: "*General Political Character*: Fed., 13 [named persons], and many others; Anti-Fed., 9 — Samuel Adams, Elbridge Gerry, William Heath, Henry Dearborn, William Hull, Benjamin Hichborn, Perez Morton, John Bacon, Phanuel Bishop, and some others. *The Reverend Clergy*: This much respected body are almost wholly Federal; some whispers have existed to the disadvantage of the pastors of Rowley and Mendon, but we believe that they do not merit the disgrace. *Mercantile Characters*: Fed., 11 [named], and an host of other much-respected characters; Anti-Fed., 5 — Nathaniel Fellows, John Brazier, Samuel Brown, Capt. J. Crowninshield, Josiah Bacon, and a few others less distinguished. *Medical Characters*: Fed., 11 [named]; Anti-Fed., 6 — Charles Jarvis, William Eustis, Dr. Kitteridge, William Aspinwall, Nathaniel Ames, Eliphalet Downes, cetera desunt. *Law Characters*: Fed. 7 [named] and 100 others; Anti-Fed., 6 — Levi Lincoln, Thomas Edwards, George Blake, Ebenezer Bacon, James Bartlett, Joseph Blake, and no others. *Mechanic Interests*: Fed., 7 [named] and innumerable others; Anti-Fed., 5 — Benjamin Austin, Abijah Adams, Ebenezer Rhoades, Joseph Eaton, Andrew Oliver — cetera desunt."

The *Independent Chronicle* paid its respects to the Junto on the occasion of a dinner to the American Minister to England, Rufus King, in Boston in 1804, as follows: "A political Cabal who associate under the banner of Bacchus to give publicity and circulation to the most inflammatory, seditious, and abominable opinions. Subtlety, malice, falsehood and treason, seem to form an association for the exercise of their fullest power, and to challenge the unprecedented moderation of the Executive Authority with every species of irritation and insult. . . . These voluptuous sneering wretches, these political pharisees . . . who manifest their piety by toasts and sentiments that would dishonor a pagan in his orgies. . . . They are eternally insisting that Religion is in danger. . . . If Religion is in danger, it will arise from the hypocrisy, malignity, and wickedness of the Royal Faction who are impiously using the name of Heaven for the furtherance of their own traitorous designs against the Republican Institutions of their country." [1]

Throughout his Diary, Dr. Ames could find no adjectives strong enough to express his hatred of the men composing this Junto and their "traitorous policies," and in this respect again his Diary resembles the more famous diary of John Quincy Adams. Against Alexander Hamilton, and against his own brother, Fisher Ames, he was especially violent in denunciation; and the following entries on Hamilton (who visited Boston and Dedham in 1800) show the Antifederalist hatred of the man:

June 24, 1800. A. Hamilton, the high adulterer, run after a tiptoe thro' Dedham.

July 11, 1804. Alexander Hamilton killed in a duel with Aaron Burr, V. P.

[1] See *Independent Chronicle*, October 18, 25, 1804.

July 22. Ridiculous parade at death of A. Hamilton, Champion of the Junto.

July 25. H. G. Otis, Speaker of House of Representatives, in praise of duelling! !

July 31. The Champion of the Essex Junto killed in a duel at New York by the Vice President, makes the main subject of conversation. But Bonaparte made Emperor of France without any stipulation for Rights of Citizens is of more importance! The abject condition of the French, after such high-toned pretentions to liberty, strikes the world with astonishment.

The death of Hamilton was the signal for an outpouring of eulogium from the Federalists, and for unbridled license of attack from Republican organs. The oration delivered by Harrison Gray Otis was the subject of particular assault by the *Independent Chronicle*, which said that: "As the Royal Faction in the United States have considered necessary to their cause, to give a theatrical air and costume to all their public demonstrations of woe on account of the untimely death of the late General Hamilton, we have deemed it equally necessary to make some remarks upon the probable effect that such a series of overstrained ceremony may have upon the public mind; and how far the morals and happiness of the people may be improved by such an exhibition of party pageantry upon such an occasion." [1] And it attempted to dissuade the delivery of the eulogy by Harrison Gray Otis in King's Chapel, alleging as its reasons: "first, because it may be detrimental to

[1] *Independent Chronicle*, July 26, 1804; and see *ibid.*, August 6, 1804, quoting the *Norwich Republican* as follows: "Why this pompous display of funeral obsequies? Will they serve as a memento to warn others against the detestable practice of duelling? . . . Will those men, whose opinions are governed more by shew than reason, be capable of distinguishing, amidst such pageantry, between the tribute of respect intended for the memory of the deceased, and the eulogizing the manner of his exit?"

The *Columbian Centinel*, July 18, 1804, lined its columns with black; and see *Ibid.*, July 21, 25, 28 for accounts of funeral exercises.

popular morals to deliver a methodical, and in all proba-
bility, an elegant apology for the practice of duelling by
praising the unfortunate gentleman who has fallen in the
barbarous act; secondly, because the permission to deliver
such an eulogy, in the interior of a Christian Church con-
secrated to holy ordinances, may be contemplated with
horror, as a prophane intrusion upon the Almighty and as
an indelible stain upon the hallowed character of his
temple."

Perhaps nothing better illustrates the bitterness and
scurrility of the politics of the period than a savage poem
published by "Anthony Pasquin" (John Williams) in Boston in 1805, entitled *The Hamiltoniad*, copies of which are
now extremely rare, owing to the efforts made by the
friends of Hamilton to buy up and suppress the edition.[1]
The poem was called forth as a counter-attack to an article
written by the Federalist Joseph Dennie in the *Portfolio*,
assailing Hamilton's opponents as "rancorous Jacobins,
scoffing deists, snivelling fanatics, and imported scoundrels." In retaliation, *The Hamiltoniad* referred to "the
torrents of blasphemous trumpery . . . of a nature so
irrational, indecent, and insulting, both to God and man,"
which had flowed from Federalist pens after the death of
Hamilton; and the author paid his respects to his Federalists newspaper opponents in the following choice language:
"It is impossible to peruse the ensuing heterogeneous mass
of distorted encomium, self-congratulation and daring
falsehoods without a smile. . . . The rhetoric of Billingsgate and the snarling of 'Bavius' become charming and
liberal in comparison. But personal scurrility is the only

[1] *The Hamiltoniad, or An Extinguisher for the Royal Faction of New England,
with Copious Notes, Illustrative, Biographical, Philosophical, Critical, Admoni-
tory, and Political, Being Intended as a High-Heeled Shoe for All Limping Republicans* (1804), by Anthony Pasquin, Esq.

weapon of Anglo-Federalism, and they are so familiarized
to the prostitution of decency that they believe it is classi-
cal. The Hottentot does not sicken over his offals, though
the rest of the world would. They have little wit and less
breeding, and if they are not scandalous, they are nothing."
The poem itself was a burlesque on the grief of the "Royal
Faction" over Hamilton's death, and these extracts are
illustrative:

> Like Cybele's mad priests, these royal Feds
> Rear, rave, and growl, and dance upon their heads.
> T' alarm our constancy, they Wit assail,
> And shake their bloody tresses in the gale;
> Burst in the nursery, with hideous yells,
> And frighten gossips with their horrid spells;
> Till Jedidiah shudders at their looks,
> And the King's Fisher flies from Dedham brooks.
> Our General's gone, the sobbing varlets cry;
> Our General's gone, the echoing hills reply.

The "King's Fisher" in the foregoing lines, and the "Old
Lady of Dedham" in the following, were both references to
Fisher Ames, and must have greatly delighted his brother,
Dr. Nathaniel: "The sedition bill has been expunged with
national execration, and the malversation of John Adams'
tadpole nobility shall have no more quarter from us than
the mechanic or farmer whom they spurn and would put in
chains, if they could secure another reign of terror. Nay,
start not, Old Lady of Dedham — the asseveration is just,
and you shall be answerable for your arrogance and your
hypocrisy; you shall be tied upon the fatal wheel of your
party, and made to repent in volumes of prayer your of-
fences to liberty and your country."

Noah Webster, the famous dictionary writer and also
the editor of a strongly Federalist and Hamiltonian news-

paper, the *American Minerva*, was treated in the poem as
follows:

> Like an old skunk, squat, trodden down, and lame,
> Swelling with rage and interdicted fame —
> Verb-murmuring Noah sat, like Envy's nurse
> Scowling at Phoebus! — levelling his curse;
> In anguish brandishing his goose-drawn pen,
> The first of coxcombs, and the last of men!

The supposed preference for English and monarchical
forms of government and the disbelief in democracy, of
which Hamilton and the Essex Junto were constantly accused, were referred to in vigorous language in *The Hamiltoniad* as characteristic of those "persecutors of human
freedom who suborned every press that could be corrupted
and established others to confound and destroy the civic
privileges of their fellow citizens."

We know that a confederacy was formed for the abolition of
an equality of rights, and he [Hamilton] was at the head of that
political association. The hisses of these traitors may be heard
in every Federal echo of New England, and we will not repose
until the hydra is crushed. The varying arts which they practice to undermine the privileges of the Farmer and the Mechanic
are of the most subtle nature. They know that the base of human freedom is affixed upon the liberty of the press, and under
this conviction they violate and stain that liberty upon every
possible event, in order to make that privilege odious, which
they are so eager to destroy. Every reasoner in the cause of the
people, however learned, polite, and kind, is denounced by this
Royal Junto as a Jacobin, Infidel, and a Republican villain!
He is assailed by a hideous clamor, to traduce his honor and
annul his morals. They will depict him as an Atheist, because he
opposes an hierarchy; and they will exhibit him as a popular
flatterer because he is unwilling to see the useful classes despised,
and the weaker orders of his fellow-citizens in misery! . . . Mr.
H. might be a proper instrument to hold up as the idol of the
Essex Junto; but he was very far from being a great man,

unless they take the measure of endowment by the altitudes of Lilliput.

Hamilton's Anglican views were also the subject of bitter comment in the *Independent Chronicle*, and other Antifederalist papers: [1]

Mr. Hamilton may justly be regarded as the founder of the Royal faction of this country. He raised it from the dregs and embers of Toryism and placed it for security in the circle of Anti-Gallican antipathies. He certainly had the credit of being contributory to every evil that threatened our liberties with ruin. His great moving principle of action was passive obedience and non-resistance to the will of his political momentum at St. James. . . . In return for this docility, he was to be upheld by every Tory agent in America, sustained by the *aurum potabile* while living, and deified when dead — at least so far as deification is dependent on illiterate journalists and monarchic scribblers. On this contract, the Federal Parcae of New Haven, Dedham and Charlestown chanted Amen! . . . The toad was not more inimical to the morals of our original mother than he was to Republicanism, at the ear of his credulous military master [Washington]. . . . He was the Cis-Atlantic echo for that tyrant, Pitt, around whose legislative neck he clung and hung, and who is the most pernicious instrument that ever desolated a nation or blighted human joy! . . . The aristocracy which he would have formed would have been an aristocracy of wealth, the most repulsive of all, as it would have embraced the pride of distinction, without its refinements. . . . He boldly declared to the author of these comments that "liberty was the highest note in the gamut of nonsense," and we have no hesitation in believing that he was sincere in that unconditional and ruthless assertion. . . . It is an objection, with the Royal Faction, particularly in New England, that every citizen may be a legislator; but we rejoice that he has this power, and hope he will always retain it

[1] See "Illustrative Comments upon the Character and Influence of the Late Gen. Alexander Hamilton, No. IV," in *Independent Chronicle*, August 23, 1804.

The *Columbian Centinel*, August 25, 1804, said: "A malignant writer still continues to insult the memory of Gen. Hamilton in the *Chronicle*. It is hoped, for the honor of our country, it will shortly be proved that the calumniator is not an American."

while his plain but sound intelligence is correspondent with the simplicity of the governing law.

Language like the above, while violent, was not wholly without justification. The charge that the Junto were monarchists and disbelievers in democracy was firmly believed by all the radical Republicans like Dr. Ames, and by the majority of the more conservative. It is certain that the individual members of the Junto gave considerable basis for this belief through the general pessimistic tone of their letters and speeches. Thus, to Dwight, Fisher Ames wrote in 1803: "Our country is too big for union, too sordid for patriotism, too democratic for liberty. What is to become of it, he who made it best knows? Its vice will govern it, by practising upon its folly. This is ordained for democracies." In 1805, he wrote: "As great geniuses snatch the sceptre from the hands of great little rascals, the government rises; though liberty rises no more. Ours is gone, never to return. To mitigate a tyranny is all that is left for our hopes. We cannot maintain justice by the force of our Constitution." [1] To Josiah Quincy, he wrote in 1806: "I have long thought a democracy incapable of liberty"; and referring to Jefferson as "our illustrious Caesar," he wrote: "Let us, however, be just to this man. Is he not a very good chief for us? Would any man, who was free from the lowest passions and prejudices of the lowest mob, manage our affairs with success?" [2] To Timothy Pickering, he wrote, in 1806: "Our disease is democracy. It is not the skin that festers — our very bones are carious and their marrow blackens with gangrene." [3] These doleful, pessimistic views of American

[1] Fisher Ames to Dwight, October 26, 1803, November 29, 1805.
[2] Fisher Ames to Quincy, February 12, 1806, see also December 11, 1806.
[3] Fisher Ames to Pickering, March 10, 1806, see also March 24, 1806, and January 12, 1807.

democracy were paralleled in the writings of George Cabot, the close friend of Fisher Ames. Writing in 1795, he said: "After all, where is the boasted advantage of a representative system over the turbulent mobocracy of Athens? If the resort to popular meetings is necessary, faction, and especially faction of great towns — always the most powerful — will be too strong for our mild and feeble government." Again, replying to Timothy Pickering, who had written in 1804, "I do not believe in the practicability of a long-continued Union. A Northern Confederacy would unite congenial characters and present a fairer prospect of public happiness," Cabot said: "All the evils you describe and many more are to be apprehended; but I greatly fear that a separation would be no remedy, because the source of them is in the political theories of our country and in ourselves. . . . We are democratic altogether, and I hold democracy, in its natural operation, to be the government of the worst. . . . While I hold that a government altogether popular is in effect a government of the populace, I maintain that no government can be relied on that has not a material portion of the democratic mixture in its composition. . . . If no man in New England could vote for legislators, who was not possessed in his own right of two thousand dollars value in land, we could do something better." [1] Others of the Junto unquestionably entertained serious and often-expressed doubts as to the permanent success of a democracy and of the government of the United States if it should continue to be administered by the Republican party. In consequence, there was never any set of politicians in this country — unless it was the extreme abolitionists — who were so hotly denounced by

[1] See *Life and Letters of George Cabot* (1877), by Henry Cabot Lodge, Cabot to King, August 14, 1795; Cabot to Pickering, February 14, 1804.

their opponents, day after day, in the newspaper press, and in all political writings.[1]

There was still another set of men who, even more than the Junto, called forth the bitterest denunciation and contempt from Dr. Ames and from other Republican writers. This was the "law craft" or "pettifoggers," as Dr. Ames termed them in his Diary; in other words, the lawyers in general. The antipathy displayed towards lawyers as a class, and especially by the Antifederalists or Republicans, is a very curious and striking feature of the history of the United States during the twenty years succeeding the War of the Revolution. During the period of readjustment, between 1785 and 1789, the hostility towards the legal profession was chiefly due to the financial trouble in which the people found themselves. Debt was universal. The courts were clogged up with suits for collection of claims; the jails overflowed with imprisoned debtors. Exasperated beyond measure by litigation, by mortgage foreclosures, and by the system of fees and court costs established by the bar associations, the people at large mistook effects for causes and attributed all their evils to the existence of lawyers in the community. Thus, the town of Dedham itself, in its instructions to its representatives in the General Court, in May, 1786, attacked "the order of lawyers" as follows: "We are not inattentive to the almost universally prevailing complaints against the practice of the order of lawyers; and many of us now sensibly feel the effects of their unreasonable and extravagant exactions; we think their practice pernicious and their mode unconstitutional. You will therefore endeavor that such regulations be introduced into our courts of law, and that such restraints be

[1] See especially, *A Poetical Dictionary of Popular Terms Illustrated In Rhyme — for the Use of Society in General and Politicians in Particular* (1808), by David Hitchcock.

laid on the order of lawyers as that we may have recourse
to the laws, and find our security and not our ruin in
them. If, upon a fair discussion and mature deliberation,
such a measure should appear impracticable, you are to
endeavor that the order of lawyers be totally abolished; an
alternative preferable to their continuing in their present
mode." The neighboring town of Braintree, the home of
John Adams, voted in town meeting: "We humbly request
that there may be such laws compiled as may crush, or at
least put a proper check or restraint upon, that order of
Gentlemen denominated Lawyers, the completion of whose
modern conduct appears to us to tend rather to the destruction than to the preservation of the town." Many
towns and many writers in the press were much more extreme in their denunciation of lawyers. Benjamin Austin, Jr. wrote a long series of letters to the *Independent
Chronicle*, in 1786, under the name of "Honestus," [1] in
which he urged: "This order of men should be annihilated.
. . . No lawyers should be admitted to speak in court, and
the order be abolished as not only a useless but a dangerous body to the public." These letters had a tremendous
influence on the public mind, which is referred to in two
interesting letters from John Quincy Adams, written when
a Senior in Harvard College, in 1787, in which he said:
"At a time when the profession of the law is laboring under
the heavy weight of popular indignation — when it is up-
braided as the original cause of all the evils with which the
Commonwealth is distressed; when the Legislature have
been publicly exhorted by a public writer to abolish it entirely, and when the mere title of lawyer is sufficient to
deprive a man of the public confidence, it would seem this

[1] *Observations on the Pernicious Practice of the Law*, by Benjamin Austin, Jr.
The *Letters of an American Farmer*, written in 1787 by H. St. John Crevecoeur,
also express similar sentiments of the times.

profession would afford but a poor subject for panegyric; but its real ability is not to be determined by the short-lived frenzy of an inconsiderate multitude, nor by the artful misrepresentations of an insidious writer. . . . The popular odium which has been excited against the practitioners in this Commonwealth prevails to so great a degree that the most innocent and irreproachable life cannot guard a lawyer against the hatred of his fellow citizens. The very despicable writings of *Honestus* were just calculated to kindle a flame which will subsist long after they are forgotten. . . . A thousand lies, in addition to these published in the papers, have been spread all over the country to prejudice the people against the 'order,' as it has been invidiously called; and as a free people will not descend to disguise their sentiments, the gentlemen of the profession have been treated with contemptuous neglect and with insulting abuse."[1]

Dr. Ames from the outset of his career entertained a very low opinion of the legal profession; and as early as 1765, in the first almanac which he edited, he had expressed vigorously his opinion of the pettifogging "attorneys," as distinguished from the "barristers," then practicing:

There is another herd of these drones as troublesome to the Gentlemen of the Bar as the other is despicable in the eye of a regular bred physician, which are called Pettyfoggers; this is a Race made up, for the most part, of the Dregs of Misfortune and Misconduct, joined with a Deal of low Wit and such a Sip of Learning as just intoxicates the Brain, as Pope has it, who, having suffered a Court of Law repeatedly in Actions of Debt, Trespass, and perhaps Criminal Actions too, at last get the Form of a Declaration pretty perfectly by Heart, run off to some different Part of the Continent, fill up Writs in the most trifling Causes, exciting Quarrels,

[1] "Diary of John Quincy Adams," in *Massachusetts Historical Society Proceedings* (1902), vol. XVI.

thereby becoming downright Barrators, the very Pest of Society.

In 1793, Dr. Ames was appointed by Governor John Hancock Clerk of the Inferior Court of General Sessions and Common Pleas. This Court was opened for the first time in the new Courthouse in Dedham in 1794, that town having just been made the shire town of the newly established Norfolk County.[1] His peppery temper and his Republican point of view kept Ames in continual hot water with the Court, the suitors, and the members of the bar in general. The action of the latter, in cutting down the Clerk's fees, aroused his particular ire; and his entries in his Diary display his frank opinions on the subject:

Oct. 31, 1793. The puppyism of Sam Haven or of his father, conspicuous in engrossing Law business to himself while clerk in H. Townshend's office.

March 31, 1794. Too much of my time engrossed by public concerns.

Sept. 29, 1795. Sundry medicines and attendance on sick, uncharged by reason of perplexities.

Sept. 30, 1796. By decision of the Judges of Common Pleas, I am prevented from endorsing writs for anybody, on the objection of Thomas Williams and a decree of the Conclave of Jesuits or Junto of the Dogs of Law in one of their Bar

---

[1] Dedham was now becoming a town of some importance. In 1794, when Norfolk County was set off from Suffolk County, Dedham became its shire town, with a new Courthouse and jail. Several handsome dwelling houses were erected about 1795, one by Fisher Ames himself, and another, adjoining Ames', by Samuel Haven, a student of law in Ames' office and then Registrar of Probate (later Judge of Common Pleas). The town had a population in 1790 of 1659 and in 1800 of 1973; and in 1793 there were in it 215 dwelling houses, 180 barns, 25 shops, 8 grain, flour, and sawmills, 1 potash works. Fisher Ames wrote to Dwight, July 3, 1794: "The politics of Dedham are interesting. Be it known to our friends at a distance, that the squash town is the capital of Norfolk. A court house is ordered by the worshipful Session to be erected near my territory according to a plan which Mr. Bulfinch is to be requested to draw. A jail is also to be built, which is a comfort to us. I do not perceive that our folks are much elated with their new dignity, so that if our squash vines should in future bear pineapples, they will be surprised."

Meetings, issued to our timid Judges of sudden manufacture.

Jan. 8, 1797. Sundry Land Jobbers or Speculators abscond, cannot realize Georgia lands — Judges, Priests, Lawyers, etc.

Feb. 20, 1797. Addled with do-nothings, I can make no progress in recording judgments of Court.

Aug. 21, 1797. Stigmatized as of the Seed of Jacob. Am persecuted by the Hedgehogs — yield Clerk's office of C. P. to one of the Order, and am almost exonerated from all business, as few are sick and Court business used to employ all leisure hours.

Sept. 24, 1799. Court Sessions — No lawyer will support a writ action if not filled out by a lawyer.

Nov. 3, 1801. Sessions innovating to my vexation. Particular prejudices manifested by the Judges.

April 3, 1802. A lawyer in every man's mess here; nothing will go with fools without a lawyer, but from good company, they are excluded! Or if they get in, they spoil it.

Dr. Ames had another, still stronger, reason for his opposition to the legal profession. He hated their politics; for the bar of Massachusetts was almost exclusively Federalist. Thus, one of its rare Republican members, Joseph Story, in describing his early years at the Essex bar, in 1801, wrote: "At the time of my admission, I was the only lawyer within its pale who was either openly or secretly a Democrat. All the lawyers and all the Judges in the County of Essex were Federalists and I was not a little discouraged. For some time I felt the coldness and estrangement resulting from this known diversity of opinion, and was left somewhat solitary at the Bar." And James Sullivan, another Republican, when he was Attorney-General, wrote in 1804: "I have in the day of the cockade tyranny, suffered every abuse that Dana, Thacher and Parsons and the greatest part of the Bar could give, without being called on for personal satisfaction. I have been several times driven to that disagreeable resource." It was because the lawyers constituted the mainstay of the Federalist party that Dr. Ames hated and feared the part which they were taking in the State and National Government; and he wrote, in February, 1799, of this fatal influence as follows:

> The air of a Court is poisonous and apt to change an honest man into an intriguer. However art and cunning may be thought essential to an advocate among the quirks of law, honesty and attention are the greatest attributes of a legislator. The making lawyers legislators, seems to defeat the grand principle of keeping the Legislative Department distinct and separate from the Judiciary — and where these two, or any two of any three departments of Government, are confided to the same hands, tho' the forms under the real sovereignty of the people are still observed to amuse them, the substance is gone. Fear takes the place of that noble ambition to support the dignity of free citizens, then the human mind becomes demoralized; and because you would sleep on your thrones and not watch your servants ye are doomed as unworthy, when you make yourselves so by obstinate blind ignorance and apathy, and as swinish multitude must be gagged, yoked and ringed." [1]

[1] An anonymous letter to the *Columbian Minerva* in Dedham, March 30, 1802, of which Ames was probably the author, gives these unflattering views: "The following sketches are humbly proposed to the consideration of all unprejudiced honest men, as reasons why lawyers or attorneys at law should not be considered suitable characters to fill all places in Government. 'Let the hypocrits reign not, lest the people be ensnared.' Job xxxiv, 30. Lawyers live upon the sins of the people; it is natural for people to endeavor to increase the stock which supports them. It is for the interest of the people to have laws as plain and explicit as possible, that the people might the more easily keep within their bounds in order to prevent multiplying lawsuits; but it is for the interest of lawyers to have them as complex as they can, that the people might more easily be entangled in their net, that lawsuits might be the more easily multiplied. Lawyers promote quarrels, under strong temptation to enrich themselves by assisting oppressors to take the spoils of the poor and defenceless, and by dividing the spoils with them. If the love of money, which is the root of all evil, has prevailed to so great a degree as to threaten the exclusion of all those moral and social virtues which sweeten and cement Society, can it be safe to trust the pub-

And in a letter to the *Columbian Minerva*, September 6, 1803, he wrote:

> It is not Federalist or Republican, Aristocrat or Democrat, but Lawyer and Citizen, between whom the eternal dispute really subsists on Government and its Administration. . . . Jefferson was educated a Lawyer, but despising the clubbish bar meetings hostile to citizenship, put it off long ago, and has become one of the best of Citizens. But he that is not now a Lawyer, or tool of a Lawyer, is considered only fit to carry guts to a bear in New England. So it is! So the people are deluded — and won't see with their own eyes! They love to be prig-ridden, as well as priest-ridden, in New England!

In many entries, Dr. Ames recorded his contempt for the "Aristocratic lawyers," and he cited on his side, with considerable gusto, two eminent statesmen — Jefferson and Washington:

> *Dec. 1802.* Thomas Paine, author of *Common Sense, Rights of Man*, lately returned from France to Washington, addresses his fellow citizens of the United States in 4 letters in the Gazettes in a masterly manner which sets lawyers and Federal Tories roaring and vomiting black, gives them the black vomit.
>
> *Jan. 1, 1803.* Chopfallen, indeed, under the glorious administration of Jefferson, under the guise of Federalism, the Order of Lawyers are barking destruction at all that won't submit to their domination.
>
> *April 12.* Jefferson, tho' bred a lawyer, despises the narrow spirit of Pettyfoggism, therefore the lawyers hate him.
>
> *1805.* — The most impudence dispensed with impunity from a new Gazette in Boston edited by John Park entitled

lic safety with a class of men who have been all their days trained up and habitu-
ated to cultivate the root of all evil? Then let us guard against resting the
weight of Government upon the shoulders of crafty, artful, cunning, designing,
intriguing men who have an interest of their own which stands in direct competition with the Public Good."

Repertory. The filth and spume of all the intrigueing tools of Federal attornies far outdoes the spitting under B. Russell, especially 7th May 1805, puts even American patience upon the stretch.

April 3, 1809. Washington, dupe of the Order of Lawyers while he was alive, renounced them after he was dead. I will not do so. I will renounce them now I am alive, and leave them to their luck after. [1]

During the administration of Jefferson, the lawyers as a class continued to be largely associated with the Federalist party. The views which the President entertained towards Chief Justice Marshall, in the latter's broad construction of the Constitution of the United States, naturally placed him in opposition to the most distinguished leaders of the bar, especially in New England. In 1803, Marshall pronounced the opinion of the Supreme Court of the United States in the great case of *Marbury* v. *Madison*, in which the right of the Supreme Court to decide upon the question of the constitutionality of Acts of Congress was established. This case and some of its doctrines were fought by Jefferson and his upholders; and it was natural, therefore,

---

[1] The statement as to Washington's opinion of lawyers apparently refers to the following curious passage in Washington's will: "In the construction of which it will readily be perceived that no professional character has been consulted or has had any agency in the draught; and that although it has occupied many of my leisure hours to digest, and to draught it into its present form, it may, notwithstanding, appear crude and incorrect; but, having endeavored to be plain and explicit in all the devises, even at the expense of prolixity, perhaps of tautology, I hope, and trust, that no disputes will arise concerning them; but if contrary to expectation the case should be otherwise, from the want of legal expression, or the usual technical terms, or because too much or too little has been said on any of the devises to be consonant with law, my will and direction expressly is that all disputes (if unhappily any should arise) shall be decided by three impartial and intelligent men, known for their probity and good understanding — two to be chosen by the disputants, each having the choice of one, and the third by those two — which three men when thus chosen shall, unfettered by law or legal constructions, declare the sense of the testator's intentions; and such decision is, to all intents and purposes, to be as binding on the parties as if it had been given in the Supreme Court of the United States."

that Dr. Ames should be found as one of the most vigorous opponents of Marshall's arguments. Of the lawyers who upheld the latter's decision, Dr. Ames noted in his Diary that: "It is alarming to find the Order, the would-be judges, arrogating that veto on the Laws for the Judiciary, which the people in their Constitution had so cautiously refused to their Presidents, Governors, etc."

VII

A POLITICAL MURDER

THE gross abuse lavished upon President Jefferson by the Federalists produced, of course, a corresponding flood of vituperation and calumny from the Republicans; and in Boston, in 1806, these unrestrained political passions had reached a point where open violence was a possible, even probable, outcome. In July and August of that year a series of rancorous political articles, written by Benjamin Austin, in the *Independent Chronicle*, and the publication of a violent criminal libel, resulted in murder. Austin's language may be judged from the following extracts:[1]

The arts and tricks of the Federalists are as various as the wickedness of their designs are base and infamous. . . . The torrent of defamation arises from this source — as soon as one story is worn out, another is put into circulation. President Jefferson, Mr. Madison, Mr. Gallatin, Judge Sullivan, etc., all become the objects of their infamous clamors. While the people enjoy the blessings of a wise Administration, these noisy revilers are constantly sounding the tocsin, and attempting to render every man as infamous by detraction as they themselves are by conduct and practice.

Calumnies have been adopted for evidence; slanders are received as full proof; lying falsehoods and even perjuries, have, in the eye of Federalism, lost the turpitude of their nature; and morality is no part of the political system it maintains. . . . The Federalist papers have had a number of important objects on hand, all tending to the same end, the overthrow of the government, the raising sedition, and the introduction of a monarchy.

[1] See *Independent Chronicle*, July 17, 21, 24, 1806.

Federalism mounted the sacred theatre of devotion and many of the clergy, with an idea that sedition clothed in the robes of religion would have a more powerful effect, refused to lead their assemblies in prayer for the Chief Magistrate of the Nation. Federalism, wrapt in corruption, crept into the Courts of justice.

On August 4, 1806, Austin wrote the following editorial in the *Independent Chronicle*:

Federalism, the curse of our country. The Federalists have become the greatest nuisance in society; they are constantly endeavoring to injure the country in every foreign and domestic concern. Our affairs in Europe are kept in a perpetual state of uncertainty by the daily publications fabricated among a junto, for the sole purpose of perplexing all the transactions of government. The Federal papers are the vehicles of defamation against the administration. . . . They are *conspirators* against the happiness, peace and prosperity of the United States. . . . The Federalists, if possible, are worse than the Tories, for they were avowed enemies and the former are pretended friends though in reality the most desperate and implacable foes. . . . We then had a set of canting, jesuitical hypocrites who, under the cloak of religion, were describing the country as infested with a band of demoralizers and destroyers of every religious institution.

On the same day, the *Centinel* referred to it as an instance of "the reptiles of Democracy"; and on the same day the son of its writer was shot and killed in Boston, as a result of a quarrel between the writer and a Federalist lawyer. This famous case — the murder of Charles Austin by Thomas O. Selfridge — has been often described in histories and law books, but its political phase has been scarcely noticed. It was certain, however, that Dr. Ames would not overlook this phase, and his Diary, accordingly, records it as establishing "the reign of pettifogarchy," Selfridge being a member of the bar. His entries are as follows:

August 4, 1806. T. O. Selfridge assassinated B. Austin's son by shooting in State Street, and Dec. 2, Grand Jury at Boston bring in a bill of manslaughter only, to the abhorrence and consternation of Good People at the Reign of Pettifogarchy established here.

Nov. 30. Thomas O. Selfridge, for the murderous assassination of young Charles Austin, 4th August last, at S. J. C. now sitting in Boston, is charged only manslaughter and bailed in 2000 dollars. People agast!

Dec. 2. News that the Assassin and Murderer is liberated at Boston S. J. C. Reign of Pettifogarchy established.

Dec. 23. Selfridge's trial begun.

Dec. 29. Most interesting trial, it seems, to whole Continent. All passions moved, threats and grumbling!

Dec. 25. Selfridge still trying.

Dec. 26. Selfridge brot in not guilty! Mobs. Pettifogarchy establishing, another reign of terror begun.

The story of the case presents a striking picture of the times. As the thirtieth anniversary of the Declaration of Independence approached, elaborate preparations were made in Boston to observe it; but each political party determined to conduct its own separate celebration.[1] The Federalists (or Federal Republicans, as they now termed themselves) had a procession, and a dinner at Faneuil Hall. Christopher Gore presided, and the guests of honor were Ex-President John Adams and Robert Treat Paine.

---

[1] In 1806 Dr. Ames noted in his Diary that the Federalists in Dedham were so opposed to the Government that they would not celebrate the Fourth of July with the Republicans: "*July 4, 1806.* Dedham refuses to read Declaration of Independence. Jabez Chickering spurned at Declaration." The *Columbian Minerva* of June 14, 1806, said also: "American Independence is to be celebrated on the 4th of July at Walpole by the Republicans. If the Federalists join them, it must be a forced compliance"; and in its issue of July 22 it cited instances in Connecticut where the Federalists declined to read the Declaration; and cited the *Albany Centinel* as saying: "We were sorry to see the wicked practice of reading the Declaration of Independence continued." The *Independent Chronicle* of August 4 noted that in Abington, Massachusetts, the day was celebrated at a combination dinner, but with two orators — one from each party; see also *Independent Chronicle*, July 17, 1806.

The occasion was especially notable for being the first time that Stuart's great picture of "Washington at the Siege of Boston" was displayed, quaintly described in the *Centinel*: "At his side is his favorite white charger whose expanded eye and features tell the story of the picture. The noble animal, though agitated by the din of the scene, appears perfectly at the command of the master's hand which holds the reigns." The usual attacks on Jefferson were made at the dinner, to which the *Chronicle* referred, in its account describing "the insolence and impertinence of the orator" and "the vileness of the defamation against the Man." The ambiguous toast to the President of the United States — "May the people be discerning and history impartial" — was strongly contrasted with the flowery and eulogistic toasts to the Federalist Governor and other party heroes. A minor celebration and dinner were held by the young Federalists at Association Hall in Elm Street.

Meanwhile, a more pretentious celebration was being held by the Republicans, advertised extensively in the papers, the day before, as "the Order of the Day is Hilarity, Philanthropy and Fraternity." In view of the state of political feeling, the word "Fraternity" must have been highly sarcastic. Unusual interest was given to the procession by the presence in line of "His Excellency the Tunisian Ambassador," Melli Meli, who "in his turban and long gray beard, with his showy oriental costume and a number of his attendants in rich Turkish and Moorish dresses, attracted to a high degree the curiosity of the public." The *Chronicle* described the occasion as follows: "The order and regularity of the march was highly pleasing, as curiosity had excited a great number of the inhabitants to assemble in the streets through which they passed, to see a stranger whose customs and habits were so novel in our country. The Ambassador was gratified with the civility and respect paid him, and expressed his warmest attachment for the citizens of Boston. The day was remarkably favorable for the accommodation of the company within the tent. The brilliancy of the scene was enlivened by the crowds of citizens assembled on the hill; the prospect from the height was magnificent; and hilarity, philanthropy, and fraternity was expressed in every countenance and exhibited in the conduct of every individual. In the evening, rockets were exhibited, and the whole business of the day closed with that display of friendship and mutual cordiality which will ever add to the reputation of Republican citizens." At the dinner, which was held in a decorated tent on Copp's Hill, Benjamin Austin, one of the editors of the *Chronicle*, presided; and among the toasts were the following attacks on the opposite party: "The good people of Massachusetts — In harmony with the Federal Government, may not their Executive long continue at variance with them!" "Federalism! Alas, poor Federalism! We war not with the dust; peace to the reliques which must repose forever in the tomb of the Capulets." A second dinner was held by the "Young Democratic Republicans" at the Green Dragon Tavern.

The quarrel which later resulted in the murder arose from circumstances connected with the main dinner. Owing to the unexpected crowd who were drawn to the tent by the presence of the Ambassador, a large number of extras (including "seven roast pigs, ten bushels of green peas, twenty-four meat pies, and forty plum puddings") were supplied by Mr. Eager, the landlord of the Jefferson Tavern,[1] and regarding the payment for these a dispute

[1] This was an old tavern in Back Street (now Salem Street). About 1803, Eager had purchased the effects of an old public house on Cambridge Common, and amongst other things a sign bearing a portrait of President Adams. When he

arose a few days later. Eager consulted a Federalist lawyer, Thomas O. Selfridge, who advised him that the Committee of Arrangements were personally liable; and suit being brought, the bill was finally paid. Unluckily, shortly after, Benjamin Austin, who was noted for his sharp tongue, stated to several persons gathered at an insurance office that "everything would have been all right if it had not been for the interference of a damned Federal lawyer," and he hinted that the suit was brought at the lawyer's instigation. Although no man was named, it is evident that all present understood Selfridge to be meant. The latter, hearing of the remark, at once demanded from Austin a retraction. Austin then made inquiries, and, ascertaining the falsity of his information, corrected his statement to those to whom he had previously made it. Selfridge was not satisfied with this, and demanded a written retraction; this being refused, he wrote to Austin: "The declarations which you have made to Mr. Welsh are jesuitically false, and your concession wholly unsatisfactory. You call the author a gentleman, and probably a friend. He is in fact a liar and a scoundrel. If you assume the falsehood yourself to screen your friend, you must acknowledge it under your own hand, and give me the means of vindicating myself against the effect of your aspersion." Austin, being naturally much irritated at this insulting letter, refused to make any further concession. Selfridge then said to a friend who acted as an intermediary that only three courses remained for him to pursue — "a prosecution, chastisement, or posting," and that, by the latter course, "the facts would come fairly before the pub-

---

swung this sign in Boston, his Republican neighbors refused "to have that old face stuck up," but offered to make up a purse to pay to have "Adams' face brushed out and a good likeness of Tom Jefferson put in its place." This was the origin of the Jefferson Tavern, regarded for some time as the headquarters of the Republican party in Boston.

lic, and the infamy of barratrously stirring up law suits would be justly laid at his door, or transferred to the villain who engendered the lie or who screens the liar from his merited deserts." Accordingly, on Monday, August 4, he caused to be published in the *Boston Gazette* the following advertisement:

Austin Posted.

Benjamin Austin, loan officer, having acknowledged that he has circulated an infamous falsehood concerning my professional conduct in a certain cause, and having refused to give the satisfaction due to a gentleman in similar cases — I hereby publish said Austin as a coward, a liar, and a scoundrel; and if said Austin has the effrontery to deny any part of the charge he shall be silenced by the most irrefragable proof.

Thomas O. Selfridge.

P. S. The various editors in the United States are requested to insert the above notice in their journals, and their respective agents in this town.

Austin, having obtained knowledge that this outrageous libel was to be published, had inserted in the *Independent Chronicle* of the same morning the following:

Considering it derogatory to enter into a newspaper controversy with one T. O. Selfridge, in reply to his insolent and false publication in the *Gazette* of this day; if any gentleman is desirous to know the facts, on which his impertinence is founded, any information will be given by me on the subject.

Benjamin Austin.

Those who publish Selfridge's statement, are requested to insert the above, and they shall be paid on presenting their bills.

Austin, further, on the same day, on meeting a friend of Selfridge, said: "If Mr. Selfridge attacks me, I hope to have such support from friends at hand as I shall be able to avoid any injury"; or (as testified to by another witness) "he should not meddle with Selfridge himself, but some person on a footing with him should take him in

hand." This remark, being reported to Selfridge, was regarded as a threat that Austin proposed to assault him.
The fact seems to have been quite the opposite, as Austin
only intended to guard himself from any assault by Selfridge. Nevertheless, unknown to Austin, his son, Charles
Austin, took upon himself the defence of his father's honor.
This young man was then a student in Harvard College, of
remarkable promise, a universal favorite, and only eighteen
years of age. Chancing to be in Boston that morning, he
read the *Gazette*, and immediately purchased a long hickory
cane. About one o'clock in the afternoon, he was talking
with a friend on the sidewalk in front of what is now the
Worthington Building on the corner of State and Congress
Streets. While there, he saw Selfridge coming round the
northeast corner of the old State House, Selfridge's law
office being in that building. As Selfridge reached a point
in State Street just opposite what is now the Merchants
Bank Building, Austin stepped out towards him and,
raising his cane, dealt him a heavy blow on the head, which
cut through his hat and through his scalp. Selfridge at
once drew a pistol which he had pocketed on leaving his
office, and shot Charles Austin through the breast. Austin,
after dealing him several weaker blows, finally sank on the
pavement, and was carried into a shop, where he soon
died. Although it was a time of day when State Street and
the Exchange were thronged with merchants, so rapidly
did the affair take place that no one had a chance to inter-
pose. Selfridge quickly surrendered himself into the
custody of the civil authorities, and, as he later wrote, "for
safe-keeping I was literally obliged to escape into prison to
elude the fury of democracy."

Though Harvard College then was intensely Federalist,
Charles Austin's funeral was attended by the whole senior
class and by the president, professors, and tutors of the

College, as well as by a long procession of citizens of Boston and the neighboring towns. The following obituary appeared in the *Chronicle*, August 7:

> When the beauty of youth, blooming in science, excellent in virtue, and rich in expectation, is taken from life in the ordinary course of mortality, the tears of sympathy flow spontaneously; but when the grave reluctantly receives its untimely prey from the hand of violence, gloomy silence burdened with astonishment denies to sorrow the usual utterance. . . . The young man visited a number of his friends and families where he was acquainted, in the forenoon as usual, and appeared very cheerful and gay; he left one of their houses about ten minutes before he was killed. His breast, glowing with filial piety, received the fatal ball which probably had been prepared for the fond bosom of his father!

It is impossible to exaggerate the excitement which this event caused in Boston and its neighborhood. Both Benjamin Austin and Selfridge were prominent men — the latter at the bar, and the former as a veteran newspaper writer, an Antifederalist leader, and an official of the United States Government. The murder at once became a political issue, notwithstanding the fact that Selfridge, in a pamphlet published later by him in his defence, stated: "Nothing of a political nature ought, even in the remotest degree, to have been connected with the transaction; for it was a mere personal controversy. But unprincipled men, who ever keep a cat-like watch for disastrous occurrences to turn to their own account, have, by base and factitious means, tinctured the cause with the spirit of party, and given to the question a political turn." As soon as the coroner's jury rendered the verdict of "wilful murder," the Antifederalist papers, terming it "a Federal murder," published detailed accounts.[1] The Federalist papers, how-

---

[1] See especially *National Intelligencer* (Washington), August 13, 15, 1806.

ever, only made mention of the event in the briefest manner. Thus, the *Centinel* of August 6 had an article of only
seventeen lines about the murder, ending: "The particulars of this unfortunate and melancholy affair are so vari-
ously represented by contradictory reports that, were it in
any respect proper, it would be impossible for us to give
any correct detail." The *New England Palladium* published, on August 6, the day after the murder, the barest
reference to it, and on August 8 said: "The late melancholy catastrophe ought not in any shape to be made the
subject of discussion or controversy. . . . Public should
suspend their judgment until they are in possession of all
the evidence. Meanwhile, we confidently trust that any
endeavour to poison the fountains of justice, to pollute our
Courts of law, to inflame a jury with political and party
rancour in the trial of a fellow citizen for his life, will be
reprobated by every honest man of whatever party." The
Boston Gazette, in which Selfridge's original libellous
"posting" had been published, said, August 7: "The melancholy event of Monday last which terminated in the
death of Mr. Charles Austin is universally deplored; and
those most sensibly afflicted by it are objects of general
sympathy. It is, therefore, much to be regretted that a
desire should anywhere be manifested to increase the public feeling or to give an improper direction by any perversion or particular interpretation of the coroner's inquest.
. . . Justice to the life and reputation of the person now
most interested requires that no judgment should be passed
and no colouring given to the unfortunate act for which he
is hereafter to be tried by the laws of his country." The
Chronicle, however, of which Benjamin Austin himself was
an editor, did not intend that the people of Boston should
forget the "late savage assassination"; and it at once began a series of articles which, as the autumn progressed,

inflamed the political passions of the public to a high degree. An article in its issue of August 11 attacked the Federalist newspapers for their practice of publishing libels, to which the whole unhappy affair was attributable (an attack which would have been more just and more effective if the *Chronicle* itself had not been as serious an offender in this direction as its rivals, the *Gazette*, the *Centinel*, and the *Repertory*): "'You must stop this shooting about newspaper slanders,' says the Federalist, 'or we are undone people.' 'But,' replies the Republican, 'lay the axe at the root of the tree, stop the newspaper slanders, let character and the peace of families be regarded by the Federalists, and there will be no occasion for shooting.' . . . There is something insolent and audaciously impudent in this exclamation of Federalists. Their papers teem with lies, slanders, and atrocious abuse. . . . Neither age, sex, character, or standing in life can be shielded from the outrageous and groundless calumnies born universally and constantly in the gazettes they issue. . . . The leading Federalists openly declare that lies and slanders for political purposes are not unmoral. But they have a very disagreeable and distressing effect upon the subjects of them and upon society." Ten days after the murder the *Chronicle* again attacked the silence of its opponents: "Why are the Federal papers silent on the late atrocious murder, committed in open day in the midst of our capital, and which will be recorded on the historic page as a dark spot in the annals of New England? . . . So powerfully do the persons who compose the factions in this town feel the public indignation kindled against them that they observe a sullen silence, and repine only because the *first object* of their wicked designs is not accomplished." Again, on August 25, it referred to "the almost total silence of the Federal editors in this town on the horrid murder," and asserted that "in private circles they palliate and even justify the culprits" in order to create a favorable public opinion prior to the trial; and that "friends of the youth are obliged to counteract their wicked designs. . . . Art, intrigue, and deception are the grand weapons of Federalism, that now recommend moderation, when murder is committed." "When before," asked the writer, "have they ever shown moderation? Suppose that the facts were reversed and that the killing had been done by a Republican. Would they not then have flared forth with attacks upon him?" It might be supposed that the editor of the *Chronicle* would have been so impressed with the fatal results of newspaper vituperation that he would have refrained from being guilty himself of similar action at that particular time. On August 21, however, he wrote the following violent attack upon the publishers of the *Gazette*:

The Federal papers are anxious to impress an idea that the remarks on the late murder in State Street are intended to excite an undue irritation in the minds of the citizens of this Commonwealth. We scorn such a design. *Irritation* is not the wish, but *reflection* is the sole object contemplated. Do the citizens of Massachusetts need any excitements to reprobate murder? . . . Party spirit may operate to give a silent countenance to inferior events; but when murder stalks predominant in places of such mutual resort, it becomes the duty of the whole community to portray it in all its horrors. . . . If the friends to silence are sincere, why have so many false reports been propagated in papers at a distance from the scene of action? Why has an unfortunate young man, whose life has paid the forfeit of his filial attachment, been represented as a ruffian pursuing his antagonist after repeated warnings of his danger, barbarously fracturing the skull of his opponent? The writers knew it was false. They knew it was calumniating a youth whose manners could never warrant such charges. They knew the whole detail was false in every particular, and yet were so cruel in their malignity as even to wound afresh the helpless victim who laid prostrate at the feet of his assailant. Further, how malicious must those printers be who first published the scurrility which gave rise to this cruel catastrophe. They are now among the foremost to have every observation subside. They became the principals in the event by their wanton publication; and after the evil had taken place, they have the baseness to censure every remark on the sequel. ... Will they throw about firebrands, arrows and death, and when the fatal effect of their conduct is experienced, say to the injured public "Peace, be still "!? The wickedness of these printers is most abominable.

On August 30 the *Centinel* broke its silence by publishing a letter from Selfridge, written from jail, in which he asked the public to refrain from forming opinions until all the facts should be brought out at the trial; and he complained of "attempts to deceive the weak by false statements and to influence the violent by declamation." He asked the *Chronicle* to publish his letter, to which the *Chronicle* replied, the next day, saying that it would comply with the request if the *Centinel* would reciprocate by publishing the various *Chronicle* articles on the murder. The *Chronicle* returned to the attack again, on September 11 and 15, by commenting on Selfridge's effort to gain credit for having voluntarily surrendered himself to the authorities; and it reviewed the law of the case in two long articles, saying: "Who is secure in his life if he may fall by a man secreting a pistol, killing at noonday, and then from his prison telling the world that he could have escaped if his innocence had not induced him to surrender!!!" A month later, the publishers of the *Gazette* announced their intention to publish a pamphlet containing a full account of the approaching trial:

The feelings of the public have been deeply agitated by this melancholy event beyond what we recollect them to have been by any occurrence within the compass of our memory. When we consider the high legal character of our State Court, but more especially of the Chief Justice who for many years has worn the complimentary title of "The Giant of the Law," — when we consider Mr. Selfridge as a counsellor at law in great practice, raised in a short time, by his industry and talents, unassisted by the intrinsic aid of personal friends or family connections, standing fairly with the Court and Bar and possessing a cool temper and a determined resolution — when we consider the distinguished eminence of the counsel (who have gratuitously embarked on the defence), such as Messrs. Otis, Ames, Gore, and Dexter — and when we consider that the trial involves a principle, viz: the right of self defence with a mortal weapon — there cannot fail to be an immense demand for the volume.

On November 6 the *Chronicle* savagely assailed this announcement and its wording as the height of impropriety, and as an attempt to prejudice the public by lauding Selfridge and the Chief Justice and lawyers who were to be engaged in the trial.

The Supreme Court began its sitting in Boston at the end of November; and when the grand jury convened, Chief Justice Theophilus Parsons — an ardent Federalist and a prominent member of the "Essex Junto" or "Brittish Junto" — delivered the charge, in the course of which he laid down the principles of the law of murder, manslaughter, and justifiable homicide. While no unprejudiced man could believe that the great Chief Justice would for a moment have been influenced by partisan motives in delivering a judicial charge, it cannot be denied that he neglected to state the law as fully and with as many qualifications as should have been done; [1] and the charge at once

---

[1] Although Theophilus Parsons, Jr., in his *Memoirs* of his father, asserts as to the disputed part of the charge that "there can be no question whatever that this was a careful and perfectly accurate statement of a principle which rests upon the most uniform and indisputable authority," nevertheless it is undoubtedly true that Thomas C. Amory in his *Life of James Sullivan* writes more accurately as follows: "In laying down the law of murder and manslaughter, Parsons omitted certain maxims of general recognition bearing on the case. . . . One of the rules thus omitted was that the party justifying killing from necessity

became the object of a fierce attack (probably written by Attorney-General James Sullivan) in the *Chronicle*, December 1.[1] "If this is law," wrote Sullivan, "we should be glad to have it written in capital letters and placed in every family, in every house of worship, and read in every town meeting. Under color of this law, what murders may be committed!" In a later issue, December 6, the *Chronicle*, professing to hope that the charge had been incorrectly reported, said: "In the name of humanity, in the name of common sense, in the name of Christianity, we call on Judge Parsons to be more explicit and not leave the citizens in this dreadful state of insecurity of their lives or suffer every trifling fracas to end in death. We consider the charge, as published, an affront on the humane principles which have ever characterized the honorable Judge. Would a Blackstone suffer himself to stand pledged for so superficial a performance? Certainly not."

To the astonishment of everyone, the grand jury, headed by Thomas Handasyde Perkins, a prominent Federalist merchant, instead of finding an indictment for murder, brought in an indictment for manslaughter only. Such unusual action taken by the grand jury without consulting the Attorney-General naturally gave rise to violent criticism, inasmuch as the coroner's jury had found a verdict of "wilful murder." The *Chronicle* was bitter in its comments. On December 11 it said: "Sudden thought — a

---

must be himself wholly without fault; another, that he had no possible, or at least probable, means of escape; a third, that the crime prevented by the killing would have been itself capital; and a fourth, that no provocation will avail, if sought."

[1] The following passage was especially objected to: "If the party killing had reasonable ground for believing that the person slain had a felonious design against him and under that supposition kills him, although it should appear that there was no such design, it will not be murder but it would be either manslaughter or excusable homicide, according to the degree of caution used and the probable ground of such belief."

Federalist on hearing that a bill for manslaughter only was found against T. O. Selfridge exclaimed, 'He is cleared, by God!' 'No, sir,' replied a boy, 'he is not cleared by God, though he may be by man.'" And on December 15, the Supreme Court having just tried a negro named Hardy who had been indicted for murder of an infant child, the *Chronicle* published this anecdote: "As Hardy, the black man, was passing from the prison to the Court house, a black woman said to him, 'Ha, you Hardy, you no lawyer — you fool! Why you no take 'em down 'tate 'treet and shoot 'em — den you be clear?'" Dr. Ames' view of the grand jury's action was expressed by him in characteristic fashion in a letter to the local Dedham newspaper as follows: "The news of the massacre at Boston 1770 scarcely gave a greater shock and consternation than now, Dec. 2, that the assassin and murderer is set free at Boston! The people are agast, petrified at first with fears, but soon the silent embers of indignation break out in flame. The long dark conspiracy has burst — a revolution commences. The petty craft prevails as it did in France." [1]

After indictment, Selfridge was released on bail; and the trial was fixed for December 23. At that period, all cases of capital crimes were tried before three Judges of the Supreme Court. Manslaughter, however, being a lesser offence, was tried before a single Judge. Chief Justice Parsons, under the plea of illness, declined to sit, and assigned Isaac Parker, a newly appointed Justice, who now sat in Boston for the first time. For this action more criticism was bestowed on the Chief Justice, which was voiced by the *Chronicle* a few weeks later, in commenting on the "propriety of leaving a cause of such vast expectation to the decision of one Judge (however adequate in legal knowledge), while the person on whom the public eye was prin-

[1] *Norfolk Repository*, December 9, 1806.

cipally fixed, in consequence of his charge, absented himself during the whole trial. He was well enough to attend an entertainment, the day previous; it would, therefore, have been pleasing to have seen him on the seat of justice discharging those sacred functions attached to his station. . . . We call on the whole fraternity of lawyers to produce a similar charge and a similar bill from the grand jury. Would it not be reasonable to expect that a Judge who had promulgated this principle would have been desirous to vindicate his opinion by officiating at the trial?" [1] Five days before the opening of the trial the *Chronicle* sounded the following note of warning: "Should the death of Charles Austin merit no atonement, yet his remains will sleep quietly in the grave; and when posterity shall ask how he came to his end, the faithful record of history shall recite his unhappy fate, and fill the eyes of honest men with tears. . . . The decision of that day [of trial] will be important to society. Should the stern equity of law justify the deed, future mothers may weep the untimely death of beloved sons, and society deplore the loss of its most promising members."

The trial began on Tuesday, December 23, only three weeks after the finding of the bill of indictment, and four and one-half months after the killing. Samuel Dexter and Christopher Gore, two noted Federalist lawyers, appeared in court as counsel for Selfridge, while Fisher Ames and Harrison Gray Otis, also Federalists, acted for him in the background. The Commonwealth was represented by the aged Attorney-General, James Sullivan, and the Solicitor-General, Daniel Davis, both Antifederalists. An extraordinarily large number of witnesses testified, chiefly on the question whether Austin had struck the blow with his cane prior to, simultaneously with, or after Selfridge's

[1] See *Independent Chronicle*, January 8, 12, 1807.

shooting, and also on the question of previous provocation to Selfridge. The intricacies of the law of manslaughter and justifiable homicide were discussed at such length, and such perplexing problems were presented, that it was felt by everyone to be the most difficult criminal case over which any American judge had ever presided up to that time. In view of the extreme jealousy with which modern courts view any comments on a case during its trial, it is interesting to note that the *Chronicle* did not stop its criticisms, and on December 25, in the midst of the trial, it published another long assault on the "dangerous principles" of Chief Justice Parsons' charge, and also the following comment on the attitude of the Suffolk bar: "In attending the trial of Selfridge, we cannot but be struck with the number of lawyers who appear aiding and assisting in the cause. It is a melancholy reflection that the death of an innocent young man should excite so much anxiety among individuals in the bar to exculpate an offender." The *Centinel*, however, of December 24 preserved unusual self-restraint, and said: "We deem it improper to give any part of the evidence until the trial is over." The evidence was closed on Christmas Day morning. The defendant's lawyers argued four hours in the afternoon; the Attorney-General argued three hours on the next day, Friday; the Judge charged the jury for one hour. The jury retired, and in fifteen minutes brought in a verdict of "not guilty."

While such a verdict was undoubtedly justified by evidence introduced in behalf of the defendant, nevertheless Selfridge probably owed his acquittal to the powerful argument of his counsel, Dexter, and to the surprising latitude which was allowed to him in introducing the question of politics into his plea, in attacking the character of Benjamin Austin, and in arguing the right of a libelled man to protect his honor by killing his libeller. Gore, in opening the case for Selfridge, said: "I cannot but feel some apprehension from the various measures taken to preoccupy the public mind, nor is it surprising that I should be thus apprehensive, when I call to mind the cruel, unjustifiable, and illegal conduct which has been resorted to through the newspapers to influence the judgment, to inflame the passions, and cause such an agitation throughout the whole community that its effect might be felt even here. . . . It will not be strange that I should feel something like apprehension, something like dismay when I behold the effect of this incitement in the immense multitude that throng around and the crowd assembled in this Court." Dexter, in his impassioned and able argument beseeching the jury to leave all their political opinions behind them, showed clearly, however, his view that such bias might influence them: "When a cause has been a long time the subject of party discussion — when the democratic presses throughout the country have teemed with publications fraught with appeals to the passions and bitter invective against the defendant — and when on one side everything has been done that party rage could do to prejudice this cause, and on the other, little has been said in vindication of the supposed defender . . . the necessary consequence must be that opinion will progress one way. But to those of you who are democratic republicans I say that liberty which you cherish with so much ardor depends on your preserving yourself impartial in a court of justice." After arguing along in this strain, he devoted a considerable portion of his speech to the provocation received by Selfridge, and his right to defend himself, saying: "Men of eminent talents and virtues, on whose exertions in perilous times the honor and happiness of their country must depend, will always be liable to be degraded by every daring miscreant, if they cannot defend themselves from personal

insult and outrage." In the course of his plea he drew a
bitter and insulting picture of a supposititious libeller,
which was recognized by everyone as intended for Benjamin Austin himself: "Suppose a man should have established his reputation as a common slanderer and calumniator, by libelling the most virtuous and eminent character
of his country, from Washington and Adams down through
the whole list of American patriots; suppose such a one to
have stood for twenty years in the kennel and thrown mud
at every well-dressed passenger; suppose him to have published libels 'til his style of defamation has become as notorious as his face — would not everyone say that such
conduct was sore excuse for bespattering him in turn? I
do not apply this to any individual."

The Attorney-General, replying to the political references made by Dexter, said: "The counsel for the defendant has addressed you with warmth and energy as a politician, and with elegance of manner and strength of language peculiar to himself has conjured you to lay aside all
political impressions. I will not invoke you to put aside
your prejudices, for if you will not obey the obligation of
your oath, you are not to be reasoned into it by the power
of rhetoric. I, therefore, consider it as improper to attempt it." He ridiculed the argument that the defendant
was driven to such an awful crisis that he could not extricate his honor except by killing; or that the punishment of
libel should be the shooting down at noonday of the
libeller. His whole speech was impressive and dignified,
and was rendered the more pathetic from the fact that he
himself, now pleading the cause of a father for a son slain,
had lost his own son, from illness, only a few days before
the trial.

Judge Parker instructed the jury that if the defendant
had no view but to defend his life and person from attack,

did not purposely throw himself in the way of the conflict, but was merely pursuing his lawful vocations, and could not have saved himself otherwise than by the death of his assailant, then the killing was excusable homicide, provided the circumstances of the attack would justify a reasonable apprehension of the harm he had a right to prevent. He thought the fact that the blow was first inflicted was of importance to the defence. The Judge's whole charge was remarkable for its impartiality and clearness of statement. It rejected, with considerable force, most of Dexter's arguments, and stated emphatically that "no man can take vengeance into his own hands; he can use violence only in defence of his person. No words however aggravating, no libel however scandalous, will authorize the suffering party to revenge himself by blows." The Judge, further, condemned Selfridge's conduct before the killing in vigorous terms: "To call a man coward, liar and scoundrel in the public newspapers, and to call upon other printers to publish the same, is not justifiable under any circumstances whatever. . . . Indeed, I believe a court of honour, if such existed, to settle disputes of this nature, would not justify such a proclamation as the one alluded to. A posting upon change or in some public place we have heard of; but I never saw such a violent denunciation as this in a public newspaper." Referring to the political atmosphere of the trial, he said: "Nor do I believe that any general apprehension is entertained that a man accused of crime is to be saved or destroyed according to the political notions he entertains." [1]

[1] It is interesting to note that, twenty-five years later, the great jurist Lemuel Shaw, who succeeded Isaac Parker as Chief Justice of the Supreme Court of Massachusetts in 1830, and who had himself been a witness at the trial, being an occupant of the same office with Selfridge, paid the following high tribute to Parker's conduct at the trial: "The parties held high positions in society, and a prominent rank in the opposite political parties; and the prejudices and passions

The verdict of "Not guilty" by the jury was followed by a storm of disapproval in Boston; and party passions were still more inflamed by the ill-advised action of the Federalist press, and of Selfridge himself, during the ensuing two months. To its credit, the *Chronicle*, immediately after the trial, appeared to be willing to drop the whole matter, though saying in a bitter and unresigned fashion, December 29: "If the individuals of party are satisfied, they are welcome to all the benefits resulting from their acquisition and to all the triumph attached to an innocent youth falling a victim to the cause of filial duty. They are welcome to the honors of a bloody arena, exhibited through the dastardly medium of a secreted pistol. Mothers and fathers can never behold the scene with delight and satisfaction. We shall make no remarks on the trial nor presume to censure any part of the proceedings or decision of the jury. Their wisdom can never be questioned. We reverence the Judge who presided and revere the venerable Attorney General for his talent and fidelity." Unfortunately, bitter and taunting language used in the Federalist papers reopened the fight with renewed vigor. On December 31 the *Centinel* said, referring to the forthcoming printed report of the trial: "When read, the public will be able to judge on evidence and oath from whom have proceeded the numerous falsehoods which have been spread abroad to prejudge the same. And the consequence will be, the detestation of the community will fall on the guilty heads of those who fabricated those falsehoods." The *Chronicle* at once dashed back into the arena, saying,

connected with the prosecution were not a little inflamed by the excited party politics of the day. Yet such was the dignity, the impartiality, the skill and ability with which the newly appointed Judge, then comparatively a stranger, conducted this trial that it is believed he gave universal satisfaction, and made himself most favorably known . . . as a jurist of great promise." See *Address before the Berkshire Bar*, September, 1830.

January 1, 1807: "The late trial, however it may have been considered by the Federalists as a party question, yet embraces considerations of a more serious nature than the mere political triumph of a few desperate associates." On January 5 it said, with reference to statements circulated by Selfridge's friends as to Charles Austin: "Falsehood again detected! The statements of the conduct of Selfridge have assumed such a variety of shapes, in order to impose on the public, that those who are desirous to do justice to an injured youth are obliged to watch for the infamous falsehoods propagated at a distance. Are not the friends of Selfridge satisfied that he is now at liberty to patrol the streets of Boston? Are they not content that this 'weak, feeble,' manslayer is now able to go where he pleases? Why then should he wish the publication of such villainous paragraphs?" On January 12 it published an article which might well have been construed as a threat or an incentive to retaliation on Selfridge: "As to the man who killed the innocent youth, he may be released by the authority of Puffendorf and others; but there is an Authority which declares that 'he who sheddeth man's blood, by man shall his blood be shed,' and there is a Judge who says, 'Vengeance is mine and I will repay it.'"

Meanwhile the general public in Boston was at a fever heat. "Murder is no crime in a Federal lawyer," exclaimed the faction opposed to Selfridge, and there were frequent riots, burning of effigies, and threats, reference to which was made in Dr. Ames' Diary:

Jan. 1, 1807. Selfridge's effigy hanged in Boston.

Jan. 10. Selfridge still hung in effigy various places. People grow indignant at the reign of Pettifogarchy.

Jan. 31. Selfridge and Chief Justice Parsons hung in effigy in divers parts of continent, New York, Salem, etc.

To these public disorders the Federalist papers, notably the *Boston Gazette* and the *Boston Repertory*, replied in savage articles referring to the "same malignant spirit" still menacing Selfridge; "the spirit of Jacobinism"; "the disgraceful scenes exhibited in our public streets". "The same spirit in all its haggard and detestable forms is still poured forth against the Federal party at large."[1] An accusation by the *Repertory* that Austin himself was an instigator in exciting these disorders was replied to by that gentleman himself in the *Chronicle*, January 12, in words which went to the limit of scurrilous vituperation: "It is distressing to encounter with savage brutality. A man destitute of humanity is a wretch the most despicable in society. He is viewed with abhorrence by everyone who possesses a mind susceptible of sympathy. To describe such a being in all his deformities requires a language too coarse for the refined ear of civilization; it is sufficient to say, in order to excite a just abhorrence of the man, that the traits of such a character are strongly marked in the editor of the *Repertory*. This brutal calumniator has, with an impudence unparalleled, dared to mention in his scurrilous

---

[1] See also an interesting editorial in the Federalist *New York Evening Post*, March 6, 1807, referring to "the most unwarrantable attempts made to connect a mere private affair with Federal politics and in the most wicked and wanton manner to fasten a stigma on the party itself. . . . See the lengths party malice will carry our Eastern Democrats . . . perceive . . . a public press devoted during the whole time to influence the community by partial statements and malignant comment to prejudge his case, so as to render it difficult for him to obtain an impartial jury; while an attempt was made by the Court itself, whose jurisdiction was thus violated, to interfere and put a stop to this horrible conspiracy against life, by a process for contempt. And to wind up the outrageous proceeding, they will see with equal astonishment, indignation, and abhorrence that the probable authors of this newspaper assassination were no other than the father of the man whose life was forfeited to the law of self defence and the Attorney General who was to conduct the trial. A case which we venture to say will serve abroad to bring greater disgrace on American manners and morals than anything that has been invented by the most slanderous European that ever visited our shores for the purpose of defaming the Nation's character abroad."

paper the names of two gentlemen as the principal agents in exciting commotion and causing the erection of the late effigies. To use the term Lyar is scarcely sufficiently expressive of the villainy of his assertion, and falls vastly short of the detestable criminality attached to so base a falsehood. He is too debased in political reputation to seek redress by a prosecution, and too notorious in detraction to excite any other emotions than detestation and abhorrence. The late movements of the people are expressive of those humane feelings which will ever operate on the number of a sympathetic community. The regularity of their procession proves that no hostile measures were intended; it was a mere display of pageantry which all who saw it could duly appreciate, according to their different sensations." The *Centinel* called forth equally savage attacks from the Republican side, by publishing extracts from Dexter's speech at the trial, including his onslaught on Benjamin Austin, and by praising it in the following extravagant language: "When the English language shall be numbered with the dead, and our orators and illustrious literary characters become classics to posterity, this speech will rank both of reason and rhetoric, among the first forensic efforts of New England." [1] To this "preposterous, sycophantic adulation" the *Chronicle* replied with picturesque, characteristic abuse of the speech and "the fulsome, puerile panegyric on the eminent talent of Mr. Dexter. . . . We shall not waste our time in noticing the absurdity of the eulogium, as it must appear to every candid person a mixture of insolence and impertinence. The speech is a poor, feeble attempt at the sublime, arrayed in the ridiculous garb of bombastical pathos. It is the feather of a goose absurdly intended to be inserted in the pinion

[1] See *Columbian Centinel*, January 14, 1807; *Independent Chronicle*, January 19, 22, 26, 1807.

of an eagle. The speech is more congenial to the principles of a gladiator than a lawyer. It is more consonant to the feelings of a bravado than a parent . . . a display of cowardice and brutality over the tomb of an innocent youth, which no man susceptible of humanity would indulge."

Into the midst of this libelling fury Thomas O. Selfridge now flung an additional firebrand by publishing a pamphlet presenting his views of his own case.[1] Although there was at once an excessive avidity of the public to purchase this pamphlet (an edition of three thousand being quickly bought up), and it "excited more public attention than any pamphlet ever issued in the town," [2] Selfridge would have done better to remain silent. For he now not only reiterated his old, but also added new and offensive, libels against Benjamin Austin, in a manner which would have justified the latter in going to almost any extremities. When one recalls that Selfridge was thus attacking again the father whose son he had just shot, one marvels that anyone, even the most prejudiced or partisan, in the town of Boston could have excused or defended such language as the following, contained in this pamphlet: "They [the editors of the *Chronicle*] are, indeed, poor beings, so far as intellect is concerned; their ignorance exceeds and almost excuses their perversity. Whether James Sullivan or Benjamin Austin furnished the infamous publications of which I complain, I do not certainly know; but I have strong suspicions against them both. . . . Many persons have suggested that I ought to have disregarded the aspersions of a man so lost to honor and dead to shame as Mr. A., of a man who had been spit upon, whipt or kicked upon the

---

[1] *A Correct Statement of the Whole Preliminary Controversy Between Thos. O. Selfridge and Benj. Austin, also a Brief Account of the Catastrophe in State Street, Boston, on the 4th August, 1806, with Some Remarks* (1807).

[2] See *Columbian Centinel*, February 4, 1807; *Boston Gazette*, February 2, 1807.

public exchange — of a man who, after having the meanness to sue for it, had his feelings, his honor, and his injury
estimated by a righteous jury of his country at the moder-
ate sum of twenty shillings.[1] . . . Now it by no means follows that because a man possesses an intrinsic baseness of
spirit and a radical defection of character, both confirmed
by inveterate habit, that he is incapable of external annoyance; although a man debase himself to a reptile, yet,
unresisted he may be formidable as an enemy. A lion may
perish by the puncture of an asp. . . . A good man's sorrows should be sacred and his feelings respected; but when
personal and political rancor overpowers parental grief and
even seems to induce a malignant joy over a departed son,
in the miserable hope that his untimely end will promote
political purposes, he renders himself the alternate object
of sorrow and scorn, of derision and detestation. . . . The
fiends of anarchy, night after night, have prompted the
perpetration of the most wanton outrages against liberty,
security, and the legitimate rights of man." Selfridge's
pamphlet, further, contained an elaborate defence of his
deed in fact and in law, with little sign of any contrition.
The self-restraint shown by the *Chronicle's* editor in regard
to this outrageous publication is shown by the fact that his
most extreme comment was the following, January 29:
"T. O. Selfridge, with effrontery unparalleled, has endeavored to vindicate his base and cowardly action by a
long train of abusive remarks and ex-parte certificate. . . .
If Selfridge is anxious for a preservation of his honor, why
does he charge a man two shillings sixpence for the evidence?" In a long series of able editorials, probably writ-

[1] The editor of the *Centinel* had in 1793 been embroiled with Benjamin Austin, had spat in his face at the Exchange on State Street, and been sued for
damages for a thousand pounds, tried, and had a verdict rendered against him
for twenty shillings. See interesting account in *Specimens of Newspaper Literature with Personal Memoirs* (1850), by Joseph Buckingham, vol. II.

ten by Attorney-General Sullivan, however, the *Chronicle*
continued to analyze and criticize the accuracy of Selfridge's statements and of his witnesses at the trial. These
criticisms were warmly resented by the Federalist newspapers, which now indulged in even more extreme libels
than any that had previously been published. The *Gazette*
of February 2 described Austin's writings as "the ravings
of a man who, we really believe, requires the regimen of a
strait waistcoat and a spare diet." The *Centinel* said, February 14 and 18: "For four months the public have been
abused with the canker-hearted assertions of the man
whose falsehood was the sole cause of the controversy and
its lamented consequence — a man whose slanders are as
well known as his face. . . . All the mean and dirty personalities in the *Chronicle* are known to proceed from that
discredited calumniator, who has made that paper a common sewer of scurrility for the last twenty years. Where
the miscreant is known, his assertions and insinuations are
harmless; for such a posted 'scoundrel,' such a recorded
'liar' (who can lie and prevaricate with the oath of God
upon him) is considered as a nuisance to society and
treated with scorn and contempt by every honest man in
it. We ask pardon of our readers for the language of the
above paragraph, but no other can be applicable to the
perjured villain who is the subject of it."

It is an extraordinary comment on the legal conditions
of the times that no indictment for criminal libel followed
such articles as the foregoing. Austin, however, took no
action in the courts, and the Government law officers, apparently sceptical of their success in persuading a grand
jury in Federalist Boston to bring in an indictment for
libel, remained passive. Instead of seeking to avenge his
personal wrongs, Austin memorialized the legislature to
define by statute the crime of murder, so as to avoid a

repetition of a charge like Chief Justice Parsons'; but a committee of that body reported that such legislation was unnecessary and injudicious, and the matter was not pursued further.

So far as the newspapers were concerned, the case dropped out of public view. Nevertheless, the *Chronicle* published some reference to Charles Austin's death on its anniversary in each year until as late as 1812, and printed, on August 5, 1807, the following "tribute of annual remembrance:"

Austin, Farewell.
Thou early martyr in a dutious cause.
Time was, when those whose hearts could prompt their hands
To deeds of darkness sought the suited time —
— The time of night — But now, O sad reverie,
Vice stalks triumphant in the Judgment Hall,
Tramples on virtue, justice, reason, life;
And murder rears on high his blood-stain'd arm
At broad noon-day! Father of all,
Spare not the guilty — let thy wrath descend
Where wrath is due — but save an injured town.
Let thy destroying angel wing his flight
Far from the threshold of our peaceful homes.
Lay not this sin to us — and of thy mercy
Avert thy judgments from a suffering land.

If this famous case had been an ordinary murder case, so long and detailed a description would not have been warranted; but such were the partisan dissensions and the personal passions which it evoked that Boston society and Boston politics did not recover from its influence for many years. It therefore deserves prominent mention as an active factor in Boston history during the exciting era of the Embargo and of the War of 1812 which closely followed it; for, without question, part of the confirmed bitterness of the leaders of the opposing political parties is traceable directly to the supporters of the two figures in this murder. Its lasting impression may be seen from the fact that, twenty-four years after, upon the death of Judge Isaac Parker in 1830, Reverend John Gorham Palfrey preached a funeral sermon in which he spoke of the Selfridge case as "a trial involving questions of the most abstruse, delicate, and painful nature, as fresh now in the memory of many of us, as events of yesterday." [1]

The unbridled license of the newspaper press in personal abuse and libel once resulting in murder in this notable fashion, it would be supposed that some effort would have been made to curb the press by criminal proceedings or by statutory enactment. Little, however, was accomplished in this direction for many years; and an interesting commentary on newspaper conditions is to be found, as late as 1812, in a special message sent by Governor Elbridge Gerry to the Massachusetts legislature, calling its attention to this evil which for twenty years had been rampant in the State — the alarming prevalence of libellous articles

---

[1] In the "Trial of Mrs. Hannah Kinney" (in *Law Reporter* [1841], vol. III, p. 411), Attorney-General J. W. Austin said, referring to Franklin Dexter, counsel for defendant: "I approach this topic with reluctance. The closing counsel has seen fit to make it the occasion or the cause of imputations, as gratuitous as they are uncourteous and untrue." *Dexter*: "Do you mean to state that the facts are untrue?" *Austin*: "I mean to say the imputations are totally untrue, and I must beg your attention, gentlemen of the jury, while I explain. . . . I confess I am restrained by the respect I feel for the Court, and for the solemnity of the occasion, from retaliating upon him as such discourteous, ungenerous, and unjust conduct deserves. It is Christmas day, and rarely are our Courts open on this day; but I well remember, thirty-four years ago, when they were open on this anniversary for the investigation of a homicide, committed at the hour of noon, upon the public exchange. It was a time of high excitement, of emotion, of feeling, of party. I remember the conduct of the defence on that occasion, by one of the most gifted and eloquent counsellors ever known at this bar; and I remember the civility, the consideration and kindness with which he treated my predecessor. All the sensibilities I then may have in relation to that trial were long since buried in the grave, and I only regret that the learned counsel who appears in this defence today, while he has somewhat of the ambition and much of the talent, has not inherited the courtesy of his father."

in the newspaper press and the defective condition of the
law of libel as laid down in the courts. At that date, 1812,
under the old Common Law and the decisions of the Massachusetts Supreme Court, a person indicted for criminal
libel was not allowed to defend himself by proving the
truth of his statements, except in one instance, namely,
where the statement was made regarding the qualifications
of an elective official. This exception did not apply to
articles regarding appointive officials, and only a few
months before Gerry's message the editor of the *Independent Chronicle* had been convicted of criminal libel on Chief
Justice Parsons in spite of his claim that he could prove the
truth of his statements. With his message Gerry submitted a report signed by the Attorney-General and by the
Solicitor-General, giving the results of their investigation
of the Boston newspapers between June 1, 1811, and
January 6, 1812. After excluding all libels, "scandal or
calumnious publication against any foreign government or
distinguished foreigners" and "any aspersions of the editors of the different papers upon their brethren of the
type," these law officials of the State found 262 instances
of libellous articles published in seven months, 25 of which
were found in Republican papers and 237 in Federalist
papers. The libels were divided into two classes — those
articles in which, under the law, truth could be pleaded as a
defence, and those articles in which truth could not be
pleaded. The detailed results were as follows. Of the Republican papers, the *Independent Chronicle* published 8
libels of the first class and none of the second, total 8; the
Boston Patriot, 7 and 2, total 9; the *Yankee*, none. Of the
Federalist papers, the *Columbian Centinel* published 13 of
the first class and 38 of the second, total 51; the *Repertory*,
13 and 21, total 34; the *Scourge*, 71 and 28, total 99; the
New England Palladium, 5 and 13, total 18; the *Gazette*, 6

and 27, total 33; the *Weekly Messenger*, 1 of the second class. Notwithstanding this licentious condition of the public press, in this same period only six indictments had been found by the grand juries, four against the *Scourge* and two against the *Chronicle*. "Such are the principles and effects of the Common Law in regard to libels," said Governor Gerry. Though no definite action was taken by the legislature to ameliorate this deplorable state of affairs, the episode is of interest as an illustration of the result of the political passions then prevalent. The Republican party, however, very wisely did not attempt to imitate the old Federalist effort to stop political libels by a National "Gag Act."

VIII

EMBARGO DAYS AND A POLITICAL FUNERAL

IN 1807 and 1808 the United States was roused to a high pitch of excitement by British aggressions — the impressment of American seamen, the search of American ships, the *Chesapeake* episode, and the disregard of the rights of American neutral traders. A vivid picture of the antagonism towards England which thus developed was given by Dr. Ames in his Diary entries. Having reached the age of sixty-six, and having taken part in the Revolutionary struggles when a young man of thirty-five, it was natural that a man of his temperament should again burn with indignation against England, and against those in his own State who took the English side.

Jan. 7, 1807. Upon news of Bonaparte's decree blockading the British dominions, etc., all insurance stopped in Boston. All Europe except England and Russia are now bowed before him, our invincible conqueror, but humane and generous hitherto. However, some brand him as a tyrant, which is not yet determined; for he only leads on the nation as yet to chastise the tyrant invaders of France, to establish a firm peace, after which his character, whether tyrant or patron of his generation, will be settled. He doth not seem, like petty tyrants, to exult in havoc, but in making all his conquests coöperate with the vast plans he has conceived, part of which is to curb the tyrants of the ocean and restore the rights of nations to unmolested neutral trade. So that it seems very possible that after a general peace in Europe is settled Bonaparte may yet shine out greater than Alexander or any other hero as the greatest benefactor of all nations by securing to all their common rights upon the ocean — and yet rival Washington nearly, by convincing the people of the Old World that they are not in right, however in fact, their own worst enemies, and that they may yet render themselves capable of their own government, there, as Washington did here.

June 30. Country raised to indignation at conduct of British Squadron at Virginia [*Leopard-Chesapeake*].

July 2. British insults and murder of 5 men on June 22 now heard of.

July 11. President's proclamation of 2nd instant, banishing British war ships and vessels of all kinds from our coasts and harbors, and prohibiting succours and intercourse. War impending! All parties join in indignation at English insult and murder, as bad as Selfridge's! ! !

July 31. Resolves blazing against Britons from one end of United States to t' other.

Dec. 27. Embargo laid by Congress! War expected! Clamor in seaports! Notwithstanding such repeated murder and insult, a contemptible party for Britain often show out as much as they dare! Even in Congress, there is Pickering, a Massachusetts Senator; began with Hillhouse of Connecticut in justification of the British; but J. Q. Adams soon silenced them, and appears completely converted to the American Republic . . . and fully justified Jefferson's Administration — to the confusion of the Federal or Hamiltonian Junto. We may soon look for foaming and rage vomited from the Feds now against J. Q. Adams.

The references to the Embargo Act only mildly recall the fierce opposition to that statute, — that "abominable measure," as George Cabot wrote of it, — which, from the moment of its passage in December, 1807, the Federalists of Massachusetts maintained, under the lead of Senator Timothy Pickering, and the even fiercer attacks which they made on President Jefferson — whom the young poet, William Cullen Bryant, in his poem on "The Embargo" at this time thus addressed:

And thou the scorn of every patriot name,
Thy country's ruin and her council's shame. . . .

. . . .

Go, wretch! Resign the Presidential chair.

As early as January 2, 1808, the *Centinel* said: "The Embargo which the Government has just laid is of a new and alarming nature. War, great as the evil, has less terror and will produce less misery than an embargo on such principles"; and the whole Federalist press, from this time, explicitly and audaciously urged the citizens of the State to set the law at defiance. The enforcement of the Embargo Act was opposed in town after town. Assaults on Government officials became common; and those who acquiesced in the Act were denounced as bad citizens. Although the Act had been held constitutional by Judge John Davis (himself a Federalist) in the United States District Court, in a famous case argued by Samuel Dexter,[1] it was almost impossible to obtain a Massachusetts jury which would convict any violator of it, even on the clearest evidence of guilt. The more openly recreant the conduct of a jury in these cases, the more was it applauded by the Federalists. In fact, the whole course of the Federalist leaders carried them very near the border line of secession and disunion, if not of treason. The project of a union of the commercial States was boldly talked of and advocated, and by no one more vigorously than by the Senator from Massachusetts, Timothy Pickering. The attitude of members of the Essex Junto in this direction, both at an earlier date and at this time, was so dubious as to lead John Quincy Adams to report to President Jefferson that these leaders were "engaged in a plot to dissolve the Union, and to re-annex New England to Great Britain,

[1] See *The Supreme Court in United States History* (revised ed., 1928), by Charles Warren, vol. I, chap. VII.

and that he possessed unequivocal evidence of that most solemn design."[1]

So widespread were the reports that Massachusetts and its neighbors were preparing to initiate a separate confederacy that Lieutenant Governor Levi Lincoln (who succeeded Governor Sullivan on the latter's death in December, 1808), in his address to the legislature, January 26, 1809, said: "The New England States have been represented, to their injury and to the injury of the United States, as distracted with divisions, prepared for opposition to the authority of the law, and ripening for a secession from the Union. Such suggestions, we trust, are unfounded." He urged that union and forgetfulness of past dissensions were needed in the citizens; and he deprecated "the cultivated reports that the Administration and the Southern people are hostile to commerce and unfriendly to the Eastern States, as calculated to produce uneasiness, jealousies, and dissensions" and based on no evidence. The legislature made answer to this comparatively mild and nonpartisan address by a decidedly pungent series of resolutions. In formal and tart answers made by the Senate and House to the Lieutenant Governor, the legislature, with sarcastic repetition of his language, protested against his "alarming doctrines and arbitrary measures," together with hardly veiled contempt of the administration's policies. A few weeks later, a committee of the legislature, after referring to "the picture of private distresses" and "disgusting catalogue of publick wrongs," reported four

---

[1] For account of this interesting episode, see *Diary of John Quincy Adams*, vol. VIII; *Report of a Trial in the Supreme Judicial Court, holden at Boston, Dec. 16 and 17, 1828, of Theodore Lyman, Jr., for an Alleged Libel on Daniel Webster* (1828); *A Notable Libel Case* (1904), by Josiah H. Benton, Jr.; *Documents Relating to New England Federalism* (1877), by Henry Adams; *Life and Times of George Cabot* (1870), by Henry Cabot Lodge; *Familiar Letters on Public Characters* (1847), by William Sullivan; *Appeal of Massachusetts Federalists to the Citizens of the United States*, January 28, 1809.

resolutions, which recited that "the new Embargo Act of 1809 is, in the opinion of the Legislature, in many respects unjust, oppressive and unconstitutional, and not legally binding on the citizens of this State." After urging, however, the citizens to abstain from forcible resistance, the resolutions stated that Massachusetts "will zealously coöperate with any of the other States in all legal and constitutional measures" to procure amendments to the Constitution "necessary to obtain protection and defence for commerce, and to give to the commercial States their fair and just consideration in the government of the Union." They urged that copies be sent to "such of our sister States as manifest a disposition to concur with us in measures to rescue our common country from impending ruin, and to preserve inviolate the Union of the States." While thus professing a desire to preserve the Union, these resolutions came perilously near, if indeed they did not go beyond, the doctrine of nullification announced by Kentucky and Virginia in 1798, and so bitterly condemned by the Massachusetts legislature itself in 1799. Not content with this, however, the legislature proceeded to assail with vehemence the action of the Lieutenant Governor in issuing orders to militia officers to aid the United States collectors in enforcement of the Embargo Act, as provided by that law. It also issued a Memorial to Congress in protest against the Act, and an Address to the People. In the latter document it set forth in extremely violent terms the "affecting picture of the publick distress." It asserted that the "present leading men in the Southern States have beheld with jealousy your increasing prosperity, and feel neither respect for your pursuits nor sensibility for your sufferings. . . . Politicians of yesterday, from the backwoods and mountains, vie with each other in the language of insult and defiance; and the men whom you delight to honor . . . are stigmatized as a corrupt and seditious party of the community." It closed by stating that "a perfect union and intelligence among the Eastern States" was necessary to prevent Massachusetts from being "in fact enslaved by sister States," and that the Constitution must be amended so as to reduce the slave representation at the South, and to prevent any future Embargo Acts. The whole of these proceedings were officially published in a widely circulated pamphlet entitled (with considerable inversion of the truth) *The Patriotick Proceedings of the Legislature of Massachusetts.*[1]

Dr. Ames' Diary presented with great vigor his Republican view of the political situation during the year 1808:

> *Jan. 1808.* Embargo and non-importation and non-exportation, maritime enterprises stopped, causes much clamor against our Gov't. But it saves our vessels from both French and British fangs. Mr. Monroe returned from St. James, and Mr. Rose special ambassador here from London arrived to make reparation for insult and murder *Chesapeake*, but said not to have full power to satisfy our demands as to search and impressment of Americans. War seems impending — Traitors among us plead for Britain and revile our government. Nothing yet transpires of Rose's mission, nor of Monroe's communications of the disposition of the British Court — only we hear of unusual politesse of British naval officers to American masters and seamen. Now, 22d, *Palladium* announces Rose's favorable reception at Washington on the 13th, and that the President Jefferson is willing to treat with him separately in the *Chesapeake* affair!

[1] For striking contemporary examples of Republican and Federalist viewpoints as to the embargo and the attitude of Massachusetts, see *The Olive Branch or Faults on Both Sides, Federal and Democratic, A Serious Appeal on the Necessity of Mutual Forgiveness and Harmony to Save Our Common Country from Ruin* (November, 1814), by Mathew Carey; and *Pills, Poetical, Political and Philosophical prescribed for the Purpose of Purging the Publick of Piddling Philosophers, of Puny Poetasters, of Paltry Politicians, and Petty Partisans, by Peter Pepperbox, Poet and Physician* (1809).

Jan. 27. Mr. Rose well received, which is said to make Tur-
reau, French Ambassador, threaten and demand his pass-
ports. Because Congress preferred Embargo to War or
submission to France or Britain, a purse-proud Junto at Boston, by their seditious publications and conduct, have excited rebellion and murders in various ports and resistance
to the laws too generally in New England; and have planned
and plotted and threatened a separation from the Southern
and Western States, prancing on princely fortunes lured
from the people here by that British trade which is the
death blow to native genius; and manufacturers, shipowners, seem determined to rule landowners; and sacrifice
honor, independence, internal industry to maritime craft,
smuggling, and all the evils of disunion so much reprobated
by Washington! Civil War seems imminent, unavoidable!
Unless the Farmers in Massachusetts threaten to beat their
ploughshares into swords to support their own laws and
Government. But while the influence of the overgrown fortunes of different kinds of speculation — for it is not all
maritime — thus threaten us with anarchy, while some are
aspiring to monarchy, others to hierarchy, hoping to glut
their tyrannic ambition in the destruction of our democracies, there is another archy which is the mainspring of all the
others. It has long been prevalent in many nations as well
as here. And grows daily more insolent, always aspiring at
the same domination in every country over law as well as
men — to which kind of archy all our difficulties may justly
be imputed; and hereupon some exclaim: Monarchy I hate.
Hierarchy I despise. Anarchy I dread; but of all archys,
good Lord, deliver us from Pettifogarchy.

It was in the midst of such excited political conditions
that Dr. Ames' famous brother, Fisher Ames, died, in his
fiftieth year, on the morning of the Fourth of July, 1808.
He had been in poor health for ten years, but his uncon-
querable spirit had kept him in the forefront of the town's
activities, in spite of his despondency over political conditions in the Nation and his mourning over the downfall
of his cherished Federalist policies. In 1806 he had been

offered but had refused the presidency of Harvard College; and he had continued to practise law actively up to the last. By his party associates this death of "the American Burke" was regarded as a National calamity, and preparations were made for an elaborate public funeral under strictly Federalist auspices, and for an oration by Samuel Dexter, the leader of the Massachusetts bar and one of the ablest of the Federalist statesmen of that Commonwealth. Dr. Nathaniel Ames, at this time, had become personally reconciled to his brother, but he still retained his bitterness against his brother's party, and he had just recorded in his Diary his determination not to celebrate the Fourth of July in company with Federalist "traitors":

> *June 30.* Great parade of Dedham Federalists or Aristocrats to increase their triumph in appointing a Fed. Orator for 4 July and draw in Republicans to join, but rubs hard. The Republicans agree to read Declaration of Independence by themselves without noticing them. It is now the Federal Aristocrats that are disorganizers and seditious. True Republicanism cannot unite with treason and rebellion. I hope none of our Dedham patriots will be deluded to join!

When, upon his brother's death, Dr. Ames learned that the public funeral was to be managed by Federalist party leaders, with an oration by Samuel Dexter, he absolutely declined to have anything to do with it, and, together with his mother and other members of the family, he refused to attend the funeral ceremony in Boston.[1] It would seem that political rancor could go no further. His statement of his position is set out in the Diary in the following extraordinary fashion:

[1] See *Columbian Centinel*, July 6, 9, 1808, for elaborate accounts of the funeral and funeral procession.

July 4, 1808. My only brother, left, died of a lingering atro-
phy, 5 A.M., and funeral first ordered by the widow here on
Wednesday in the Episcopal form — Aetat. 50.

July 5. My Brother's body snatched by the Junto, deluding
the widow to order the funeral at Boston. Early this morning comes a servant of [George] Cabot from Boston with a
billet requesting his funeral to be in Boston from Cabot's
house, and that the Junto had provided an eulogium to be
said at his funeral, etc. And the widow, immediately deluded by such party political proposal, assented and coun-
termanded orders to the Dedham printer of yesterday,
announcing his death and funeral here, and made him alter
his types conformably to her sudden compliance with the
requisition of Junto aforesaid 3 times. And in the afternoon
comes Geo. Cabot to allure me into a sanction of ridiculous
pomp of pretended apotheosis, and then went and told our
mother that I should attend, but none of the relations will
attend. In the night, they took off his body in a superbly
trimmed mahogany coffin in a coach, and on the 6th sundry
coaches from Boston came for the family. The Bakers, only,
go as relations, besides his widow and children. The *Centinel* of this day has an eulogium equal to the ceremonies of
apotheosis. Dagget gone with the herse to bring back the
putrid corpse, after their mummery over it in Boston, to
stigmatize the town of Dedham, which is the principal intention of the Junto, to blast Republicanism. But making a
farce of a Funeral will rebound on their own heads, unless
perhaps it may be the introduction of a Fashion to make
political funerals.

And the following extraordinary anonymous "Communication," which appeared in the *Independent Chronicle* of
July 7, deploring the intrusion of politics and "pageantry"
into the funeral, was without question from the pen of
Dr. Ames:

Appropriate Reflections. Cities contended for the body of
Homer after his death, because the place of his nativity was
uncertain; but if he had died in a respectable village, on the

books of whose church his baptism and the baptism of his
father and mother were recorded together with the baptism
of his children, would it have exhibited the affection of his
friends to have had his funeral obsequies withdrawn from
that place to the distance of twelve miles? Pageantry may
answer the purposes of party; but when it is displayed to the
outrage of every domestic sensibility, we pity those who
sincerely mourn the loss of friends that they are made sub-
servient to such cruel exhibitions. We are commanded,
as Christians, to go to the house of mourning; but, as partisans, mourners are to come to those who wish to profit in
their political views by sacrificing the tender feelings of a
widow, the poignant reflections of an aged mother, and the
affection of weeping children. O Federalism! how art thou
at war with every sympathy of the human heart!"

While history has recorded Fisher Ames as one of the
most talented and patriotic of the early American statesmen, and in doing so has corroborated the verdict of his
Federalist associates, it is interesting to note that, at the
time of his death, many of his contemporaries held a con-
siderably lower opinion of him. Thus John Quincy Adams,
writing in 1809, in the *Boston Patriot*, a review of the *Collected Works of Fisher Ames*, spoke of the book as "that
strange medley of wit and weakness, of reason and dotage,
of benevolence and rancour, of ardent spirit and childish
terrors," and proceeded to excoriate the dead man as follows: "The last half of this volume might be denominated
the political bible of the Junto — the scab of this political
leprosy — threefold cord of Prostration to Britain, Horror
of France, Contempt for America. . . . Mr. Ames was a
man of genius and of virtue — he meant well to his country and served her with fidelity according to his best judgment. But, at a very early period of his public life, he
connected himself with Hamilton, his bank and his funding system, in a manner which warped his judgment and
trammeled the freedom of his mind for the remainder of

his days. . . . He became a convert to the English school, and with all the opinions of the anti-revolutionist mingled all the fear-engendered fancies of the anti-gallican. . . . He lived in a perpetual panic that America would be finally only the last morsel for the voracious maw of the monster Bonaparte. He was continually but ineffectually laboring to impart his terrors to his countrymen; they grew stronger upon him as they proved inefficacious to others, until he worked himself up into a sort of reasoning frenzy compounded of adoration of British power, abhorrence of France, and contempt of his own countrymen." And a writer in the *Independent Chronicle* termed Fisher Ames "the most illiberal, if not the most unbenevolent that ever appeared among us . . . every page of whose political writings breathes contempt and execration." [1] Such criticisms, however, were fully matched by the tartness of the replies from Ames' friends; and Joseph McKean, in especial, replied to Adams: "The malignity of this sarcasm is precisely characteristic of the merciless and unfeeling attack on the memory of exalted worth. It was chiefly the unfeigned and unexampled respect which provoked the deadly resentment of Mr. Adams. That any man out of his own distinguished family should call forth the tears and regret of a whole community, was an outrage upon the feeling of jealous pride not easily to be forgiven. Mr. Adams, who with crocodile tears followed the remains of the illustrious sage to the grave, was composing as he went this letter phillippick on a man whom he had not the courage to attack when living." [2] Thus, missiles flew back and forth over the grave of the departed Federalist, equalling in violence the political abuse of the living.

[1] M. C. D. in *Independent Chronicle*, November 18, 1811.

[2] See pamphlet entitled *Remarks on the Hon. John Q. Adams' Review of Mr. Ames' Works, with Some Strictures on the Views of the Author* (1809).

The local attitude towards the Embargo and the Jefferson administration in his native town absorbed Dr. Ames' attention in August:

> *Aug. 20, 1808.* Mann's Dedham paper filled with a flaming Federal slanging philippic against Government and B. Austin, which I reprobated in manuscript of Harrington, a student in law here, before publication, and told him I would not take his paper if he filled it with such stuff; and this morning went to remonstrate against publishing it — but he regarded not me, but H. ——, seemingly enjoying my defeat by the hands of a lawyer and himself in underhand way!
>
> *Aug.* Beyond conception, almost, is the impudence of the pettifog faction in sedition and slander against the best administration of Government ever blessing men. They, the Pettifogs, have already raised rebellion, murder, and treason in some parts in July and August.
>
> *Aug. 28.* At a convention of Republicans from all the towns in the county of Norfolk, Cohassett excepted, James Mann, Nathaniel Ames, Nathaniel Ruggles, Samuel Bailey, Abner Crane, John Ellis and John Swift, Esquires, were appointed a County Committee to communicate with the Central Committee of the State viz. Hon. Aaron Hill, Perez Morton, Samuel Brown, Charles P. Sumner, William Jarvis, Esquires, and Town or sub-committees to watch over the Republican interest both in State and National Governments, especially as to elections and appointments — convey intelligence — confute false rumors — confirm the wavering in right principles — prevent delusion of weak brethren — and fight that most formidable enemy of civilized men, political ignorance, a task, mighty, endless and insuperable without funds to excite, support and disseminate the fruits of patriotic genius—and with the most ample funds will prove a Herculean labor enough to stagger common undertakers to combat the pulpit, the bar and host of superstition, vanity, pride, and selfish wretches under foreign influence, that never had a conception of searching out principles or seeking the truth, and will neither read, see nor hear anything contrary to their own narrow prejudices, wholly actuated by the impulse of the moment.

At the same time, Ames kept a keen eye upon the attitude towards the Embargo in Europe and in Washington:

July 31, 1808. Insurrections in England of Mechanics out of employ. Effects of American custom withdrawn, effects of Embargo!

Aug. 1. Revolution in Spain not relished by people. They rise *en masse* against Bonaparte in favor of old dynasty of Monarchs. Why one set of tyrants is not as good as another, I would enquire, before fighting for either.

Oct. 25. Wild geese fly. News that Bonaparte has declared war against U. S., but from England! A Gull Trap! to prevent Madison, President! And proves so since.

Nov. 30. Both natural and political atmosphere hazy, drizzling with all pestilent drops of maritime or mercantile sedition and slander of the best administration of Government, trying to extricate maritime enterprises from piratical fangs of two lawless belligerents, England and France.

Dec. 1808. Giles' two speeches in Senate, with Macon's, Burwell's, Clopton's, Montgomery's, etc., in the House of Congress, against Hillhouse, Pickering, Quincy, Livermore, etc., are masterly, luminous, convincing upon Embargo and complete justification of Jefferson's Administration.

Dec. 5. John Randolph, naturally and originally a firm Republican but disappointed of an embassy, turns all his resentment against President Jefferson and the Government; this day, makes a speech in direct hostility to his own patriotism and pretends to persuade Congress to open trade, involving submission to British tribute and French confiscation, as if the honor and dignity of the U. States was nothing in comparison to the benefits of the little trade the belligerents might allow us, or that the sacrifice of manufacturing and internal industry was nothing in comparison of such trade. His resentment carries him to the utmost bounds of extravagance. But, 6th December, Mr. Gholson gives him a delicate trimming in an excellent speech reprobating the idea of immolating internal industry to commerce, etc. Also Mr. Eppes makes another excellent speech showing the repeated insults of Britain, many years back as well as lately, etc. But Giles' speeches make the debates of this Congress worthy.

Dec. 13. Men detached from militia to make 100,000, equipped, accoutred, and ready at a moment's warning to march anywhere to defend against invaders, as Britain has now more troops in Canada and Nova Scotia than ever they had in America before at once. 17 men detached from this company. 30 all Dedham's quota of 100,000. Town votes bounty at 2 dols. each, and to make up pay 12 dols. per month if called out.

The spirit of insurrection produced in Massachusetts by the new Congressional legislation in enforcement of the Embargo is strikingly shown by Dr. Ames' entries in the early part of 1809:

Jan. 6, 1809. This morning, 1/2 past 6, new Embargo passed, after Congress sat all night.

Jan. 14. Gholson makes excellent speech in Congress against New England merchants.

Jan. 18. Boston rebels against Federal Government.

Jan. 26. Excellent resolves of Kennebec in support of Government — as good as 10,000 persons at Philadelphia.

Feb. 1809. This Rebellious winter session of General Court is a blast on the honor of Massachusetts, and must be worse than a blot on the historic page of our country. It is all, I think, an attempt to establish the reign of Pettifogarchy.

Feb. 9. In *Patriot* an excellent essay taken from *Aurora,* headed "Original Restraint of Commerce and Tribute," shows that the French Decrees cramping neutrals are founded on British restraints of neutrals and contain a provision that when the British Government relax those restraints, the Decrees cease to operate — which makes evident that the British began, before the French, to cramp us!

Feb. 20. Topsfield: This town some months ago was conspicuous as the seat of a seditious Fudderal meeting, belching rebellious Resolves against President Jefferson and

Congress for Embargo,[1] but this day the largest meeting
ever known in Essex County of real citizens of all the towns
issue excellent Resolves in a voice of thunder, shaking Fudderalism into growling insignificance.

March 4. In *Centinel* are flaming Lawyer Resolves of the
town of Oxford or several towns of South district of Worcester, there met, 8th Feb. 1809, against Embargo and Congress, signed Benjamin Heywood, Chairman and Francis
Blake, secretary — also town of Jaffrey, N. H.

The defiant tone of these town resolutions, termed by
Dr. Ames "eggs of sedition," might well have alarmed any
serious lover of the Union. Thus, in the town of Gloucester, January 12, 1809, it was "Resolved that we will mutually watch and protect what little property we have still
left, — that we will use all lawful means 'to arrest disturb-
ers and breakers of the peace, or such others as may (under
pretence of authority from government) go armed by
night' or utter any menaces or threatening speeches to the
fear and terror of the good people of this town. And that
we will ever hold in abhorrence pimps and spies and night-
walkers, who fatten on the spoils of their suffering fellow
citizens. Resolved that to our State government we look
for counsel, protection, and relief at this awful state of
general calamity." The town of Bath asked the legislature
to take steps to relieve the people either alone "or in concert with other commercial States, as the extraordinary
circumstances of our situation may require." The town of
Topsfield expressly endorsed Great Britain's position, and

---

[1] John Adams wrote to Benjamin Rush, September 27, 1808: "The Union, I
fear, is in some danger." And on December 26, 1808, he wrote to J. B. Varnum:
"I have been constantly anxious and alarmed at the intemperance of party
spirit and the unbounded license of our presses. In the same view, I could not but
lament some things which have lately passed in public bodies. To instance, at
Dedham and Topsfield, and last of all in the Resolution of our Massachusetts
Legislature."

resolved that "neither the honor nor the permanent interests of the United States require that we should drive
Great Britain, if it were in our power, to the surrender of
those claims so essential to her in the mighty conflict in
which she is at present engaged; a conflict interesting to
humanity, to morals, to religion and the last struggle
of liberty." The town of Augusta resolved in favor of
open resistance to law, saying: "With submission almost
amounting to criminal apathy, we have suffered privations
and restrictions, never before expected or endured by a
free people. Now that even the means of subsistence is at
hazard, and the sacred asylum of our dwellings is no longer
held inviolable, silence would be a crime, and resistance
would become a virtue of the first magnitude." Boston
went so far as to formally declare that "we will not voluntarily aid or assist in the execution" of the Enforcement
Act, and that all who did so assist "in enforcing upon
others the arbitrary and unconstitutional provisions of this
Act ought to be considered as enemies to the Constitution
of the United States and of this State."

While many Massachusetts towns on the seacoast undoubtedly were sufferers from the effect of the Embargo, a
disposition to aid them as far as possible prevailed in other
parts of the State, and the following entries concern this
somewhat unique episode — to which little allusion has
been made by historians:

Feb. 9, 1809. Norfolk County consultation; among other business, agreed to make a donation to Marblehead of pork, to
eat with their dry fish, which they generously refuse to
smuggle, etc. ($94.50 pd. to Ames as Treas.)

March 16. Donation to Marblehead from Norfolk, inland
County.

March 18. 8 loads of meal and pork, etc., went off thro' Boston, 15th, to Marblehead, to their high satisfaction.

The situation which occasioned these entries was an interesting one. While many of the towns of Massachusetts were in flat rebellion, others were patriotic in their support of the government, despite the ruin caused by the Embargo Acts. Few towns in the Commonwealth were more hardly hit by the cessation of commerce than Marblehead, yet no town was more vigorous in its Republicanism. On December 7, 1808, it had passed resolutions upholding the Embargo as "a law of wisdom," and on February 9, 1809, still further resolutions reciting: "We view with the utmost abhorrence and indignation the conduct of a party among us who are continually endeavoring to excite the good people of this Commonwealth to a disobedience of the laws of the Union." [1] The patriotic fishermen and merchants of Marblehead did not stop with words, but they acted up to them. They refused to become smugglers and lawbreakers, as the Federalists of most New England seaports had. Naturally, among a people whose whole livelihood was maritime, there was great suffering. To relieve this condition, and to provide for the families of these law-abiding citizens whose trade was destroyed and who were actually in distress, Republicans in inland towns were called upon to contribute the provisions which the Marblehead men had scorned to obtain by unlawful means. Dr. Ames quotes in full an extract from the *Salem Register*, describing the arrival in Marblehead of these provisions: "The Genuine Reward of Principle! We understand, and we rejoice in the information, that the Republicans of several towns in the county of Norfolk on Thursday last presented a donation by the hands of a committee selected for that purpose to the poor of Marblehead. It consisted of 20 barrels of pork, 30 barrels of meal, etc., etc. On the news of the approach of the Committee with

[1] *History and Traditions of Marblehead* (1880), by Samuel Roads, Jr.

the waggons, the inhabitants of the town immediately
assembled, and with drum beating and colors flying,
formed a procession of about 500 persons, and at the en-
trance of the town met the Committee and escorted them
to the Town House, where they were received with three
times three cheers. The waggons were not driven by hired
men, but by independent farmers who determined that the
whole should be a voluntary offering to the noble spirit of
patriotism which has characterized the incorruptible
citizens of the 'Pride of the Fisheries,' in times which try
men's souls. In the evening, a handsome entertainment
(consisting of salt fish and potatoes) [1] was given by the
citizens of the town to the Committee and Independent
Farmers, which was conducted with one genuine spirit of
hospitality. We do not know which most to admire — the
persons giving or the persons receiving the donation. It is
truly honourable to all concerned, and will remain a lasting
testimony to the character of a town which stands un-
shaken in its principles.

> The storms and tempests thunder round its brow
> And oceans break their billows at its feet."

As the presidential election approached, the Federalists
of Massachusetts, who controlled the legislature, determined to have presidential electors chosen by that body
instead of by the people in districts — the Constitution of
the United States having vested power to select the method
of choice of electors in the respective States. On this
Federalist action Dr. Ames commented bitterly as follows:

June 7, 1808. Comes Gov. Sullivan's speech, the keenest lash
of England and the Feds, but Feds are determined ring us
and choose electors themselves. Israel Thorndike ought to

---

[1] The following note is added in the original Diary by Dr. Ames: "This was
added by a rank, envious Fudderalist!"

be caught and try the yoke and ring first that he wishes to fix on us forever.

Nov. 14. Senate and House Representatives at Boston, by vile, treacherous usurpation upon us the Sovereign People, arrogate appointment of electors of President without even the Governor's assent or notice to him. If the People patiently submit to this, they will readily bow their necks to yokes and noses to rings! The Constitutional mode rightly pursued is in my opinion a sort of stigma on our Majesty, but this usurpation of our choice of electors is a treacherous usurpation on us. Now we ought to raise our voice like Jove and demand an alteration of Constitution and resume the direct appointment into our own hands as of Governor without the intervention of Electors!

The events of the spring of 1809 and after Madison's inauguration as President were noted by Dr. Ames, as follows:

Feb. 21. Embargo divides the People into parties — Northern States nearly in open rebellion against Congress and Southern States. Pettifogarchy governs N. Eng. men, who charge Southern States as Frenchified enemies to Commerce.

Centinel relates from Plymouth, England, that an insurrection of the Spaniards since the 4th December when the French took it (Madrid) 26,000 of them have been butchered! ! At an ordination in Boston lately, one of the Reverend toasts was "Spanish Clergy, now militant, may they soon be triumphant! !" 26,000 Frenchmen butchered by Spanish patriots will cheer up the Boston Clergy and holy Inquisition. But official documents may reverse all — and, very soon, really do.

March 8. Rebellion at New Haven, burning vessel of U. States by mob, etc., etc.

March 15. Embargo yields to Non-Intercourse (in Congress).

March 22. John Adams' letter shows him still American.

March 23. News of rebel mob at New Haven.

March 31. Election of Governor here and in New Hampshire, seems more interesting than ever and great exertions made. Arms at last likely to decide!

April 8. English army in Spain said to have arrived in England — what remains. Bonaparte has settled affairs of Spain, and an Envoy sailed from England to treat with U. S. Haughty tone of England lowered!

April 15. Another letter of J. Adams published. Still a Patriot!

April 17. British army whipped and home from Spain. Truckles.

April 19. John Adams' letters confounding the Fudderal opposition, highly approving Congress. British Government more compliant.

April 21. President Madison's proclamation of adjustment with Britain, 10 June next. But the impudence of the Federals arrogating the merit to their rebellion is too much!

June 24. Austrian army destroyed by French; 50,000 killed and taken! Napoleon triumphant still! to great grievance of a British party or Pickering's Junto here! ! !

June 31. British Government got supplied, then refuse to perform agreement with Erskine and put even Fudderalism to blush for their baseness! ! Americans without number rush into Bull's throat.

The description by Ames of the Fourth of July celebration held in Dedham in this year, 1809, by the Republicans depicts the opposition felt by that party to the clergy and its Federalist efforts:

July 1. Preparations making to keep natal day, 4th July, divers places as well as here, to mortification of British faction who hoped now for calm of Despotism! At Dedham, celebration of Independence; an excellent oration, or statement of facts as the orator called it, was given to a full Meeting-house of Ladies and Gentlemen, with which all enlightened Republicans were highly gratified; but some weaker breathren, under an idea of uniting all parties by soothing milk and water, affected displeasure: Col. Geo. Ellis, Major Abn. Ellis, Luther Richards, Lem Gay, are of this milky class; but David Dana, a still weaker tool of the Fudderalists, was outrageous, and says that Worthington, the orator, for coming here to make such a disturbance ought to be drummed out of town, and yet cannot allege a single falsehood he uttered.

July 21. Clergy confederate to run down 4th July orator here, but the People in general pleased to run him up the more!

At Dedham celebration 4th July, one toast is: "The whore of Babylon — a check to her seductions at head-quarters of good principles — at least among our clergy who might now command veneration as with our pious ances-tors, by beating up for volunteers against the man of sin, as well as that queer old Demi-rep."

As an offset to this Republican toast, it is interesting to note that at a separate celebration and dinner in Dedham held by the Federalists, at which Theron Metcalf (later Judge of the Supreme Court) gave the oration, the follow-ing toast was given: "Thomas Jefferson — his promises were, as he then was, mighty; but his performances, as he now is — nothing." In Boston there were three sepa-rate processions to celebrate the day, a Municipal proces-sion, a Democratic procession, and a Federal Republican procession, and each with its oration and dinner.

Sept. 6, 1809. Jackson, British Minister, arrived.

Nov. 18. Handbills about British insolence of Envoy.

Nov. 19. News of Jackson's dismissal for insult to Govern-ment, but other British Envoy may be sent.

Dec. 3. Attempts of Young Men of Dedham to form into Tammany Societies.

March 16, 1810. While our Junto traitors justify Jackson's insults to our Government, in England Jackson is blamed for the same.

March 17. Junto traitors likely to be foiled every way.

March 30. Most flattering assurances, all quarters, of restora-tion of Republic — but boast not too soon.

March 31. Chronicle of March 29 states the fact that lately in State Senate, Col. [Israel] Thorndike "declared that Brit-ain had the right to impress from our vessels and he hoped she would never give it up!"

At this time, in the spring of 1810, Dr. Ames had become so wrought up against British acts of aggression that he indulged in the following extraordinary diatribe with reference to a committee report which was accepted by the Massachusetts State Senate, on February 8, by the close vote of 20 to 17:

> However staunch patriots may be shocked and astonished at the Lying Report of the heavy laden blunderbuss, signed Elijah Brigham per order, upon second thoughts I cannot but have doubts of the sincerity of this attempt to bring back this country to court, caress, and hug that corrupt old whore of a step-mother that we rejected forever, after she had starved and poisoned about 11,000 of her children on board the Jersey prison-ship and as many more perhaps in the Sugar-house at New York (as Elihu Pond knows), flogging Giles and Jessup at the gangways of her warships, etc. And latterly coming fawning into our own jurisdiction to insult, kidnap, press, rob, plunder and murder U. S. American citizens! And pretend to control our navigation and trade by pretended paper blockade and Orders in Council! After these and innumerable other infractions of national law, to pretend to set her up as a barrier against Bonaparte who keeps his distance — and whom British tyranny and aggression caused to be made the dreaded commander he is, it must, I think, be a finesse of the present Fudderal majority to try what sea-monsters country throats can be made to gulp down — or else to excite the Lords of the soil to find a champion of the country interest against cent per cent importers, speculators, bank-directors! and make independent Farmers swear they will no longer offer abominable sacrifice to seagods, rivergods, or strange foreign idols! ! We stand in need of a barrier against tyrants that can come to our doors to rob and murder — the tyrants of ocean, I should repeat.

The clergy and the lawyers continued to be Ames' pet bane, in 1810:

Feb. 17, 1810. High road to profit and honors among Yankees since Hamilton's reign has always been through a Lawshop. Have we no civilians? No Philosophers but pettifoggers?

Apr. 19. Samuel Fisher, George Morey, George Homer, John A. Haven, Committee, prostitute the Honour of old Harvard in complimenting David Osgood, D.D., priest of Medford, for a seditious sermon preached at Cambridge, April 8, 1810.

Aug. 10. Received a note from an anonymous cub imputing to me a character as being an imp of Hell, because I oppose pettifogarchy, and my cautious purity defeats the purposes of the pettifoggers.

The aggressions of both France and England on American commerce, the outrages on American shipping, and the intensity of public feeling against England and the gradual approach of war through the years 1810 and 1811 were interestingly detailed with much force by Dr. Ames:

June 9, 1810. Jefferson's policy proves best. Noisy merchants caught in their own trap! Unshackled as they desired, most of their vessels taken and condemned.

July 4. Independence. Two orations here, fireworks, etc.

July 8. French aggressions on Americans increase.

July 13. American trade or smuggling nipped by Buonaparte!

Aug. 3. Spain dismembering, some parts may fall to United States — Florida about declaring independence and coming into our Confederacy.

Sept. 4. Louis Bonaparte abdicated throne of Holland, on Napoleon's lawless aggression, and said to be coming to America.

Sept. 15. France relaxes from late severity. Berlin and Milan Decrees now declared will be repealed from November, if England revokes her Orders in Council and paper blockade.

Oct. 31. The spirit of revolt of American Spaniards from the tyranny of Old Spain has took firm hold. And Lucien Bonaparte, immensely rich, has embarked for the United States, it is said — to evade the ire of his brother Napoleon! No, he has thrown himself into the arms of the Old Prostitute, England!

Nov. 8. Madison's Proclamation renews intercourse with France.

1811. Mrs. Anne Seward's Life of Dr. E. Darwin is one specimen among the finest genii of England condemning their own Government, both with respect to France and United America. She says: "Its belligerent spirit overlooks the Atlantic, shorn of her continental beams, a spirit to whose unwarned and persisting violence in later years the lives of her soldiery and the comforts of millions of families are sacrificed, in defiance of the Gospel which preaches peace on earth and good will towards men." But here we have plenty of ape-ish miscreants and English agents that excite sedition and rebellion against the best of Government in our own country!

Congress have much business, this winter, with close doors — supposed about Florida, as the President has ordered force to recover possession of West Florida, the title to which is plain from the debates, especially by the lucid speech of Mr. Clay in Senate. And it appears, the inhabitants, Spanish as well as Americans therein, wish to join the United States. And all the Spanish Colonies in South America and North are struggling for Independence. It seems decreed that it is time that Americans break all European shackles! Even Cuba is said to begin to shake off its Spanish mother's shackles. Embargo has raised a spirit of factory enterprize in this country that never will be extinguished. Cotton factorys continually rising up in various parts of United States. And some woolen, but wool is yet scarce, tho immense numbers of merino sheep continually importing from Spain promise a prolific supply of wool for future factorys. I am informed that the cotton factory in Medway netted, last year, 56% and that the Dedham factory averages 33% or 200 dollars on a share which they say have cost 600 dollars but will now sell for 900 or 1000 dollars.[1]

---

[1] A later entry, of May 25, 1812, as to another cotton mill, shows that the stock was not as profitable as Ames had expected: "Norfolk Cotton Factory shares now 2 years run, still assessed, now 30 dollars on a share — instead of

Last year, 1810, G. Britain imported 11,096,163 bushels of wheat, besides flour and other grain. Of this wheat, 2,678,448 bushels were imported from France, tho' in open war. From America, only 278,632, tho' neutral and in peace. But British envy of American enterprise has really created War in disguise, to discourage our agriculture and rather promote that of their open enemies.

Jan. 18. Florida about acceding to U. S.

Jan. 19. Trade with France relieved and open.

Jan. 28. News of West Florida restored to U. S. proves abortive.

In the spring of 1811 Dr. Ames' entries mingle his view of legal politics with world politics. At this time, he had some thought of being a candidate for the office of Registrar of Probate, then held by a Federalist, whose supporters referred to the doctor, in the newspapers, as "that most violent and tyrannical aristocrat." [1]

March 4. At Dedham Town-meeting, a splitting of Republicans and the Fudderalists. And I hear since that on declaring the vote, the Fudderalists clapped in Town-meeting.

March 6. Samuel Haven's malignant slang at me in Town-meeting shocks good folks.

March 8. Non-intercourse with England passed, until her Orders in Council revoked. Passed, 1st inst., in Congress, after 2nd midnight session! ! !

March 11. French Decree of 13 December. The Berlin and Milan Decrees are the answer to British Orders in Council. Neutral flags make free goods. And nothing short of actual

dividends to reward the undertakers or Proprietors — it has run more than 3 years. They were incorporated by Act dated Nov. 12, 1808, but it was near a year after before worked it and have been continually making improvements and additions ever since, so that besides all its great earnings, sundry assessments on shares, and interest computed on money advanced, makes my shares No. 39 amount to $884.69 on May 25, 1812. And if a dividend on the profits to each share before the year is ended doth not exceed more than $53, it is no more than simple interest, vastly short of great profits contemplated. That is, the mill must clear above 2654 dollars in the year."

[1] *Columbian Centinel*, March 9, 1811.

blockade shall authorize seizure of vessels entering a port!
say Buonaparte and conservative Senate.

March 16. T. Pickering, now at leisure, addresses the citizens
at large in full slang of Junto against Jefferson, Madison,
France, Bonaparte, etc., to little purpose, I hope, to allure
us into the fangs of England again.[1]

March 20. French vessels use Americans as friends again now,
and we will make our rights respected.

April 22. Samuel Haven [in Dedham] gives a flaming political
charge to Grand Jury.

May 13. French losing in Spain and Portugal.

May 17. Spat with one Wainwright, at Smith's Tavern, who,
railing at Democracy, said we had been governed long
enough by the rabble; he wanted good men brought in but
would neither say who were of the rabble nor who was a
good man. I told him if he was of the United States and not
a Democrat, he was a traitor, for our Government is clear
Democracy; and not Lobster-princes but Lords of the soil
were to rule us, as we are not a nation of shopkeepers.
This "W" is said to be an Englishman, a Boston shop-
keeper!

May. British war vessels, swarming on our coast, annoy
our coasting trade intolerably. They press even passengers,
and seem to threat to send their press gangs into our streets
next! Whereupon President Madison orders Commodore
Rogers, commander of our frigate the *President*, of 44 guns,
to go in pursuit of these pirates. He returned to Sandy
Hook and gives account that on 23rd May in the morning
saw a strange sail, pursued, and about 9 P.M. came up with
her and hailed her, but received no answer; on enquiry
again who she was — what ship — received for answer two
cannon balls, one of which wounded one sailor, on which
Rogers sent a single shot which was answered by a whole
broadside by the other, without damage; then Rogers let
fly an American broadside which settled the contest. Com.
Rogers stayed by till daylight, sent his boat and found it was
British sloop of war, *Little Belt*, Capt. Bingham, who had

[1] See "Letters of Mr. Pickering to the People of the United States" in
Columbian Centinel, March 16, 1811.

30 men killed and sundry wounded by American shot, and vessel much shattered. The Briton pretended regret for not answering, as he supposed Rogers a French frigate, etc. But since, we have accounts that sundry broadsides were exchanged before the Britons were subdued, as above.

June 30. Remarkably cold, begins storm, hay caught out. French perfidy as to Berlin and Milan Decrees disgusts all, and dissolves confidence in any but our own Government. We must consider ourselves Americans. And the voice of all America now seems to be that all European shackles on this quarter shall be broken.

July 19. French restore sequestered American vessels since 1 Nov.

July 31. Accounts of another great battle in Portugal. Massena out-general'd Wellington, 12,000 British left dead — but proves fudge.

Aug. 22. Much irritation of J. Bull at Rogers' chastisement of British insolence! (see 27 May last).

September. Dull time for news. The contest now seems to be between the Lords of the Soil and Lobster-princes — One party says there is free trade for us to France, the other, no.

Oct. 31. English insolence at sea and abuse of Americans is without bounds, and incessant clamour for Congressional vengeance against both belligerents at their session, next Monday!

Nov. 4. Congress convene.

Nov. 9. President's Message arrived yesterday, in 62 hours from delivery.

Nov. 13. Augustus James Foster, British Envoy to U. S., beat all hollow by Monroe, our Secretary of State.

Nov. 18. British Government, now too late, tender indemnity for *Chesapeake* murder, etc.

Nov. 22. The *Scourge,* a blackguard Lawyer Paper at Boston, has excited caneing of the printer, nearly come to selfridging.

Nov. 30. 2 French vessels at Savanna, Georgia, burnt to the water's edge in retaliation for insolence of their sailors, rushing into street of Savanna and armed with swords, etc.; cutting, abusing American sailors, one of whose hearts they stabbed, a mate of a Philadelphia vessel. The two ves-

sels burnt were picaroons — *La Vengeance* and *L'Agile.*
Since, hear some of the French sailors were killed; 120 of
them are put in gaol for protection.

During these exciting years of controversy over the Embargo and the French and British maritime aggressions,
the political situation in Massachusetts was white-hot.
Never, even in Jacobin days, had State politics been more
violent. While the Presidential and Congressional elections in the country had been strongly Republican during
the eight years of Jefferson, Massachusetts had remained
rock-bound in her Federalism; and no Republican had been
elected Governor since Samuel Adams, in 1796. Dr.
Ames took a most lively interest in the details of Massachusetts politics, and a State election lost by the Republicans in 1805 had caused him to record pessimistically:

> *March 31, 1805.* Great election efforts made for next Mon-
> day. One party holds James Sullivan and Gen. Heath for
> Governor, etc; the other, [Caleb] Strong and Robbins; but
> many think Gerry instead of Sullivan would have been most
> likely to succeed, but Gerry refused his name to be again
> bandied. And now it appears evident to me we are plunging
> into the vortex which has always engulphed men and citi-
> zens in all ages, and fixed on them yokes and rings as swin-
> ish multitude, and dominion of pettyfoggers, or drove them
> to court monarchy as a protection against pettifogarchy! ! !

In 1806 the Massachusetts State election was particularly heated; and the campaign literature of the times is
illustrated by the title of a pamphlet widely circulated by
the Federalists attacking the Republican candidate, James
Sullivan, who was an old Revolutionary patriot and long
the State Attorney-General: "The Sham-Patriot Un-
masked — Being an Exposition of the Fatally Successful
Arts of Demagogues to Exalt Themselves by Flattering
and Swindling the People." The years 1807 and 1808

brought a political revolution at last in Massachusetts, Sullivan being elected and reëlected Governor. His death, shortly after his reëlection, threw the State into the hands of the Federalists again in 1809, Christopher Gore being elected Governor. In 1810 and in 1811, however, the Republicans returned to power, with Elbridge Gerry as Governor.

Dr. Ames commented on these events in characteristic language, as follows. Of the 1808 election he wrote:

March 20, 1808. Electioneering opened. Pamphlets flying like wild geese in a storm.

May. In May great consternation among Repub. at amount return of Reps of British, Fed. hue. Both Houses Federal; Bigelow Speaker, and Otis President of Senate. The Republican Governor's election expected yet to be set aside, when Devilism reigns. Many Republicans say they wish it that the spirit of the sovereign People may be roused into energy — but never so, their spirits are broken down!

May 25. Very dark Election! Devilism reigns! Federalism triumphant. House, 31 Fed. Majority, and Senate ditto. Feds astonished at their own luck!

May 30. Sullivan, Gov'r. [Levi] Lincoln, Lt. Gov. Fed. Houses cast off all votes they dared.

May 31. A Revolution in General Court; 2 Houses Fed. by small majority — not from alteration of public sentiment but from negligence of Repub's and great exertion of Federalists. Some have owned or boasted of the sums they paid to runners over the State to delude Republicans into security and prompt Federals to exertion to send utmost number of Representatives.

Of the 1810 and 1811 elections he wrote:

April 9, 1810. Gerry, Governor of Massachusetts by more than 3000 majority, but the Pickering Junto secretly alledge he is not qualified in property or estate! [1]

[1] Dedham voted for Gerry by vote of 397 to 129.

April 13. New Hampshire and Vermont returned to '75 principles.

April 17. Rhode Island returned to '75 in all branches.

April 22. Connecticut approximating Union. Fudderalism upon its last legs. Hamiltonian, Pickeronian faction declining.

May 1. Much parade of militia. Roxbury troops of horse came prancing round, set all the children a running — every eye straining to see wonders.

June 1. Gerry declared Governor, Gray Lieutenant Governor. But Senate equal 20 and 20. House Republican. Senate clogs the wheels of Government.

May 29, 1811. Election, all branches Republican. House 21 majority. Gerry Governor by near 300.

June 7. Governor's speech this day keenly lashes Boston Feds., Otis, etc., as seditious rebels.

June 9. Gov. Gerry's speech excellent!

Jan. 11, 1812. Governor Gerry's speech spunky, good.

Jan. 12. Governor's Communication at opening this session much approved in different States. A Governor without the pettifog bias can display patriotism if not talent.

IX

THE WAR OF 1812 AND THE
BOSTON REBELS

DURING the spring of 1812, when it was evident that the country was drifting inevitably into a war with England, the attacks of the Federalists on President Madison's policies became increasingly bitter, and tremendous efforts were made to redeem the State from the control of Gerry and the Republicans. A characteristic answer to these attacks was made by Dr. Ames who, as chairman of a Norfolk County convention, March 12, penned the following resolution: "That we view with extreme indignation and contempt that vile and outrageous abuse which, proceeding from a party decidedly hostile to the Constitution and principles of a free government, has endeavored to impede and embarrass its operation, by assaulting with every possible indignity the men who are entrusted with its administration; and that, in this violence, we see the systematic attempts of a party to erect a monarchical system on the ruins of our republican institutions." [1]

To counteract the efforts of the Massachusetts Federalists, President Madison now exploded a bomb in their

[1] Dr. Ames' sympathy with republicanism extended to the efforts of the Spanish colonies to escape from monarchical rule:

> *Jan. 1812.* Declaration of Carthagena, a Spanish province of S. America, of their Independence dated Nov. 11, 1811. Inquisition, at the sovereign People's demand, abolished! Which confirms hopes that all America may soon be self-governed, without European or other foreign control.

> *Feb. 3, 1812.* South American provinces successively declare independence of Old Spain, and, greater still, abolish the cruel holy Court of Inquisition! ! !

ranks by sending a special message to Congress, March 9,
1812, which aroused the Republicans from one end of the
country to the other to a white heat. In this message
Madison stated that he laid before Congress certain documents proving that at a recent period a British secret agent
was employed "in fomenting disaffection" in Massachusetts "and in intrigue with the disaffected for the purpose of bringing about resistance to the laws, and eventually, in concert with a British force, of destroying the
Union and forming the Eastern part thereof into a political
connection with Great Britain." These documents, which
had been recently bought by the Government for $50,000,
were a series of letters, written in 1808 by an Englishman
named John Henry, for the information of the Governor
of Lower Canada. In them Henry had described the political situation in New England as he viewed it, and also his
meetings with various Federalist leaders. In one letter, he
had written from Boston: "The men of talents, property,
and influence in Boston are resolved to adopt without delay
every expedient to avert the impending calamity, and to
express their determination not to be at war with Great
Britain, in such a manner as to indicate resistance to government in the last resort"; in another: "In a few months
more of suffering and privation of all the benefits of commerce, the people of New England will be ready to withdraw from the Confederacy, establish a separate government, and adopt a policy congenial with their interest and
happiness. For a measure of this sort, the men of talents
and property are now ready." In April, 1808, he wrote:
"I attended a private meeting of the principal characters
in Boston where the questions of immediate and ultimate
necessity were discussed. . . . Every man whose opinion I
could ascertain was opposed to a war, and attached to the
cause of England." The letters gave seeming reinforce-

ment to the charges, long made by the Republicans, that
New England was ripening for secession. The Federalist
newspapers, however, treated them as of no significance
and as a joke. The *Centinel* (March 18) said as to Henry:
"All the information he gave was the echo of the falsehoods which then circulated from the polluted press of the
democratic party, or fabricated by his own mischievous
invention." Three days later, it spoke of "the infamous
and silly plot of John Henry," and declared: "The opinion
of such a wretch as John Henry, the Federalists held in
unutterable contempt." In its headlines, during the succeeding two weeks, it termed the matter "The Paltry
Plot," "Fifty Thousand Dollar Plot," "Madison's Hard
Bargain"; and it claimed that Madison had been sold and
deceived, and that the word of a venal spy was worthless.
The Republican papers, however, made vigorous use of
this communication against their old foe, the Junto. The
Chronicle said (March 12): "The Republicans in the Eastern States have long been satisfied of the existence among
men of a small but dangerous and desperate Faction devoted wholly to England. So inveterate has been their
hatred of our happy constitutions and Republican form of
government that they would not scruple forcibly to separate the Union and annex the Eastern part to England (the
God of their idolatry), if they could but succeed in establishing Monarchy, Aristocracy, and British Dominion. A
small but artful, intriguing, and ambitious set of men has
long existed in these States, and are well-known under the
appellation of the Essex Junto. . . . The film is fast falling
from the eyes of good men; they begin to perceive that they
have been basely deceived by a desperate Faction, whose
entire devotion to a Foreign Power has now become open,
clear and explicit. But it gives us great pleasure to state
that what the Republicans have always affirmed is now

proved to be correct, viz: that the great body of Federalists were Americans at heart, but would not follow their leaders in any disorganizing project."

In spite of the Federalist denials, it is probable that Henry reported with reasonable truth the general character of talk by some Federalist leaders; and the nearly contemporaneous letters of Timothy Pickering to the British envoy, Rose, and the language and actions of the Massachusetts legislatures of 1808 and 1809, gave considerable support to the charge of seditious sentiment.[1] It is not surprising that a hot Republican like Dr. Ames should have boiled with indignation at the disclosure of such sentiments on the part of his hated Junto, and at the defeat of Governor Gerry and the return of the Junto's party into power at the State election in April, 1812, despite such disclosures. He invented the curious epithets of "Lobster-princes" and "Henryites" as applied to the members of the Junto. His Diary entries also gave an interesting picture of the gradual approach and declaration of war:

March 14, 1812. Henry's disclosure of secret Villainy of Boston rebels. Fudderal traitors of 1809 exposed.

March 25. Electioneering stuff. All the papers now excluding other matter.

April 1. A caucus or consultation of Democrats, pretty full from all parts of the town except South Parish, appoint committees from each squad to hunt our Republican voters and get their conveyance to poll, if lame or unable — at Marsh's Tavern.

April 2. Ditto — Fudderal at Lem Ellis's [Tavern].

April 16. Sovereign voice — Dedham: Gerry, 299; Strong, 172. Gain, Republican 46, Fudderal 56.

[1] See *History of the United States*, by Henry Adams. For an entirely different and contemporary view, see William Sullivan's *Familiar Letters on Public Characters* (1847), pp. 328 *et seq.*

French and Britons both vile pirates. Make prize of Americans! Britons took, from January 28 to February 25, eighteen of our vessels of immense value!!! War must ensue!

On the first returns of votes here April 7th for Governor, etc., the prospect was gloomy (so it was last year), when afterwards it appeared Gerry was chosen — but now even General Heath today says, Strong is chosen!... I had felt a confidence that Henry's disclosure would reduce Fudderalism to the few traitors that joined him — but now I find that the herd are conducted only by their prejudices, not at all by principle or reason. I entertained too honorable an opinion of my own countrymen — they are mere geese running in the foxes' jaws.

April 17. William Ellis, on return from Penobscot, informs that General Cobb told him some time past "that there should be but one Governor of New England, send no members to Congress, take care of our own commercial interests as required, leave the other States to take care of their interests, they would soon unite with us again and consolidate a firmer union!!!" Ellis says Republicans have greatly increased in Maine; that even in Portland, so Fudderal, they expect to gain Repub. Representatives in May! But we find there is no dependence to be placed on the multitude, almost as shifting as the wind. It is curious to behold the dupes of Lobster-princes among some Lords of the soil. The Henryites of Boston have seized some Country Asses by their ears, and set them on braying against their own Government. However that may clog the progress, it will defeat the success of our gaining the complete control of N. America or our own resources.

May 4. Dedham Town meeting choose Representatives — old ones — tho' Fudds intended to steal a march.

May 5. 19 men detached for Army!

May 24. Recruits for Army brisk, even in Connecticut.

May 26. All Fudderalists concentrating at Boston today.

May 30. [Caleb] Strong declared Governor by majority of 600! and not near so many as the illegal vote of Boston.

June 2. The despatches from [Joel] Barlow at Paris by the *Hornet*, tho' they show nothing yet carried into effect, shew the comity of Duke Bassano that the French Government is well disposed to us.

June 10. Talk of war stronger daily, and Britain persists in her tyranny, seizing our vessels. Both belligerents live on U. S. Piracy, and Plunder, as if in collusion! Insurgency in England against their Government or Prince Regent and Ministry. Many killed, under Riot Act.

June 16. Various reports of war, but papers don't come.

June 21. War, War, decided on, Congress vs. England. Federalists aghast!

June 24. Declaration of War vs. Britain by U. S. in Congress, 18th inst., arrived.

June 26. Massachusetts House of Representatives makes false, furious electioneering address to the People vs. President and Congress, for not still submitting to British piracy!

From the moment of the declaration of war, Massachusetts steadily threw obstacles in the way of its successful prosecution. The Federalist newspapers denounced the war in unbridled terms. The *Centinel* said, on the day of its declaration: "Predictions verified. The awful event so often anticipated by us as the inevitable effect of the infatuated policy of the Rulers of the American people has now been realized — and the worst of measures has emerged from its secret womb in the worst of forms. A naked and unqualified War is declared to exist." And, in almost every issue, it termed the war "unjustifiable," "needless," "bloody," "destructive," "objectless," "hellish." The clergy of the State also united in fulminations against it, as "impious," "unrighteous," and "Godless." Republican members of Congress who voted for the war were publicly insulted on their return to the State, as noted by Dr. Ames *infra.* Congressman Ebenezer Seaver of Norfolk County was hissed on the Exchange in Boston; and Congressman Charles Turner of Plymouth County, Chief Justice of the Court of Sessions, was assailed in Plymouth and (as stated in a Court order adjourning its session) "was violently assaulted by a mob, seized, kicked and pushed through the streets in a most shameful manner, his person injured and his feelings insulted" — an example, said the Antifederalist papers, "of the principles of mobocracy of Plymouth Federalism, aristocratic in appearance, monarchic in sentiment, but anarchic in action." The house of Benjamin Austin, a leading Republican of Boston, was stoned. As to these acts the *Chronicle* commented as follows: "Further prostration of all law, order and decency — or — progress of Federal Mobocracy in Massachusetts. Such outrageous acts of cowardice and insolence serve to produce all those evils they deprecate. . . . We hope also that certain clerical demagogues will be reprobated, whose sermons are wholly calculated to raise rebellion, excite mobs, and disturb society." [1]

A project, favored by Timothy Pickering and Harrison Gray Otis, for the calling of a State Convention to consider measures of resistance was dropped, after a vigorous debate at a Boston town meeting, August 16, several prominent Federalists, like Samuel Dexter, breaking away from their party on this course of action and terming such a convention illegal and unconstitutional. Dr. Ames' own town of Dedham was heartily in favor of the war. With very slight Federalist opposition, the town absolutely refused to follow the lead of Boston, and adopted the following resolution at a town meeting, held July 20, in which the peace resolutions of the Boston Federalist meeting were denounced on the ground that they "openly and without disguise recommend a general combination to counteract a just and necessary war waged for the protection of our violated rights and liberties; and, as the report

---

[1] See full and dramatic accounts of these attacks in the *Independent Chronicle*, August 6, 10, 13, 17, October 15, 1812.

and resolutions contain statements false in point of fact, disgraceful to freemen when considered as an exhibition of their feelings and spirit, erroneous when viewed as opinions of public measures, hostile to their design to the National Union, and highly disorganizing in their tendency — therefore, *Resolved* by the citizens of Dedham in legal Town Meeting assembled, that the above report and resolutions of Boston, being in substance an exhortation to submit to the insults and aggressions of Great Britain, and an attempt to suppress that manly spirit and patriotic enterprise which is now displaying itself in the prosecution of a just and necessary war, ought to be dismissed with the indignation and contempt which proceedings and sentiments so disgraceful will ever excite in the minds of a free, enlightened, and virtuous people; *Resolved* that since Congress has thought it necessary to declare war for the protection of commerce, for the liberties of our citizens, for our national sovereignty and independence, for a republican form of government itself, we hesitate not to declare our firm resolution to prosecute it with all our energy." The *Centinel* assailed these Dedham resolutions as "violent, indecorous, and disgraceful," and said "the Friends of Peace were confounded at the vulgar impudence, indecency, and servility, as well as falsehoods they contain."[1]

The legislature of the State went on record in violent language as denouncing the war. The Senate said: "The war was founded in falsehood, declared without necessity, and its real object was extent of territory by unjust conquest, and to aid the late tyrant of Europe in his view of aggrandizement." The House of Representatives, in like vehement tone, resolved: "The real cause of the war must be traced to the first systematical abandonment of the

[1] See *Columbian Centinel*, August 1, 1812; see also *Independent Chronicle*, July 23, 1812.

policy of Washington, and the friends and framers of the Constitution — to implacable animosity against those men and their universal exclusion from all concern in the government of the country — to the influence of worthless foreigners over the press, and the deliberations of the Government in all its branches — to a jealousy of commercial States, fear of their power, contempt of their pursuits, and ignorance of their true character and importance — to the cupidity of certain States for the wilderness reserved for the miserable aborigines — to a violent passion for conquest." In addition to this legislative declaration, the counties (except Norfolk County) held conventions and adopted long resolutions in opposition to the war.[1]

By energetic use of a social machinery still almost irresistible, the Federalists and the clergy checked or prevented every effort to assist the war, by either money or enlistments. The Supreme Court, through Chief Justice Theophilus Parsons, himself a member of the Junto, formally advised Governor Strong that neither Congress nor the President, but the Governor alone, had the right to decide when the exigency existed under which, in accordance with the United States Constitution, the President could call the State militia into service. Governor Strong decided that neither foreign invasion nor domestic insurrection existed, and declined to comply with the President's request for militia to defend the seacoast. For these actions the Court and the Governor were hotly attacked by the Republicans; but they were entirely consonant with the whole Federalist attitude. Organized efforts were made to discourage and throw obstacles in the way of enlistment. One of the main devices was to cause a person enlisted to be arrested and bailed on action for a fictitious debt, the

---

[1] See resolution of Norfolk County in *Independent Chronicle*, August 20, 1812.

courts holding that a person so bailed was the property of the bail and could not be called into military service. This hostile attitude of Massachusetts was graphically described by a contemporary, Mathew Carey, in his *Olive Branch*, published in 1814: "From the hour of the declaration of war, a steady, systematical, and energetic opposition was regularly organized against it. The measure itself, and its authors and abettors, were denounced with the utmost virulence and intemperance. The war was unholy, wicked, base, perfidious, unjust, cruel, and corrupt. And every man that in any degree co-operated in it or gave aid to carry it on, was loaded with execration. . . . Those who were unacquainted with the causes that led to this war might, from the publications that appear against it, believe that the United States had been wholly the aggressors — that England had been a tame and submissive sufferer of depredation, outrage, and insult; and that our rulers had been wantonly led by inordinate and accursed ambition to engage in a ruinous and destructive war, to enrich themselves, squander away the public treasure, and impoverish the Nation. They were, it would appear, actuated by as unholy motives as ever impelled Attila, Genghis Khan, or Bonaparte, to perpetrate outrage and cruelty to the utmost extent of their power. These allegations are made in the strongest language in the public papers in London. . . . The Federal papers re-echo and magnify the accusations of the British writers, and have succeeded so far as to inflame a large portion of the public with the most frantic exasperation against the rulers of their choice."

On these seditious conditions in Massachusetts Dr. Ames' Diary contained most pungent comments; at the same time, in his peculiarly graphic style, he entered many picturesque references to the prominent events of the war:

June 27, 1812. Burr came to take Henry's place at Boston. Reports that our Com. Rogers has took prizes.

June 30. Terrible threats and manoeuvres of submitters to Britons. Dutton and Thorndike gone to Hartford to excite disunion with Governor Griswold, revive Gore's Northern Confederacy of 1809. All anxious to hear from Com. Rodgers on cruise, of whom variety of vague reports of a battle with the *Belvidere*, British frigate, whose Captain got wounded; but no certain intelligence yet.

July 2. The War declared to exist. No effects yet break the maze!

July 4. Independence. Fudderal display! Bissextile and July completes 36th year of independence and sovereignty of the United States. But independence not realized, until British tyranny drove us into manufacturing — and although many factories have been burnt and various other impediments of the British faction, agents, and importers of British goods, in Boston especially, have occurred — factories, wool, etc. are here in irresistible progress; and further, this year, the naval superiority of citizen-sailors over the slave-sailors of England is sundry times illustriously manifested in contest of our hostile ships! ! ! The trident of Neptune falling from the British gripe! The charm is broken.

July 10. Handbill that French Decrees repealed 18 months past, under Bonaparte's hand.

July 22. Prizes brought in, fears our squadron be taken by English.

July 23. Boston Junto outrageous, seditious, hiss Seaver and other Congress Members in streets of Boston.

July 24. Various prizes, each side.

July 29. Maritime pedlars and their dupes enraged at war — Plymouth, Newburyport and N. Hampton.

Consultation of towns of Norfolk. Agreed to hold Norfolk consultation at Marsh's [Tavern], Dedham, 3rd Monday of August at 9 A.M. Thence to join Suffolk and Middlesex in Address to President.

July 31. Good prizes arrived at Boston today!

Aug. 5. The war on Canada progresses. United States standard waves in Upper Canada, and many Canadians join U. S. General Hull's good proclamation to them.

Aug. 7. Junto in Boston town meeting vote to call State Convention to resist Congress, break Constitution! But Dexter deserts them — a death blow! They are thunderstruck at it, but must ease down.

Meanwhile, regardless of Massachusetts, the war was being prosecuted on sea and land, victories and defeats in the fall of 1812 being interestingly depicted in Dr. Ames' entries:

August 11. War rages on fresh water, as well as salt. Battle of ships, Sacketts' Harbor. Opposition to Seaver brewing.

August 14. Rejoicing in Boston at sundry prizes carried into Halifax.

August 30. Constitution returned from glorious cruise. The *Constitution* frigate, Isaac Hull, Captain, arrived at Boston from short cruise, having taken sundry British prizes and took and sunk the *Guerriere*, Captain Dacres, after short conflict in which she was cut and mangled most effectual!y by our guns — just chastisement of the bragging Dacres that he wished to engage not one but two Yankee frigates of his own force, both at once, but found more than his match in one of inferior force! His was 29, ours 44 guns! Commodore Rogers' squadron arrived in Boston, same time, 31st, but without any very brilliant success.[1]

Sept. 1. Rumor that Gen. Hull has taken Fort Malden, with loss of 200 men.

Sept. 2. Gen. Hull's army taken at Detroit! 2500 men! Confirmed! ! Not more than 800 fit for duty, the rest sick. Country indignant at the defeat of Hull. News arrived that General Hull, having entered Canada, had retreated back to the fort at Detroit; and there, having 2500 men, he surrendered to the British General Brock with only 1800 men, Indians and all, without firing a gun nor suffering Col. Miller, who offered to pledge his life to take the British Fort Malden, and afterwards to repel the Britons and Indians

[1] Dr. Ames always refers to Commodore John Rodgers as "Rogers."

marching up 12 deep before our cannon loaded with grape-shot. Every tongue charges Hull, at present, with treason! ! !

Sept. 9. Some officers arrive on parole at Boston, seem to exculpate Hull from treason! It must be gross cowardice! Even Hull's son, who was an aid-de-camp, when he saw the white flag his father displayed, exclaimed in a rage, "the meanest soldier in the army calls you coward."

Oct. 4. Wars rage. Bonaparte in Russia, and savages in America.

Oct. 15. Various war maneuvres. 200 freshwater sailors re-take the *Adams* and Schooner *Caledonia*, loss 2 killed and 7 wounded, and they took 50 British prisoners with the vessels! But the British kept up continual fire across Niagara and killed a Major. Gen. Harrison destroyed 7 Indian villages and all their cornfields.

Oct. 20. Our *United States* frigate commanded by Com. Decatur saw the *Macedonian* to windward in Lat. 30, Long. 26, and gave chase. The enemy bore down about 10 o'clock and exchanging shot at a distance, the *Macedonian* having her mizen shot away, they came to closer action. In 17 minutes after, she struck her colors to the *United States*; but one account of the action says: "The fire of the U. S. frigate was so tremendously vivid that the crew of the *Macedonian* cheered, conceiving her to be on fire!" While the British ships of war, complete for action, are kept snug in port, our little navy rides the ocean in defiance of Britain's thousand ships of war, and have sundry captures that have raised our naval glory to choke the pride of Britain!

Oct. 27. All anxious for particulars of disaster at Queenstown opposite Niagara, in eleven hours fight, Indians and English. It is said the detached militia refused, so lost us the victory 13 inst.!

Oct. 31. Astonishing is the variety of accounts of battle at Queenstown — All turned to electioneering, nothing yet official.

In this fall of 1812 occurred President Madison's campaign for reëlection. The condition of the politics of Massachusetts in this campaign and that State's final support of Madison produced characteristic comments from Dr. Ames.[1] In the Norfolk district, the Federalists, despairing of carrying it, voted for a Republican candidate nominated to oppose Seaver, the Republican, who had voted for the war.

> *October (end).* A most subtil plan of Fudderalists, this fall, is laid to dupe the people and split and divide the Republicans by pretending to condescend to meet them in one of their own party, so as to destroy the present Administration. They yell they will vote for Peace Party, and wonderfully captivate the simple [De Witt] Clinton (whom), tho a stigmatizer of Fudderalists, they fix on to oust Madison, and the like is practiced for Congressmen, confessing their own minority by joining Republicans.
>
> *Nov. 3.* Town Meeting for Representative to Congress — Seaver 229, Ruggles, 141. N. Ruggles got a hoist on Fudderal stilts.
>
> *Nov. 6.* The lying and delusion now practiced by the Fudderalist party is bold beyond conception, but the success among the vulgar is more astonishing. They become Jews or Musselmans, as Dr. Bramble, etc., say the word! ! !
>
> Such is the result of Fudderalist cry for the Peace Party, meaning submission to Britain. Pretended condescension to dupe weak Republicans. It is confession of weakness to take candidate from opposite party, to break and divide like the Devil, to conquer by division and lying and propagating that I fell off to their candidate on Fudderal Stilts. The Fudderalists try to assume a new title, now calling themselves "Peace Party."
>
> *Nov. 9.* President's Message in *Chronicle* is superlative.
>
> *Nov. 11.* The lying and delusion of the Fudderalist party exceed all bounds.
>
> *Nov. 13.* Madison and Gerry electors bear away, in spite of New England Pettifogarchy.

[1] On November 2, 1812, the town of Dedham voted in the presidential election 223 Republican, 152 Federalist; for Congressman, Seaver (Republican) had 229 votes, Ruggles (also Republican) 141; in the entire Norfolk District, Seaver had 1938 votes and Ruggles had 2426.

At the end of this month of November the doctor made an entry as to the Republican Congressman from the district and his appointees which clearly shows that the doctor was no civil service reformer:

> Hard rub for Congress — Member for Norfolk District, Seaver, having a fat office of Collector of this District, has his Deputy collectors and principal assessors of his appointment all over the District, as Eb. Fisher, Micah White, Elihu Pond, etc., who worked like beavers, against wishes of people, to perpetuate same men in office or succeed him; but all their endeavors are fruitless. According to returns obtained, either no choice or Ruggles has it! ! Many people highly disgusted with Seaver and his deputies, saying they have greased him long enough, and that he ought to have refused. By such a display of Republican principles, generously encouraging rotation of loaves and fishes, instead of monopoly of them, he would have preserved that popularity now forever lost!

In 1813 Dr. Ames' Diary was chiefly concerned with the events of the war on sea and land:

> *Jan. 1813.* A rendezvous in Dedham very successful in enlisting soldiers for army of 20,000 and others all over U. S. as successful.
>
> *March 18.* Rumor of mediation of Alexander of Russia between United States and Britain.
>
> *March 21.* What prompt Victory! Our sloop of war, 16 guns, in 15 minutes kills Capt. Peake and others and sinks the *Peacock* with 19 guns.
>
> *March 24.* News of fifth Naval victory. The *Hornet* of 16 guns, Capt. Lawrence on 13th Feb. sunk the British brig *Peacock*. Capt. Peake killed in 15 minutes, 22 men sunk.
>
> *April 27.* Gen. Dearborn and Com. Chauncey, from Sackett's Harbor, north end of Lake Ontario, take York, southwest end of same Lake, with 1000 prisoners and vast military stores, after the Britons and other enemies had exploded a mine which killed our great Gen. Pike and 300 or

400 more of our troops and many of their own. This did not retard our men, who rushed on, causing immediate surrender. But while articles of capitulation were fixing, the British Gen. Sheaf with most of his regulars skulked off with all the Indians. But this is the successful beginning of our seizing Upper Canada.

April 29. The frigates *President* and *Congress*, on the 23 or 24 April, said to have sailed out of Boston Harbor in defiance daily; but our frigates only gone below the Castle just got a supply of powder by several large Pennsylvania wagons, and wind is contrary.

May 4. Europeans boil and bubble in blood. John Bull rages at our naval success!

June 2. British frigate *Shannon*, best in British navy, long been preparing and doubly manned, came off harbor of Boston. Our *Chesapeake*, Capt. Lawrence, who took the *Peacock* lately, of superior force, could not resist the call of honor; boldly meets the *Shannon* and was boarded and obliged to yield to double force and number! Boston filled with joy! ! ! No! Only the Englishmen there — it seemed to unite all others. Scarcity of news, foreign and domestic. No news of our frigates — Rogers at sea, the *Essex* at sea, two blockaded in New London, and the *Constellation* up James River. 74 ships and frigates now building in our ports. Merchants, Junto men, professed friends to Britain, practising direct contrary to their preaching, outwitting the farmers opposed to their foreign attachments, anticipating their progress in stocking farms with merino sheep, giving the severest blows to their friends the English.

June 4. Another battle at Sackett's Harbor. Decatur blockaded at New London.

June 6. All anxious for particulars of *Chesapeake* and *Shannon*.

June 18. British account arrived of loss of *Chesapeake*.

June 19. Our Gen. Winder and Chandler surprised in Canada, 150 men and some cannon lost.

June 25. Hampton taken by the Britons, soon quitted. Women subjected by Admiral Cockburn to lust, even of blacks.

Aug. 20. Dedham Gazette published. Fudderalists' cloven hoof peeps.[1]

Sept. 4. U. S. brig *Enterprise*, 16 guns, Lieutenant W. Burrows, Commander, near Seguin took British brig *Boxer* of 18 guns, Capt. Blyth: American loss, Lieut. Burrows and one man killed, 7 wounded. British loss, Capt. Blyth, and 26 men killed and 18 wounded — carried into Portland, where both Commanders are buried and martial honors; and four or five of wounded since dead.

Sept. 25. Commodore Perry's squadron on Lake Erie took all the British fleet, superior in men and guns, after great slaughter, on 10th inst.! Particulars not arrived.

It is significant of the attitude of Massachusetts that, although Perry's glorious victory at Lake Erie was greeted with wild enthusiasm throughout the country, in Boston alone was there no festivity held in its honor. A Republican newspaper made this comment: "From almost every section of our country we continue to receive the most exhilerating accounts of spendid celebrations for the victories of Perry and Harrison. But in Boston — poor, degraded Boston — we are as mute as fish. The torpedo touch of the British faction has palsied every fibre and dulled every patriotic sensation. So entirely are we lost to all natural feeling, that events the most honorable to our public character seem to make no impression; and low abuse of our own armies appears to be the article most in demand in the Boston market. While reading the vivid descriptions of illuminations in New York, Philadelphia, Baltimore, Charleston, etc., every friend to his country feels a new glow of patriotic ardor; and we cannot but pity that cold-blooded race who can bear, unmoved, the animating details." [2]

[1] The *Dedham Gazette* was founded by Theron Metcalf, a Federalist lawyer of the town, later Judge of the Massachusetts Supreme Judicial Court.

[2] See *Independent Chronicle*, November 4, 1813.

Dr. Ames' Diary continued with the events of the fall of 1813:

Sept. 27. Rogers arrived, Saturday last, at Newport; took and destroyed 27 British vessels, took whole fleet Greenland whalemen, ransomed 11 for 20,000 dollars each.

Oct. 24. Harrison conquered Proctor's army of Indians and British, Upper Canada.

Nov. 16. Harrison and Hampton's armies joined, go down St. Lawrence to Montreal.

Nov. 23. Army gone into winter quarters.

Nov. 30. On the 11th inst. was the battle of Cornwall on St. Lawrence above Montreal, with a detachment of Wilkinson's army and British — and a bloody one. Joel Smith was killed. Our men fell into an ambuscade between cannon, and were mowed down by grape and canister shots — the worst disaster, except Hull's base surrender, this war. Gen. Covington and other officers killed. The Canada newspapers say that they took above 400 of our men, besides killed and wounded, and sundry magazines or stores. So that our army will suffer for provisions and clothing! ! ! Henryites yell more than ever! ! !

Dec. 4. Creek Indians excited by Britons and Spaniards in Florida to murder our citizens, met a second defeat by Gen. Jackson near Loose River, Indians lost 300 killed, our loss 15 killed 85 wounded. Might have extinguished the Creeks if provisions had been sent to army.

Dec. 16. Captain Porter in *Essex* frigate successful in South seas; many good prizes of whalemen, so that he has acquired a fleet of 8 or 9 sail of armed vessels from Britons', with all accommodations! His letters to Secretary of Navy, elegant.

Dec. 18. Embargo, 17th, passed 18 to 15 in Senate, 85 to 57 in House.

Dec. 24. Portsmouth, N. H. burnt. Light seen here all night last, and 100 miles off.

Dec. 25. Upper Canada lost! After Harrison's coming, British in Upper Canada, on Sunday, 19th, crossed over and took by storm Fort Niagara, with 3000 regulars and Indians. They massacred all the Americans but three, and followed up the massacre, Manchester and Lewistown and Tuscarora village, burning every house, and Buffalo like to share same fate! ! !

Of the Napoleonic Wars in Europe Dr. Ames gave an interesting criticism early in the year 1814:

> The British Government, tyrants at sea, embroil all Europe and the world by bribery and force. The Russians, Prussians, Germans, allied against France, instigated by England, prove faithless and break over their own agreement for a general peace, and invade France with Cossacks committing all manner of savage brutality. Women from 12 to 60 they ravish, burn, plunder, and kill, in January; but the yeomanry of France, grown exasperated at such enormities, closer bound than ever to Bonaparte, rise en masse in February, and exterminate their destroyers. A peace would have been concluded, if Lord Castlereagh had not gone over to the Congress and excited [it] by bribery and gold, to a breach of faith of the Allies. England is the fountain of horrors of the world! Grown rich by plundering all parts of ocean and earth, she seduces nations by gold into her vortex; but (by accounts to 20th February) France has recovered from despair! Though Murat, King of the people, and some other of Bonaparte's Generals, had proved ungrateful traitors, the good people all are loyal, and adhere to Bonaparte, all converted into volunteer heroes.

One of the economic effects of the war, the practical destruction of transportation of goods by water, owing to the Federal statutes prohibiting exports and also to the blockade maintained by the British fleet, and the consequent enhancement of the profits of carriers by land, was interestingly described by Dr. Ames in an entry at the end of the year 1813:

> Now England obstructs intercourse by water; land carriage is the only way of conveyance between the States, so that contractors for teams is now a regular occupation. Tim Gay, Jotham Richards, and Luther Eaton are a trio of con-

tractors that keep constantly in Boston an office to contract
to supply merchants with teams to Providence, New York,
Philadelphia, etc., to carry goods for a certain price per
pound or hundredweight. The price now is lower than it
was; it is now 4% to the owner of the team, who allows those
contractors 5 percent of his 4; and each team carries between 40 and 50 hundredweight. Now T. Gay, in connection with Richards and Eaton, hath contracted to carry 50
loads from Salem to New York for 4½ per cent; the ½ cent is
over what they give the teams, and make 1000 dollars into
the contractor's pockets for the 50 loads, besides which they
have their commissions of 5 percent. Lately, Richards made
1300 dollars clear, in a contract from Portsmouth to New
York. The road is full, almost daily, with covered wagons,
which land conveyance diffuses money over the country;
while coasters are near idle, and those laborers concerned
about shipping, so that it is said that many of the poorer
class of industrious people are moving off from Boston to
the Southwest country to seek a living. Such is now the
effect of our war with England.

The Diary continued at the opening of the year 1814:

Jan. 1, 1814. Embargo in operation.
Jan. 4. Sugar, coffee, etc., doubles in price.
Jan. 6. Rumor of armistice for 90 days with Britain causes
    sudden fall of the price of West India goods.
Jan. 31. John Holmes, a new champion of old principles, has
    sprung in Senate of Mass., and knocked over Quincy etc.,
    and laid the Boston rebel, Lowell, flat on his back. The
    Feds of Boston stamp, thunderstruck!
Feb. 5. Dull times for news. Embargo excites Boston Lobsters
    and their dupes to the edge of rebellion. Otis in House
    moved to raise troops against Congress!

These last entries refer to a condition of affairs which
was making Boston flatly rebellious, and an obstacle to
any successful prosecution of the war. Governor Strong, in
his address to the legislature, January 12, 1814, had indulged in the following language: "In the tumult of arms,

the passions of men are easily inflamed by artful misrepresentations; they are apt to lose sight of the origin of a contest, and to forget, either in the triumph of victory or the mortification of defeat, that the whole weight of guilt and wretchedness occasioned by war is chargeable upon that government which unreasonably begins the conflict, and upon those of its subjects who voluntarily and without legal obligations, encourage and support it." The Senate, in its answer, reinforced these mutinous sentiments by declaring that "a people can give no encouragement to a war of such a character without becoming partakers in guilt, and rendering themselves obnoxious to those just retributions of Divine vengeance, by which, sooner or later, the authors and abettors of such a war will be assuredly overtaken." The House said that only after failure of an attempt to negotiate a peace can "any voluntary support of this unhappy war be expected from our constituents." In the debate which ensued over these extraordinary pronunciamentos Josiah Quincy took a prominent part; but the most brilliant speech was made by a Republican senator from the Maine District, John Holmes, whose reply to Quincy filled the Republican press, as well as Dr. Ames, with exultation. The *Chronicle* gave the following amusing account of the debate: [1] "The violence of the Governor's speech has, as might be expected, produced a corresponding violence in the Legislative answers. While these answers were under debate, the spirit of party, by the intemperance of the opposition, was carried to as great a height as we ever witnessed, particularly in the Senate. But we congratulate the State and the country at large that the Republicans have in that body a champion so fully able to defend the glorious cause in which he is engaged. The Honorable Mr. Holmes of Alfred, with the

[1] See *Independent Chronicle*, January 31, 1819.

nerve of that warrior who carried dismay into the ranks of the Philistines, presents himself to a host of opponents, and like him, is victorious in every contest. No wonder that Mr. Quincy shrinks, and even faints, under the force of his powerful arguments. We never witnessed a more eloquent speech than that of Mr. Holmes. From the countenances of many of the opposition, it was evident that this speech had forced conviction on their mind, although a false pride prevented them from acknowledging it. 'Fee, Fie, Foe, Fum — Dead or Alive!' The boisterous declamation of Mr. Quincy in the first part of his speech in the Senate and his fainting in the midst of it are ominous as to the final result of Boston Federalism. This man vociferated with the lungs of Stentor. He drank two tumblers of cold water in about thirty minutes, to extinguish the volcano within his bosom; and yet with all this salutary cooling application, he was so far burnt up with ardent passion that he cried out 'I am gone,' and immediately tumbled backwards into his chair. But if this was a faint attempt to imitate the Earl of Chatham, it was a poor description of that sublime scene. The Earl of Chatham really expired; but Quincy on the next day was more alert than before."

The language of Governor Strong and of the legislature, given above, had great effect in preventing enlistments; but a move was now made by the Federalists which was still more fatal to the efforts of the United States Government to cope successfully with the war necessities. This move took the form of an organized effort to prevent the success of the war loan which the Government was trying to raise. The *Olive Branch* (published during this year) gave the following account: "Every possible exertion was made in Boston to deter the citizens from subscribing to the loans. Associations were entered into in the most solemn and public manner to this effect; and those who

could not be induced by mild means were deterred by denunciations. The pulpit, as usual in Boston, came in aid of
the press to secure success. Those who subscribed were
declared participators in, and accessories to, all the 'murders,' as they were termed, that might take place in the
'unholy, unrighteous, wicked, abominable, and accursed
war.'" The Boston papers were continually publishing
appeals to Federalists not to subscribe, saying: "If they
lend money now, they make themselves parties to the vio-
lations of the Constitution, the cruelly oppressive measures
in relation to commerce, and to all the crimes which have
occurred in the field and in the cabinet. Any Federalist
who lends money to Government will be called by others
infamous. It would be a base abandonment of political
and moral principles. Any man who lends his money to the
government at the present time will forfeit all claim to
common honesty and common courtesy among all the
friends to the country."[1] Such pressure and fear of obloquy
were brought to bear upon subscribers to the war loans
that official arrangements were made by which subscriptions could be filed without publication of names.[2] "Who
that has a soul to feel — who that has a spark of patriotism
or public spirit in his frame but must be fired with a holy
indignation at such a hideous, such a horrible state of the

[1] *Olive Branch* (1814), by Mathew Carey, pages 289 *et seq.*
[2] The lack of success by the government in raising money is strikingly shown
by the following facts, taken from the *Report of the Secretary of the Treasury for
the year 1814.* Under the Act of March 24, 1814, authorizing a loan of $25,-
000,000, 6 per cent treasury notes for $10,000,000 were offered at a discount, at
rates varying from 85 to 88; (in round numbers) $9,800,000 was subscribed by
45 persons, and of this less than $8,000,000 was paid in; from Massachusetts
there were only four subscribers (William Gray, Samuel Dana, Jesse Putnam,
and Amos Binney of Boston), to the amount of $325,000. On August 22, 1814,
another loan of $6,000,000 was offered, of which only $2,900,000 was subscribed
at rates from 80 to 88, and about $2,500,000 was paid in by 17 persons, of whom
two (Amasa Stetson and Jesse Putnam of Boston) were from Massachusetts
paying a total of $52,000.

public mind?" exclaimed the *Olive Branch*, reviewing the disloyal situation:

Boston, the metropolis of Massachusetts, has been for a long period, and more particularly since the reign of Federalism, the seat of discontent, complaint, and turbulence. It has been itself, restless and uneasy, and has spread restlessness and uneasiness in every direction. It has thwarted, harassed, and embarrassed the General Government, incomparably more than all the rest of the Union together. Whatever difficulty or distress has arisen from the extraordinary circumstances of the times, has been aggravated and magnified to the highest degree, for the purpose of influencing the public passions. The leaders . . . in all their movements have had, and still have, but one object — to enfeeble and distract the Government. With a population of only 33,000 inhabitants and with a commerce quite insignificant compared with that of New York, Philadelphia, Baltimore or Charleston, Boston has, by management and address, acquired a degree of influence beyond all proportion; greater in fact than the above four cities combined — a degree of influence which has been exercised in such a manner as to become dangerous to public and private prosperity and happiness, and to the peace and permanence of the Union. It has brought us to the very verge of its dissolution, and threatens us with the awful consequence — a civil war. The movers of this mighty piece of machinery — this lever that puts into convulsive motion the whole of our political fabric, are few in number. But they are possessed of inordinate wealth, of considerable talents, great energy, and overgrown influence. . . . A Northern Confederacy has been their grand object for a number of years. . . . Boston has persecuted the Government with as much virulence and malignity and violence as if it was administered by devils incarnate. She has involved in the vortex of disaffection no small portion of the population of her own and sister States, and has done England more effective service than all her armies.

During the spring of 1814 Massachusetts witnessed the actual presence of the enemy on its coast, and the seaport towns were in constant fear of attack. Boston itself was in danger, and its banks and citizens began to move their valuables into the country. An interesting picture of these "ticklish times" was given by Dr. Ames:

April 3, 1814. The *Constitution* frigate chased into Marblehead by sundry British warships.

April 4. Struggle, Boston Rebels vs. Yeomanry.

April 5. News that President recommends to both Houses of Congress a repeal of Embargo. At which Boston Junto and rebels yell, groan, and sneer.

May 5. Boston Feds try to kill Bonaparte again; and now swearing at Britain for blockading all our ports, now our Embargo is off, as far worse!

May 11. Wellington's army coming to America!

May 12. Bonaparte kicked down by the fickle, base people.

May 20. All in suspense on fate of France.

April–May. Col. Eustis's Regiment of flying artillery recruiting; have headquarters, barracks in Dedham. And the Colonel employs a young Fed. physician who curses the Government and the war with Britain, and has said he wished that every soldier marching to take Canada might die before arrival there. Such are the absurdities of squandering 40 dollars a month on such Federal enemies as this medico. If the President knew it, the Colonel's commission might flutter for employing such an internal enemy.

May 28. All on tiptoe to hear from France.

June 3. Rumor Bonaparte dethroned. Peace in Europe; English coming to swallow U. S., confirmed thro' England. Bonaparte confined to Island of Elba, and pension of 25,000 pounds.

June 9. Seditious Court [Legislature] of Massachusetts, by New York and other States despised.

June 10. Specie of State Bank said to be moved to Worcester.

June 11. Boston blockaded, rumor of entering the town! Rumors that British Admiral Cockburn has dispersed proclamations in Boston, inviting acquiescence of the inhabitants in his entering harbour and taking peaceable position in town, promising protection to unresisting people! !

June 12. Dorchester and Milton militia mustered in night; repel British landed at Cohasset and Scituate burnt, carried off vessels.

June 13. Report that Dorchester and Milton militia companies mustered at midnight to repel the Britons from blockading fleet landed at Weymouth! The specie of Mass. State Bank was removed on Saturday, 11th, from Boston to Worcester — and that of the Union Bank said to be coming to Dedham Bank Vault. Yet we hear of no order from Governor Strong nor from Major General Crane to call forth militia or hold themselves in readiness. Nor can we expect any! ! After observing the answer of the two Houses now in session to Governor's speech, applauding British conduct, the Boston Henryites, and Tallyrands now published their intention in the *Centinel* to celebrate, the 15th inst., British successes in France! However unbecoming lately to celebrate our own victories over Britons.

Political world big with events. British gold corrupts all the courts of Europe, has dethroned Bonaparte, restored Bourbon dynasty, Louis 18th, and turning all European Monarchy, Hierarchy, Aristocracy, and Kingcraft against American Democracy! !

June 15. Bourbon Feast in Boston for British success! State House illuminated and the blockading enemy join in the rejoicing with Boston rebels!

No single episode in American history is more extraordinary than the "Bourbon Feast" above noted by Dr. Ames; but few historical works have given any account of it. In June and July, 1814, the British fleet was maintaining a practically effective blockade of Boston, and was harrying the coast close to that port, to the north and to the south. Ships in the harbor of Scituate were attacked and burnt.[1] Gloucester and Salem Harbors were blocked up. Plymouth was attacked, Nantucket captured, and a factory and ships in Wareham were burned. Contributions

---

[1] See extract from letter from Scituate, April 11, published in the *Independent Chronicle*, April 13. See also issues of June 9, 16, 23, 30, July 11, 1814, and *Columbian Centinel*, July 2, 9, 1814.

It is interesting to note that at this early date a project of harbor defence by mines to be exploded by electrical current was suggested; see article in the *Independent Chronicle*, June 16, entitled "Harbor Defence by Electricity."

of thousands of dollars were levied by the British on other
Cape Cod towns. By July 11 barges from the enemy fleet
ventured within Boston Harbor itself, near Gallups Island,
and only seven miles from the town; and British frigates
lay all the time off the Graves and Cohasset. Yet it was at
this exact time that the Federalists of Boston chose to celebrate the recent victories of the allied forces of England,
Austria, Prussia, and Russia over Napoleon in Europe. No
wonder that Dr. Ames commented on the "Boston Rebels"
joining with the enemy in celebrating "British successes"!
Only a typical American sense of humor prevented arrest
for high treason of the Boston leaders in this episode. This
celebration, which was held on June 15, was termed by the
Centinel "a splendid and solemn Festival in honor of the
Restoration of Safety and Peace in Europe." John Lowell,
the most vehement opponent of "Mr. Madison's War," as
he termed it, was the leader in suggesting and managing it.
The festival began with a procession to King's Chapel;
then followed an elaborate musical service, and a sermon
by Reverend William Ellery Channing. Honorable Christopher Gore then made an address, referring "to the late
wonderful events which have delivered a great portion of
Europe from the most iron-handed despotism, which have
spread joy and gratitude among one hundred millions of
People in the Christian World, and to the prospect of
felicity held out to mankind." Resolutions were proposed,
effusively laudatory of the Czar of Russia, terming him
"Alexander the Deliverer," "the great head of the Confederacy for the Deliverance of Christendom," "dear to
every lover of national freedom." This alone would have
been a curious sentiment for citizens of a republic like the
United States to apply to a monarch of the type of Alexander of Russia; but the resolutions went close to the verge
of the ridiculous when they expressed their "affection and

respect to the late unhappy and injured possessor of the throne of Bourbons" — Louis XVI. After further praise of the victory of the Allies over Napoleon, they ended: "It is because the recent events in Europe have a direct tendency to render liberty secure, to check anarchical propensities, to restrain ambition, foster morals and religion, and to protect property and the arts, and finally give solid peace to the Christian world, that the Assembly hail them as blessings; that they bow in humble gratitude before the Almighty." After this remarkable ceremony, there were fireworks and illuminations in the evening. The *Centinel* gave a glowing account of the success of the occasion. The *Chronicle*, on the other hand, presented a jeering and probably more truthful description. Of the procession it said "there was a forced attempt to excite public applause," "emphatically a 'solemn festival.' There was not the least appearance of hilarity, not a boy to huzza, not a countenance that emitted the common radiancy of conviviality." The "performance at King's Chapel — the Te Deum" it termed "a poor, feeble attempt; chilling coldness prevailed." Of the evening celebration it said: "Scarcely a jovial huzza was heard. . . . Everyone was inquiring what the illumination was for. . . . The farce was more highly exhibited. . . . 1000 persons to assemble on the open Common to look at 2500 lamps burning in the windows of the State House, was a ludicrous display of festivity. . . . At the end, the boys determined to have some fun, and made a bonfire of the staging." From the above account it is evident that there were limits to the desire of the Boston citizens to sympathize with the British over their successes, whether in Europe or on this continent. The *Chronicle* closed its narration with a more serious comment on the ill-advised attitude of the extreme Boston Federalists: "It was a solemn mockery to exhibit marks of rejoicing in Boston by illuminations and artificial fireworks, while the enemy were illuminating our coast with the bonfires of our vessels and our adjacent villages. While our neighbors and friends were experiencing all the distresses of invasion and conflagration, it was a wicked appeal to Heaven within a house of worship of the blessings we enjoyed in consequence of events in Europe. How must Louis XVIII have respected Boston loyalty! How must Lord Castlereagh estimate Boston sincerity! What dependence could the British ministry place on the despicable junto in Boston? What hypocrites, what sycophants, what apostates are Boston Federalists!"

The months from June to October were full of anxiety to the people of New England. The enemy was at their very gates. Several of the seaport towns in Maine were captured by the British. Wellington's troops, fresh from victories in Spain, were said to be landing in Canada for invasion of the United States. Dr. Ames continued to record with much vivacity the alarming conditions: [1]

June 17. Seven loads heavy money of Union Bank lodged in Dedham Banks vaults shews a distrust of Boston rebels in their friends; the British squadrons blockading the harbor, as to plunder, however secure as to persons and houses, rapes and insults. Now rejoicing publicly, at British success in dethroning Bonaparte. British squadrons along our coast operate a complete embargo. Peace in Europe lets loose the British dogs of war in America, subsidizing the Indians, as they did the courts of Europe to dethrone Bonaparte, to destroy the United States. A crisis near!

July 7. English troops daily landing at Quebec to recolonize U. S. Wellington's veterans from Spain! ! !

---

[1] The *Dedham Gazette*, June 17, July 1, 1814, gave an account of two British frigates anchored off Cohasset rocks, sweeping the bay of craft, entering Scituate, and burning vessels there, going into Annisquam and boarding vessels, also attacking Wareham.

July 15. Rumors of armistice — but British troops daily arriving militates.

July 21. British took Eastport; treachery!

Aug. 2. Detachment of this brigade, militia, here, march to Boston, south, to oppose British invaders. And other detachments of militia marched to Boston.

Aug. 14. Wellington's veterans sent direct from conquest of France here. Our Yankees dish 'em up without ceremony! 3rd victory at Niagara!

Aug. 28. News that, on 25th, British took Washington after battle at Bladensburgh! Com. Barney and sailors nobly fought — militia shrink!

Aug. 31. London news to 20 July. No prospect of peace, but English delusion. French grumbling at Austria justly as casuse of their degradation and delusion, by their daughter married to Bonaparte to entrap him in the allied kingtrap. So the French people are caught. But British gold in subsidies was a more fatal bait than the young princess of Austria.

Nantucket in treaty with the blockaders to rest neutral during war! Alexandria laid under contribution of 2000 barrels flour to Lord Hill! Also plundered of all merchandise, thorolly stripped.

Sept. 3. Nantucket B. Bills denounced for Revolt. Boston Town meeting to fortify. Castine and Machias taken.

Sept. 5. Great war chickens hatching.

Sept. 7. Castine and all east taken. *Adams* frigate blown up by our Capt. Morris.

Sept. 9. Boston goods lodged in Dedham, and all moving out for fear 8 or 10,000 British!

Sept. 11. News just from Boston that Plattsburgh is taken, also Portland! False, turns out contrary. Troops march to Boston.

Sept. 12. Dedham and other companies march to Boston, for defence. New England tories talk of separate peace! ! ! Governor and Council of Mass. treat the President of U. S. with rebellious churlishness. The President requests Gov. Strong to aid in expelling the enemy from Castine and to advance funds for only 60 days, and to organize or aid in organizing troops. Both which Strong refused, for that the

Council would not authorize it! Then the Adjutant General, being requested to afford copies of the inspection returns of militia of Maine, he also refused!

Sept. 17. Vast stores, naval, military, lodged in Dedham. Fear of invasion of Boston. News arrived of two important victories over British invaders, veterans of Wellington's army of Spain.

Sept. 20. Two grand victories of Americans over Britons at Plattsburgh on 11th, and Baltimore 13th. Gen. Ross, Commander-in-Chief, killed, and 500 men; and at Plattsburgh, the Commodore of the fleet killed, named Donnie, and more prisoners taken than the whole of our Com. McDonough's men! Vast number killed; and by land Gov. Prevost's army of 14,000 slaughtered and repulsed by 1500 of our Gen. McComb's men! Signal favor of the Great Spirit! ! !

American affairs to mid-October in prosperous train. Deserters and prisoners by hundreds arriving. Prizes taken and many yet in. Forts building by voluntary labor of citizens from most towns within 20 or 30 miles of Boston. More union against British brutality, except in Boston where the Junto are on the verge of rebelion. F. Blake impudently moves in General Court to seize and stop internal taxes and duties of General Government, in concert with a John Low of Lynn. Otis more smooth, but full of rebellion.

The last entry made by Dr. Ames marked the first of his references to the famous plan for concerted action by the New England States which resulted in the notorious Hartford Convention. The plan was the outcome of the critical situation in which Massachusetts found herself at this time, with the enemy at her very gates. It was not until this September of 1814, after the capture of Castine in the Maine District by the British, that Governor Strong of Massachusetts had been willing to call out the militia, which he had refused to do two years before. Even then he did not consent that the State troops should act under the National Government, but placed them under command of a State major-general. President Madison, in view of this action, very naturally declined to have the Government assume the expenses of the State troops. Whereupon Governor Strong sent a message to the legislature, October 5, saying: "The situation of this State is peculiarly dangerous and perplexing. We have been led by the terms of the Constitution to rely on the Government of the Union to provide for our defence. We have resigned to that Government the revenues of the State, with the expectation that this object would not be neglected. Let us, then, relying on the support and direction of Providence, unite in such measures for our safety as the times demand, and the principles of justice and the law of self-preservation will justify." The language of the last sentence could bear but one interpretation — an invitation or suggestion that the State must take care of itself, or, in other words, practical secession. The *Centinel* had already published an article, September 10, advocating, in the boldest language, such action: "The Crisis — The present aspect of the war in which we have been so inconsiderately and wickedly plunged by our profligate rulers, is indeed appalling to every man who values the security and even the liberty of his country. The indignation of Heaven, it is apparent, has now visited our country for placing its confidence in men who have uniformly set at defiance the common rules of just policy and public morality." After thus ranging Heaven as an active ally of the Federalist Party, the *Centinel* proceeded to urge the calling of a Convention of Eastern States, which should demand that the President dismiss "his whole corps of incompetent and corrupt ministers" and make peace with England, and in default of his compliance: "If he will not do this, but will continue to prefer his party to his country, these delegates should be empowered to adjust terms of union with other States, and to make a peace for themselves. . . . The Union is already dissolved practically. The Government now cannot protect the several States, if it would. Men of Massachusetts, I say then, arise! Shake off your slumbers. Act for yourselves. For if you depend longer on the wretched rulers who have ruined you, you will indeed be restored to the grade of subjects." This was certainly strong, and very close to treasonable, language.

Three days later a town meeting was called in Boston to consider measures for the defence of that town. John Pickering wrote from Washington, October 12, urging Massachusetts to retain all its revenues, and support its own military force "necessary for our protection against the foreign enemy, and the still greater evil in prospect — domestic tyranny." The legislature now acted at once on the Governor's suggestion; and a committee, of which Harrison Gray Otis was chairman, reported that the people must provide for self-defence by withholding its revenues. And, pointing out that the present evils could not be efficiently remedied by present methods of amending the United States Constitution, the committee made the fateful recommendation that a conference of New England States should be invited to devise some mode of common defence, and "to lay the foundation for a radical reform in the National compact." To this suggestion of a convention the legislature assented by majorities of nearly three to one; and twelve delegates were chosen, to meet on December 15. Within a few weeks occurred the Congressional elections, and the State reinforced its approval of the legislature's action by choosing eighteen Federalist Congressmen and only two Republican. Such action could not fail to be looked upon with much alarm by Republicans throughout the country, and it was regarded as the legitimate fruition of all the plans for a separate New England confederacy which had been maturing, in their opinion, for ten years. Mathew Carey, in the preface to his *Olive Branch* (published in the autumn of 1814), said: "It cannot be any longer doubted that there exists a conspiracy in New England among a few of the most wealthy and influential citizens to effect at every hazard a dissolution of the Union, and to form a separate Confederacy. This has been asserted by some of our citizens for years, and strenuously denied by others, deceived by the masque the conspirators wore, and their hollow professions. But it requires more than Boeotian stupidity and dullness to hesitate on the subject after the late extraordinary movements, which cannot possibly have any other object." And Carey expressed the Republican attitude towards the State of Massachusetts in the following indignant language: "She seems determined, if she cannot rule the country herself, to send it to destruction headlong. She has been for years a curse and scourge to the Union. We should not have had war but for her. . . . Could she be made to suffer alone, it were 'a consummation most devoutly to be wished.' A strong navigation act and discriminating duties would soon bring her to her senses and convince her of the immeasurable folly and madness she has been guilty of. They would sink her to her proper level — that level which her ungrateful soil, her insignificance in point of population, and the narrow limits of her territory, prescribe — and which, I repeat, nothing but the advantages she has derived from her persecuted, insulted, outraged and inflamed sister States could have enabled her to pass."

Dr. Ames continued in his Diary with the following interesting comments, showing his contemporary Republican views of the Hartford Convention:

Oct. 10, 1814. Otis brings forward New England kingdom again! ! ! Sackett's Harbor said to be besieged.
Oct. 14. General Court, Otis in Senate brought in report to

raise standing army of 10,000 State troops, full of proud rebellion! and to consult other New England States in conspiracy at Hartford.

Oct. 16. Impudent arrogance of British Commissioners at Ghent to dock U. S.!

Oct. 18. L'd Wood, S. Richards, G. Cabot, and 11 turbulent fellows more to meet at Hartford to set up New England Kingdom. Geo. Cabot, H. G. Otis, Wm. Prescot, Tim Bigelow, N. Dane, Hodijah Baylies, Joseph Thomas, Geo. Bliss, Jos. Lyman, Sam. Wilde, Stephen Longfellow and Dan. Welch, this day appointed, in Convention of both Houses of Mass., to consult with other delegates invited from other New England States to conspire against our General Government; plot treason, etc.

Oct. 22. A session of General Court of Massachusetts to ripen treason by Otis, Blake, Quincy, Bigelow, etc., nobly combated by Jn. Holmes, etc.! ! ! Appointed an illegal Convention, 15th, at Hartford. 2 States only approve — R. Island and Connecticut.

Oct. 30. Soldiers return from garrison at Dorchester, So. Boston.

Nov. 12. 20 Privateers said to be fitting out at Boston — other ports likewise, as our privateering has proved profitable. John Bull groans!

Nov. 17. The *David Porter* arrived at Boston rich with prizes, goods, of 15 days cruise.

Nov. 23. Song in *Aurora* on Hartford's Convention.

Nov. 24. Some towns in Maine nobly display their abhorrence of rebellious Junto of Boston and Massachusetts Legislature.

Nov. 29. Report that Mr. Gerry is dead, and John Prince rejoicing at his death — and John Perry and others of Federal Junto! !

Dec. 4. Negotiation at Ghent continues.

Dec. 15. Rebels Day at Hartford!

Dec. 17. No news yet from the Rebel Convention or Conspiracy!

Dec. 21. Hartford Convention, secret conclave.

Jan. 4, 1815. Hartford Convention, intended to intimidate the whole U. S., dissolved after 20 days conference; in con-

clave, bro't forth a mouse. The rank Boston Junto Henryites in rage of disappointment for not exciting rebellion.
And John Randolph publishes his letters to Jem. Lloyd of
Boston, and displays patriotism alive with a vengeance
against J. Adams and present Administration. Yet I would
very much sooner vote for Randolph President, than Rufus
King, but I should fear he would soon burst with so hard
blowing his own horn! And since Randolph's said letter,
the whole *Daily Advertiser* is filled with Lloyd's answer.

The result of the conclave of the twenty-six men who
convened at Hartford was simply a set of resolutions calling for amendments to the Constitution of the United
States; and this issue, though applauded by the conservative men of the party, did not satisfy the bulk of the
Massachusetts Federalists. The *New York Evening Post*
said: "The tone of this report, though in our opinion sufficiently high for the occasion is, I know, from the most
authentic information quite inferior to the public feeling
in the Eastern States. The people there are in advance of
their leaders." [1] And Dr. Ames' description of "the rank
Boston Junto Henryites in rage" at the outcome of the
Hartford Convention was probably a truthful characterization of the sentiment of the more extreme Federalists.
Men like Timothy Pickering and John Lowell were frankly
disappointed at the character of the delegates as being far
too conservative, and they openly stated that immediate
action was what was needed — not words and resolutions.
The Republicans, after having so seriously attacked the
Hartford Junto for seeking to establish a "New England
Monarchy," now felt a reaction, and were inclined to treat
the Convention's actions as ridiculous. "The mountain
has been in labor," said the *Baltimore American*, "and has
brought forth something like a mouse, or rather like a mis-

[1] See *Columbian Centinel*, January 11, 1815.

chievous rat, eager to undermine the National Garner." [1]
The Massachusetts legislature "highly approved" the
proceedings of the Convention, at once adopted its resolutions, and arranged for the appointment of three
commissioners to go to Washington to urge action upon
the Government. By the time the commissioners reached
Washington, however, the battle of New Orleans had been
fought, and the news of the signing of the Treaty of Peace
at Ghent arrived.

The general sentiment during this exciting period and
the events of the close of the war were strikingly described
by Dr. Ames:

> *Jan. 19, 1815.* Anxiety for fate of New Orleans not yet
> satisfied. General Court sit. Governor's speech, old rebel
> slang!!
>
> *Jan. 20.* Nothing from Europe long, nor New Orleans.
>
> *Jan. 21.* Our privateers successful yet.
>
> *Jan. 22.* A battle at New Orleans, fate unknown.
>
> *Jan. 24.* Important news expected with anxiety. No papers.
>
> *Jan. 25.* No news. General Court prosecutes printers of
> *Yankee!*
>
> *Jan. 26.* News from New Orleans, 23rd inst., British beaten
> off Borgne; Jackson took 50 prisoners. Cold as Russia.
> Our *President* frigate taken by 4 British men of war.
>
> *Jan. 28.* No *Patriot* nor *Centinel* bro't today. Between two,
> we fail. No news from New Orleans.
>
> British forces from W. Indies as above attacked, 17th
> Dec., at New Orleans, which news arrived in January; and
> 3rd Feb., have letters from thence stating fighting every
> day. To 30th Dec. and to 6 Jan., not denied! St. Mary's in
> Georgia taken by British, Jan. 13th.
>
> *Feb. 1.* Flying news of complete defeat of Britons at New
> Orleans!
>
> *Feb. 3.* Fate of New Orleans, Jan. 6, still undecided. On Dec.
> 10, the Britons entered Lake Borgne and soon took our 5
> gun boats, skirmish every day.

---

[1] See *Independent Chronicle*, January 23, 1815.

Feb. 6. Harpy, privateer at Salem brings English papers. English petition King for Peace with U. S.!

Feb. 9. Grand news from Orleans. British army beat, 8 Jan., with loss of 2600 and 3 generals, many officers etc., and but 7 killed and 6 wounded of ours. Remarkable battle, so unequal loss.

Feb. 13. A letter from a Mr. Goodhue at New York arrived this morning to Ben Russell of Boston, with an account of the arrival of the British despatch vessel, with Mr. Carrol, American messenger, bringing a Treaty of Peace between Britain and United States of America, signed 26th December at Ghent for ratification by President Madison, which letter issued in handbills noticed in Boston, Dedham, etc. etc. by bell ringing, cannon firing, etc. And here the Peace Party now very bravely and heroically turn out with arms today, now we have no enemy to fight.

It is hoped the Eastern third part of Massachusetts may now be recovered without bloodshed! Tyrants of Ocean opposed by other nations of Europe induce those to come to terms with U. S.

Feb. 13. All rub a dub. News of Peace signed 26 Dec ! ! !

Feb. 14. Bells ringing for Peace. Land ships hauled up. Peace signed 24th Dec. — Bells.

Feb. 18. Peace ratified. Captures here within 12 days after ratification to be good prizes, different terms for other parts of the world, 120 days longest term.

Feb. 21. Peace came in night. News of its ratification with a whorah! Hostilities cease!

Feb. 22. Pompous celebration of peace in Boston and Washington's birthday. Mass. Senate mean and niggard and chétive, in address to General Jackson on glorious victories at New Orleans 15 vs. 15. The President cast the vote. Even Francis Blake despised his party and voted not with them! ! !

March 2. The Boston rebels at their dirty work again! Peace not their object!

March 3. Town caucus, did not attend.

March 5. H. G. Otis, Wm. Sullivan, Parkman disgraced as insurgents! All argue to strip President and Congress and

invest Gov. Strong with their power. Consummate arrogance!

March 27. Report to New York Assembly, capital! Fine
castigation for Massachusetts disorganization.

The entry of February 22, above, referred to a curious
episode illustrating how stiff-necked in opposition to the
administration Federalist Massachusetts remained, even
in the moment of American victory. The House of Representatives, though Federalist, presented its thanks "to
General Jackson and his brave soldiers for the valor,
talents, prudence and patriotism" by a vote of 65 to 37.
The Senate, however, in its resolve said that it "entertains
a higher sense of the achievements and valor," and then
proceeded to attribute to the Lord the victory of New
Orleans, as follows: "That while they participate in the
general satisfaction which this event is calculated to produce, they are impressed with a deep sense of gratitude to
Almighty God for this signal interposition in behalf of our
country and above all for that divine power with which he
has vouchsafed to us the return of peace." Not content
with this grudging tribute, the Senate prefixed to its resolve a preamble containing bitter reflections on the administration, which was carried, after a tie vote, by the
casting vote of the President of the Senate: "Whereas and
notwithstanding the opinion of this Senate in relation to
the injustice and wantonness of this war in its original
offensive character is unchanged, and notwithstanding that
the gross improvidence of the Administration in conducting it has been apparent, even in the case alluded to by the
proposed resolutions, and that the correctness of these
principles has been proved by the fact that the treaty of
peace between the two countries does not secure any of
the objects for which the war was originally declared."

With the close of the War of 1812, American politics played a less prominent part in Dr. Ames' Diary; but the exciting events in Europe continued to interest him greatly. The return of Napoleon from Elba, his final deposition after Waterloo, and the triumph of the "Kings of Europe venting terrible threats" were all recorded by him, together with his contempt of the Boston Junto for glorying in the victory of the "Kingcraft."

April 28. Bonaparte is said to have recovered Paris. . . .

April 29. The grand news from France confirmed, with exhilarating circumstances! On 15th June last was a Grand Bourbon feast in Boston at downfall of Bonaparte. Now the throne of France is filled by the man of the people's choice. Democrats here would not be more extravagant to illuminate, as they did, the State House, etc., joining the enemy then blockading Boston in public rejoicing in cause of Kings!

May 2. We hear all the Kings and aristocrats of Europe proclaiming war against France: and here too, our Junto and Boston rebels join the yell!

May 3. All Kings and aristocrats boiling against France! ! ! Gazettes filled even here with nothing else.

May 8. Bonaparte has quiet possession of throne of France, all parts contiguous highly gratified. But Kings of Europe venting terrible threats. Bourbons decamped. John Bull roaring. All Europe in commotion, joy and sorrow.

May 13. Foreign news all about Bonaparte's outgeneralling Kingcraft!

May 14. Boston Rebel again flames out against Bonaparte. Grand preparations and threats of the conspiring Kings to destroy France and kill Bonaparte again. All France preparing defence. Great apprehension for France by some lately from thence. Thunder having burst we shall learn the calamity! But so long threats may induce Quincy to say, as he did by our Gov! "They cannot be kicked into war! ! !"

July 4. Independence kept up with revived energy in U. S. And in Dedham with considerable pomp and large procession, fine oration by J. Bailey and prayers by Mr. Gammel.

News of a great battle between Bonaparte and Wellington on the 15th June, battle begun and continued four days. The Prussians were beaten the first two days; then, as the French were exhausted the English attacked and drove the French! Jerome, B's brother, killed, supposed! But further accounts from France give them victory. Both claim it! ! We wait particulars. 4th inst. Paris capitulation to Wellington. Bonaparte not to be found, suspected sailed for America. Whence democracy is to be hunted by traitor Kings!

Aug. 5. Report that Bonaparte, tho' successful first, but because he did not finally conquer all Europe is forced to abdicate and imprisoned by his own people, his own constituents! ! No. Bonaparte generously offers to sacrifice himself for France and abdicates! But is caressed by France! Is expected in America, as safe conduct therefor was refused.

Aug. 9. Enles's Regiment arrived and encamp on Church lot (Swets) South of Mill Creek.

Aug. 13. Time for Bonaparte to arrive — but —

Aug. 26. Bonaparte surrendered to British about 10th July. Conduct of traitor King in France execrable. Demand 500,000,000 francs paid to pay all the expenses of War. Royal Deliverers maintain foreign armies 5 years to hold them in subjection, to break down the spirit of free citizens into slaves.

Sept. 10. Vast militia parade these two days at Dedham. 1st division, Boston, Bellingham Cohasset — all meet at much expense and grumbling, only to salute a bareheaded General.

Nov. 12. Bonaparte arrived at St. Helena strictly guarded.

X

THE GREAT CHURCH FIGHT

IN Dr. Ames' Diary thus far, politics has been seen intruding upon funerals, weaving itself around murders, interfering with professional business, sowing dissensions in families and among neighbors. The Diary entries of the year 1818 depict, in a humorous vein, a great church conflict, the roots of which emerged from political soil. This was the famous struggle between the church and the parish in Dedham over the choice of a minister, which finally resulted in the epochal lawsuit in the Massachusetts Supreme Judicial Court, settling the status of the Unitarian and the Congregational churches in that State for all time.

While, in the broadest sense, the struggle in Dedham was representative of the larger conflict, then going on all through New England, between the new liberal doctrines and the old Congregational creed, — between budding Unitarians and Calvinistic Trinitarians, — nevertheless in reality the local conflict was largely fought, not on any great principle, but on differences of opinion growing out of the opposing political tendencies.

Until the year 1803 the affairs of the First Church in Dedham were reasonably peaceable. In its life of one hundred and sixty-three years it had had only five pastors (whose terms of service had averaged thirty-three years each). The church building had been erected in 1762, with fifty pews on the lower floor, the persons paying the highest parish tax rate having the first choice of pews, and all pews reverting if the owner ceased to be a taxpayer. (Incidentally, it may be noted that when the church was built Dr. Ames' father had third choice of pews.) The pulpit was in the centre of one side of the church; and very near the pulpit, along the east side, was a deep gallery for singers. In the galleries also were the free seats, the men on one side, the women on the other. Immediately under the pulpit and joined to it were the deacons' seats, and above that, and entered from the pulpit stairs, the elders' seats, occupied by the time-honored members and those hard of hearing, who thus were seated so high that their heads were on a level with the pulpit. The seats in the pews were on hinges, turning up when the people rose to pray, and at the end coming down with a great clatter, "especially if the prayer happened to be of unusual length." [1] Until 1785 it was customary for one of the deacons to read the Psalms line by line, the congregation singing them thus by piecemeal; and in 1766 a vote is recorded that Mr. Ebenezer Richards "who usually led in singing be desired to sit on the Lord's Day in the seat under the pulpit, commonly called the elder's seat and that he have the liberty to nominate a number to sit with him to assist in carrying on the singing." [2] In 1786 it was voted to sing "without the deacon's reading." No musical instrument was used until 1790, when the parish desired Mr. Abner Ellis to make use of an instrument "to strengthen the bass"; and in 1803 it was voted to purchase a bass viol. No organ was introduced until 1821, and the opposition of those who disliked

---

[1] See *Sermon preached on Oct. 31, 1858, on the Sunday after the 40th Anniversary of his Ordination*, by Reverend Alvan Lamson.

[2] *A History of the First Church and Parish in Dedham*, by Reverend Alvan Lamson (1839). In 1784 the old New England version of the Psalms hitherto in use was exchanged for that of Tate and Brady; and in 1793 Dr. Watts' version was adopted.

innovations is hinted at in an entry in Dr. Ames' Diary, March 18, 1811: "Parish Meeting grant other people's money for singing. Why not a band of music or Organ, etc?"

The covenant of the First Church in Dedham, to which all persons who joined the Church must subscribe, was unusually liberal, being practically confined to the following statement: "We profess our belief of the Christian religion. We unite outselves together for the purpose of obeying the precepts and honoring the institutions of the religion we profess"; and, as Parson Haven said in 1796, a disposition prevailed "to permit everyone freely to enjoy the right of his private opinion provided he doth not break in upon the rights of others." Certainly, with so broad a creed as this, it would seem as if dissensions in the parish on doctrinal lines would be impossible or at least extremely unlikely. A very serious dissension, however, did arise, but on political rather than on doctrinal grounds. At the end of 1802, it became necessary to choose a successor to Reverend Jason Haven, who had been pastor for forty-six years. Nathaniel Ames and others had long been restive under the old minister's domination, his "clerical tyranny" and "lulling them to sleep by the hum of dronish sermons"; and they wanted a priest that "would address the reason and understanding of his hearers, not really as a flock of sheep whose fleece he would shear unto the skin." [1] They also objected to a contract for life with the new minister, as the custom then was; and urged that he be engaged on trial for a short time. The Parish, led by Fisher Ames, however,

---

[1] As early as November 16, 1778, Dr. Ames recorded: "Parish vote 600 pounds salary to Haven occasions many protests that they never will pay the tax and a petition to the Committee to call a new meeting"; and on December 1, 1778: "Parish meeting reverse their grant of 600 pounds salary and put forth a subscription."

voted to choose a young man, of supposedly liberal views, Reverend Joshua Bates; and Dr. Ames in tart and lively phrases records the defeat of his proposal:

Dec. 30, 1802. They were first taken in by two upstart lawyers to defeat their own purpose — and F. Ames wishing to shut me out of the meeting so as to enjoy my pew, he harangued them so pathetically about pious forefathers that he cram'd the Priest down their throats, tail foremost — duped by a Lawyer.

Civil and ecclesiastical oppression and intrigue triumphant. Harangueing, arrogating, blackguarding in Parish meeting beat the people out of their senses, made them defeat their own wishes and drum good citizens out of the meeting, playing the rogues' march. But some few acted like good men — as John Dean, Calvin Whiting, Abiathar Richards, Jr., Eliphalet Baker, Calvin Guild, S. Lowden, F. Fisher, etc.; others remained indignant, mixed with their enemies in meeting — John Endicott acted the turncoat, openly deserting his own principles — others pitifully, as Weatherbee; and the smooth, double faced Deacon Bullard as usual marred his own design to bind the Priest to stay for the terms of the contract, voted, leave him at perfect liberty to carry on work of ministry here just as long as he pleases, but completely binds the parish; they are handcuffed. And we wanted mutual freedom to go to worship, unhandcuffed, not to be obliged to support a preacher after he grows disgustful, unable, or too lazy or negligent to perform his duty, as we think these terms tempt him.

Feb. 10, 1803. Parish meeting yield to yoke of F. Ames to ordain Bates 16 March, entail discord on the Parish; many discontented join Episcopal Church. The Parish, that is, F. Ames and Deacon Bullard, after midnight caucuses agree to handcuff the Parish and their children and bind them to pay an enormous salary of 1522 dollars and have Bates ordained 16 March next. I and others having joined the Episcopal Church, they exult at our departure, as I hear, as not more to be troubled with our opposition. I never troubled the Parish meetings much with my presence and cannot justly

be called a turbulent fellow. Every infamous slander against
seceders is raised to justify themselves in their oppression
and tyranny that drove us to withdraw. This is common
to unprincipled mortals.

The soreness which this split in the church produced is
made even more clear by the manner in which Dr. Ames in
his Diary entries of later dates continued to revert to and
harp upon his "excommunication":

> *June, 1803.* Preparations for noticing 4th July in various
> places, in various manners — some with orations and men-
> tal feasting — others with solid meat, wine and punch to
> please the bodies' appetite. And some have asked me about
> going to join them, the very ones that voted my excom-
> munication! ! ! At which I was astonished! ! !
>
> *Dec. 6.* B't of Elijah Fisher a heap of dung, at 20 dollars, and
> in casting away on my clover, F. Ames came and stormed
> at my presumption to my men, in buying dung without his
> leave, when I did not know he arrogated all the dung as well
> as religion in Dedham. After turning me out of the House
> of God, I expected he would allow me to grovel in dung.
>
> *January, 1806.* Fatal 30th, Dec. 1802, Saints of old Parish
> shoved out — see the particulars noted in first leaf of
> Diary for 1803. I quitted the meeting of Hypocrites and
> tyrants . . . yet they taxed and still continue to tax me to
> Bates' support, vile pirates.

One result of this parish controversy was the secession of
many of its members into the Episcopal Church, an amusing sidelight upon which episode is found in the columns of
the local paper, which printed the following sarcastic letter: "Mr. Mann — Please to give the following a place in
your paper and oblige a Customer. — It is said that Mr.
Farefame, Mr. Moreland and Mr. Mateland, and some
others, have joined to the Episcopal Church in Dedham.
If this be true, it is matter of joy that the Goats have sepa-

rated themselves from the sheep; and that the Pastor elect when he takes the charge of the Flock, will have nothing but sheep to feed." [1] To this a member of the Episcopal Church made answer: "Mr. Printer — Please to tell Mr. Altus Vertex, the bearer, and Mr. Niger Aries, the author of the information in your letter of the first instant, that to me 'it is a matter of joy' that the Flock in Dedham, over which the 'Shepherd Elect' is to be placed tomorrow, consists now only of sheep; as my young growing woodland, given for sacred use and lying in the parish where the lambs will feed, will no more be subject to the foul destructive waste of Goats. — The Ghost of Samuel Colburn." [2]

In spite of this rancorous opposition of Dr. Ames and his followers, Reverend Joshua Bates was ordained, March 16, 1803, as recorded by Dr. Ames in his peculiar vein: "Bates ordained, Clergy stuffed; vast provisions." "The order of the services was performed before a very crowded but a remarkably civil and brilliant assembly," said the local paper. "A very pleasing attention and decorum was preserved throughout the whole solemnities; and no accidents or indecent behaviour occurred in the festive hilarity with which the day was closed." It is significant that it should have been necessary to record that "no accidents or indecent behaviour" accompanied a church ordination, and such a condition boded ill for the success of the new pastor's administration. Within two years a serious dissension arose over a proposition to enlarge the meetinghouse, and Dr. Ames, with highly characteristic prejudice, attributed this new split in the parish and further secession to the Episcopal Church to the "intrigues and pettifogyies of lawyers" (the lawyers, be it noted, being Federalist in their politics). His Diary in 1805 records the following:

[1] *Columbian Minerva* (Dedham), March 1, 1803.
[2] *Columbian Minerva*, March 15, 1803.

The Old Parish of Dedham, by intrigues of lawyers bro't into a broil by an unnecessary vote to enlarge the Meeting House to accommodate F[isher] A[mes] with a pew. Many, it is supposed, wish to join the Church to avoid the expense, etc. if the Episcopal Church was not encumbered with Montague, who is a stumbling block and mars the projects of the Church. Edward Whiting, this 21st of January, 1805, says many would sign a petition to be incorporated with the Episcopal Church by General Court, and is full of the idea that such a thing at this time would be very taking with a considerable portion of the Parish; and considers it as very unfortunate that Sam Colburn's donation is not bro't under good regulation for the benefit of the Church. And Jonathan Damon yesterday proposed to me to draw a petition to the Parish Committee for another meeting, to undo what the last voted, etc.; but I had rather not interfere — let them sweat and groan awhile under pettifoggery!

March 7. Parish Committee finally refuses to obey the law as to refunding taxes assessed on different sects of worship; and add insult to injury — for Ben Weatherby, one of the assessors, told me if a law authorized a man to change his religion as his coat, it was a bad law. I told him he was as big a tyrant, or would be, as Bonaparte; and that an action would determine now he had refused Montague's orders. [1]

Dr. Ames, while intolerant in politics, abhorred bigotry or intolerance in religion, and in 1812, noting a call for a town meeting to petition for the repeal of the law allowing persons belonging to churches other than Congregational to have their parish tax transferred to such church, he termed it a meeting "to repeal the law for freedom of religion — to try to revive the sport of roasting heretics! ! !"

Meanwhile, personal antagonism to the Reverend Mr. Bates, the growth of more liberal and Unitarian beliefs, but above all political dissensions, were destroying the con-

---

[1] This entry referred to existing statutes, under which a man who joined a church other than the Congregational Church in any town or parish was entitled to have the parish tax paid by him turned over to the church of which he became a member.

cord of the parish. Federalism and Antifederalism entered into religion and rent the church asunder. The year 1803 was in the middle of Jefferson's first administration. It was a time when the clergy of Massachusetts were united in reviling the President and vied with the newspaper editors in devising new epithets against him. Their general views were summed up in the *New England Palladium*, as follows: "Should the infidel Jefferson be elected to the Presidency, the seal of death is that moment set on our holy religion, our churches will be prostrated, and some infamous prostitute under the title of the Goddess of Reason will preside in the sanctuaries now devoted to the most High." Three Congregational ministers and one Episcopalian were especially virulent — Jedidiah Morse of Charlestown, Charles Osgood of Medford, Elijah Parish of Byfield, and John S. J. Gardiner, rector of Trinity Church in Boston; but their associates, while perhaps more guarded in language, were equally opposed to Jefferson, as "an atheist," "an infidel," "a free-thinker," "a revolutionist," "a disorganizer"; and they did not hesitate to express these views, not only in their Fast Day and Thanksgiving Day sermons, but on Sundays as well. Probably nothing served to foment dissension and to enflame the public mind more than the practice, so largely indulged in by the clergy, of preaching politics from the pulpit.[1]

[1] John Quincy Adams, writing to William Plumer, October 6, 1810, referred to the "profligacy with which they were endeavoring to make religion an engine of faction, by the mountebank trick of their solemn fasts, and by goading into the pulpit every ignorant, priestly fanatic that they could employ as a tool, to pollute with the filth of personal malice and detraction the sacred desk of God." *The Writings of John Quincy Adams* (1914), vol. III, p. 508.

Pierrepont Edwards wrote to Jefferson, May 12, 1801 that in Connecticut "the malignity of the Federalists here is wholly inconceivable. . . . Our leading Federalists are all royalists; they think as our clergy do. . . . The throne and the altar have here entered into an alliance offensive and defensive." "Office Seeking During Jefferson's Administration," by Gaillard Hunt, *American Historical Review* (1898), vol. III.

The sentiment of the Republicans against this obnoxious course can be fairly seen in the following extracts from a number of letters of denunciation written at this time by Benjamin Austin to the *Independent Chronicle*: "The deceptions which have been practiced on the public, and the falsehoods propagated by those whose duty it is to study the truth, have had a great tendency to destroy the morals of the people, and to render them inattentive to the precepts of the gospel. When they find so many of the clergy deceiving them with foolish political tales, the people begin to doubt the validity of those doctrines which they preach and enjoin. When they observe more zeal to propagate political than evangelical principles, the people suspect that the apparent sanctity of such clergymen is more a cloak of hypocrisy than a garb of piety. A few leading clergymen have shown such an intolerant spirit — have acted and preached with a temper so unbecoming the mild, catholic precepts of the gospel that many serious persons have become so disaffected as to neglect an attendance on public worship. . . . The pulpit in many instances has become a political theatre, and days set apart for religious worship have been converted to party rant and defamation. The society instead of being entertained or instructed in matters of religion have been enraged against each other by the inflammatory dogmas of the preacher." Again he wrote: "This is a species of virulence and indecency of language ever used by bigots. . . . Destitute of argument, they always have recourse to hard names and scurrilous reflections — they never reason, but entrench themselves within their sacerdotals, and abuse their opponents with every opprobrious term which malignity can devise or fanaticism suggest. 'Deist,' 'atheist,' 'infidel,' 'defamer,' 'disorganizer' are weapons with which they assail their antagonists." And Austin still again adverted to this deplorable attitude of the clergy in another letter to the *Chronicle*, in which he said, with much justice and without exaggeration: "The mind of the audience, instead of being solemnized to adore the Supreme Being for all his mercies, has been convulsed with party controversy. The preacher in many instances has exhibited more the attitude of a dictator than the solemn deportment of a Christian minister. The congregation has been greatly disturbed by the inconsiderate behaviour of the priest; and the society have separated with as much personal irritation as if they had been attending an electioneering town meeting. . . . When the congregation was dismissed, instead of hearing anything which related to the business of the gospel, each one went away 'wagging his head' and insulting his political antagonist. . . . The minds of the aged have been soured and embittered, while the young have been led to contemplate them only as set apart for political controversy. . . . Contentions and bickerings, instead of love and amity, were too often the production of those solemn ceremonies."[1]

With such provocation, it is not surprising that the Jeffersonians should retaliate with objurgations against their clerical assailants. "The Jewish hierarchy," wrote Austin, "this hypocritical junto were stigmatizing the author of our religion in the same opprobrious manner as the Essex Junto now do Mr. Jefferson. . . . The fact is the whole history of our Saviour shows the hypocrisy of priests and their minions, — the dangerous tendency of Priestcraft." Furthermore, such intermingling of politics with religion by the minister was certain to produce divisions in the congregation. "The people when they settle a minister do not intend to erect a clerical inquisition within the parish. Politics were never contemplated in the articles of

[1] *Constitutional Republicanism* (1803), by Benjamin Austin, Jr.

a church compact. They are willing to hear gospel truths
but are opposed to political creeds. . . . If he employs his.
time in preaching on political subjects, he robs the parish,
as they never gave him a salary to discuss controversies of
this nature. Those clergymen therefore who have arrogated such liberties, either on the Sabbath, Fast or Thanksgiving Days . . . must be considered as heretics who have
prostituted their sacred profession and demeaned themselves to become the tools of a wicked and degenerate
faction."

From the very beginning of his pastorate, Mr. Bates,
following the course of the rest of the clergy, filled his sermons with solid Federalist, anti-Jeffersonian doctrines; and
the editor of the local newspaper noted in his columns that
one of Mr. Bates' parishioners had adopted his pastor's
advice to drop that Republican sheet and subscribe to the
Boston Palladium, as "the most orthodox and evangelical
Federal" paper.[1] The First Parish, however, was Jeffersonian in its politics by a considerable majority, as was the
town of Dedham. The results of Mr. Bates' preaching
were, therefore, what might have been expected, and they
were later described by a Republican lawyer who lived in
the town at the time, and who, being an Episcopalian,
viewed the contest from the impartial standpoint of an
outsider. He wrote that the objection to Mr. Jefferson as
a disbeliever of Christian doctrines "was so frequently and

---

[1] "A Federal man in a Republican town who did not vote for the ordination
of the present minister there has become at least so much reconciled to him as to
follow his general advice to drop the *Columbian Minerva*. His objections are
partially that the words 'old tories, federal faction,' some unfavorable things
concerning some priests, Paine's writings so much in favor of the present and so
much against the late administration and reign of terror, occur so often that he
cannot bear the very sight of the paper. This we call his taking the subjects
home! He enquired my opinion — which is the best paper of *order?* Without
hesitation, I replied, ' the *Boston Palladium* is the most orthodox and evangelical
Federal.'" — *Columbian Minerva*, June 14, 1803.

so earnestly reiterated that this circumstance produced a conviction in the minds of many men that political reasons, and not fear of danger to the interest of religion, were the real motives of this attack on the President. A respectable minority in the Parish, on the other hand, who saw their neighbors apparently uninfluenced by so serious a charge, concluded that they had already come under the influence of wickedness in high places and had acquired a strong propensity to infidelity. . . . Dr. Bates deemed it his duty to proclaim aloud his fears and apprehensions from the influence of infidelity. . . . He could not conceal his opinion that he thought many of his hearers, at best, but doubtful Christians. . . . This produced unfriendly criticism, which in turn exposed those who doubted, to the renewed charge of heresy and irreligious propensities."

When the War of 1812 began, Dedham and its First Parish were strongly in favor of the administration and opposed to the recreant moves of the peace party. But the clergy of Massachusetts were on the other side and were united and vociferous in their denunciations of the "hell-begotten" war. The rector of Trinity Church preached a sermon, July 23, 1812, which was typical. "It is a war, unjust, foolish and ruinous," he said. "As Mr. Madison has declared war, let Mr. Madison carry it on. We shall suffer enough in our property without risquing our lives in an impious contest. . . . If you do not wish to become the slaves of those who own slaves, and who are themselves the slaves of French slaves, you must either, in the language of the day, cut the connexion or so far alter the National Constitution as to ensure yourselves a due share in the government. The Union has long since been virtually dissolved, and it is full time that this portion of the disunited States should take care of itself. . . . To continue to suffer as we have suffered for eight years last, from the incapac-

ity of a weak if not corrupt administration is more than
can be expected from human patience or Christian resignation." It may easily be imagined that a congregation
which regarded such sentiments as treasonable when
uttered on the stump would not receive them quiescently
when delivered over a pulpit.

That the voice of Mr. Bates was not quiet during the
war, and that his attitude was not that of passive protest,
may be gathered from the following anecdote related of
him when the news of peace reached Dedham.[1] "Pitt
Butterfield of Dedham was a leather dresser and a radical
politician of the Republican stripe. When news reached
the town that General Jackson had signally defeated the
British at New Orleans, January 8, 1815, the excitement
was intense and the War Party or Republicans. . . at
once determined to fire a salute in honor of the great victory. The old town gun was dragged to the church green
in front of the meeting house of the First Parish. . . . The
Federalists were strong in numbers as they were influential
in character, and as the preparation for the salute went on
their opposition to it assumed an air of open hostility. . . .
Mr. Butterfield was captain of the artillerists . . . Parson Joshua Bates was spokesman for the Federalists and
headed their column with a pail of water in hand with the
avowed purpose of wetting the priming before a match
could be applied to the gun. His attitude and speech were
defiant and it was thought by his supporters that his active
opposition backed by the weight of ministerial authority
would dampen the ardor as well as the powder of the patriotic Republicans. . . . The blood of all the Butterfields
was up. Striding promptly to the front and throwing off
his coat, he faced the church militant and in language more
forcible than elegant gave the other party to understand

[1] See *Dedham Historical Register*, vol. I.

that any interference with the loading or firing of the field piece would result in a fight then and there and that the broadcloth of a priest would not protect a meddling and domineering politician. It was enough. Mr. Bates was in a false position and he had the good sense to see it. He retreated precipitately with his unemptied bucket and with the best grace possible. The grim artillery men at once loaded their piece half to the muzzle and its black lips time and time again that January afternoon voiced the exultation of the victorious villagers."

Simultaneously with the growth of this political dissatisfaction with Reverend Mr. Bates, another cause of dissension was rapidly spreading through his congregation. This new factor was the growth of that liberal outlook on religion known as Unitarianism. For a proper appreciation of the manner in which these two factors, politics and Unitarianism, brought about the great Dedham church fight some knowledge of the peculiar interrelations between the church and the parish in old New England towns is required.[1] The theory and practice of Congregationalism then prevailing in the churches of Massachusetts were based on the full and perfect right in each company of worshippers of convenient size, covenanted together, to choose, institute, and ordain all pastors, teachers, ruling elders, or deacons needed by them. "When a party of men with their families proposed to plant a new town settlement or precinct, they addressed a petition to the General Court [the legislature] for a grant of land in the wilderness. Receiving their warrant, and reaching their destination, they proceeded to allot the land to the members of the

---

[1] The following description of church and parish conditions is largely taken from *The Church and Parish in Massachusetts, Usage and Law* (1858), by George E. Ellis; and from *A Half Century of the Unitarian Controversy* (1857), by George E. Ellis.

company in parcels of upland, meadow, and woodland, according to a fair rule of division. They set aside the dreariest and bleakest spot, provided it was sandy for easy digging and worthless for culture, for a burial ground. Other lots were staked off for a meeting house, the school house, the pound, the parsonage, and the ministerial wood lot. A tax was then levied upon the inhabitants according to their property, to open roads, to build a meeting house and a school house; and a tax was annually imposed to keep these works in repair and to support the minister and to pay the school master. So far, of course, no distinction was made, founded on church relation. The roads, the meeting house, the minister, and the school entered into the public burdens. Sometimes, a covenanted body, the Church, was the original nucleus around which gathered a congregation, and the proportion of numbers in the membership of each was constantly changing. Sometimes a Church was formed within a previously assembled congregation that had maintained worship. Governor Winthrop, the Deputy Governor 'and many others, men and women' formed at Charlestown, July 30, 1630, the First Church of Boston. They had then no minister or other officers, which they directed and constituted, a month afterwards, and signed a simple covenant. In other cases, as for example, in the First Parish of Dedham, there had been worship under a tree and in a rude meeting house by a congregation within which was afterwards gathered a Church." All the inhabitants of a town or of the parish were obliged to pay taxes to defray the expenses of the town or parish minister and of the meetinghouse, as well as to attend public worship under penalty of a fine. The choice of a minister was made differently at different times — first by the church, then by the parish, then by the two concurrently, and finally under the State Constitution of 1780 by the parish, from

which he derived his support. A statute of 1754 constituted the deacons trustees of all church and parish property, the church not being a corporate body, and hence
unable to hold property in succession. The minister, thus
provided for by law, whom each town should have and
maintain was termed in the statutes "a public teacher of
morality and religion." The church, as distinguished from
the parish, contended frequently, however, that while the
town or parish might appoint this "public teacher," only
the church could give him the sacred official character of
"pastor." Hence, usage had come to require that ordination to a pastorate should be the solemn act of a church as
such, calling the chosen in the presence and with the approbation of a council of sister churches. But as the church
regulated its own membership and admitted whom it
chose, numerous occasions arose for conflict between the
church and parish. The church might have members who
were not proprietors or taxable in the parish; its members
might be women and children as well as men and adults.
The parish could only consist of taxable inhabitants of the
town. Moreover, the church — an *imperium in imperio* —
prescribed its own terms for admission to membership —
an assent to a covenant or confession of faith as framed by
it. These terms might be free or rigid in doctrinal belief —
they might vary and be relaxed or tightened from time to
time. With such materials for friction, it is easy to see
that the choice and institution of a new minister when
there were differences of opinion between the members of
the church and the members of the parish might give rise
to considerable contention. And as ministers frequently,
when once chosen, had a life tenure of office, the choice
became a matter of intense importance. Where the minister held to an unabated Calvinism and his church sympathized with him, of course, no new members could pass the

ordeal of covenant without acceding to the terms required of a member of the congregation for securing the privilege of church communion. Thus all the parishioners who held liberal views were excluded from the church.

Just such a situation was arising in the early part of the nineteenth century in many a Massachusetts town. The new doctrine of Unitarianism was gaining a rapid hold on the people. The first really Unitarian church was King's Chapel in Boston, which adopted, in 1787, the radical views of its new minister, Reverend James Freeman. Harvard College, which had so great an influence on the intellectual life of the State, had had two presidents between 1781 and 1810, Willard and Webber, both of whom, though not professedly Unitarian, tended towards the beliefs of that sect. The election of Henry Ware, in 1805, as Professor of Divinity, an admitted Unitarian, had filled the religious bodies of the State with great consternation. A set of brilliant young scholars composing the Anthology Club had published in Boston from 1804 to 1811 a review enunciating Unitarian principles. Andrews Norton, a prominent Harvard teacher, had edited in 1812 the *General Repository*, which published as a first article a "very bold defence of Liberal Christianity." So rapid was the spread of the new liberal views that in 1808 and 1809 the Andover Theological Seminary and Park Street Church in Boston were founded for the express purpose of providing asylums for the highly orthodox. Between 1810 and 1820 Unitarian societies sprang up in Philadelphia, Washington, Charleston, and New York, — "tiny islands in the broad main of orthodoxy," — but only in New England, and especially in Eastern Massachusetts, had the new faith a large following.[1]

[1] See *Life of Ezra Stiles Gannett* (1884), by William C. Gannett; *Life and Writings of Jared Sparks* (1893), by Herbert B. Adams; *History of the United States*, by Henry Adams, vol. ix.

In Dedham, the new liberal views had prevailed to some extent in the First Parish, and, combined with the dissatisfaction over the pastor's political actions and sentiments, had resulted, in 1818, in a majority of the congregation being opposed to Reverend Mr. Bates and his orthodox preaching, in spite of the fact that he was still a young man of great piety and ability who had only been settled for the then comparatively short period of fifteen years. It was, therefore, with great relief that in February the parish received the information from their pastor that he had accepted the position of president of Middlebury College in Vermont. And then arose the great church fight. One of the three candidates to succeed Mr. Bates was Reverend Alvan Lamson, who was an able and pleasing young man, but had only recently graduated from what was looked on as a hotbed of Unitarianism, the Harvard Divinity School. When the question of calling him as the new minister arose, the parish, or congregation, elected Lamson as its minister. The church — that is, those who had signed the covenant, the wheel within the wheel — voted not to call Lamson.[1] To reconcile the differences between the two bodies, a Council of Churches was called; but as the Council was composed mostly of Unitarian ministers, it sustained the action of the parish and its legal rights to choose the minister, in spite of the opposition of the church. It is of no particular interest to go further into the details, but many of them appear in the picturesque language of Dr. Ames, to whose Diary the further telling of the tale may be left:

[1] The facts were that the parish chose Lamson by a vote of 81 to 44, this two-thirds majority representing four-fifths of the taxable property in the parish. The church voted against him 17 to 15, but one vote was cast by mistake affirmatively, so that the actual vote should have been 18 to 14. Six members of the church did not vote. Amongst the eighteen opposed were two of the three deacons of the church.

August, 1818. A Mr. Lamson been preaching at the old meeting house, has a call 100 louder than Bates had, 83 majority 44 minority. Great ferment in the Parish, the major part of the Church against him, but congregation resolute to settle him.

August 31. Parish meeting voted to settle Lamson, 44 dissentients; to give a salary 100 dollars more than the last minister and while he supplies pulpit.

Sept. 27. Lamson's acceptance makes M. Newel kick and Jonathan Avery march out etc. Much grumbling of large minority!

Sept. 28. 23 vote to have Lamson reconsider his answer (in order to retract); 65 vote opposite, so that the minority grows larger.

Oct. 28. Attempt to ordain Lamson disappoints vast concourse of people. Council decide to ordain him over the Parish and Society, not Church, of First Parish in Dedham.

Oct. 29. They announce this decision, whereupon Deacon Joseph Swan first, then his stepfather Deacon S. Fales, walk out from the meeting house — also Wheaton, Messinger, and others. Ordination then completed after.

Nov. 8. Large minority of 1st Parish call Council of Churches! To find hole to creep in again!

Nov. 14. Deacon Joseph Swan died crazy! head of minority vs. Lamson. But it is said they still mean to hold Church funds, being majority of Church!

Nov. 19. Opposition Council ends, declares late ordination of Lamson wrong, mortify Chickering and Stimpson. S. Haven pleased but party not relieved.

Nov. 22. Mr. Otis preached at church. Deacon Fales and others disaffected attend church.

Matters were now at a deadlock; the parish had ordained Mr. Lamson, but the church had not. Moreover, one of the deacons of the church belonged to the seceders and had in his possession the records, the funds, and the Communion service of the church of the First Parish in Dedham. Neither party would yield — neither the "Big Endians" nor the "Little Endians," as Dr. Ames called the Lamsonites and the Anti-Lamsonites. Allegations of fraud in the holding of the election began to be made. Judge Haven, a "Little Endian," charged that, of the 81 of the parish who voted for Lamson, some were members of the Episcopal Church "who had been induced to vote by the Committee to swell the numbers and some who had transferred three or four days before" — that is, who had left the parish and joined some other church. Dr. Ames had his theory of the cause of the dissension. He characteristically laid it all to the malign intrigues of the lawyers, the "pettifogs":

> *April, 1819.* Religion in Old Parish burst out blazing so as excites astonishment of modest old-standards or "bulwarks of Religion we profess," to find the cause of splitting into so many parties and sets, damning each other with religious rancour! But the cause is manifest. It is because they blindly follow a lawyer at the head of each.
> Chick [Jabez Chickering] heads Big Endians.
> [Samuel] Haven leads Little Endians.
> [Erastus] Worthington the Episcopalians.
> But the Little Endians are divided into Unitarians or Universals, and Brimstonarians.

Curiously enough, Judge Haven, one of the lawyers whom Ames accuses as an instigator of all the trouble, himself attributed the dissensions to two other lawyers, and in a pamphlet which he wrote descriptive of the proceedings spoke of these two men "who had been for several years the chief plotters and workers of the two political parties in the place, and thus had in their control and were familiar with the use of the whole complex machinery for operating on the prejudices and passions of the people. Political disputes having become less interesting of late and being of one heart on the subject of religious order, they joined their hands to bring about such a state of things in that respect as was suited to their task — peaceably if they could, forcibly if they must."[1] And Judge Haven in his pamphlet further described the contest in the following vigorous language: "We believe that this picture of disorder, if drawn to the life, would so shock and deter the beholder as to cause him, if he belong to the Congregational Community, to cling with increased affection to the ancient, regular and pacific principles and usages of the Congregational Churches. For the honor of the Christian name, we would gladly suppress the picture; but for the good of the Christian cause, we must not." So heated had the feelings of the two factions become and so tenacious was each of what it held — the Lamsonites holding the old meetinghouse building, the others holding the records and funds, each claiming the name of the "First Church" — that no possible solution could be found except a suit in court to determine the respective rights. Accordingly, a suit in replevin was brought by the two deacons elected by those members of the church who voted with the parish against the deacon elected by the old church, to recover the bonds, securities, church records, and documents which he held. This suit — "*Eliphalet Baker et al as deacons of the First Church in Dedham vs. Samuel Fales*" — was begun in April, 1819, tried before a jury in February, 1820, and argued before the Supreme Judicial Court in October, 1820. Famous lawyers were engaged on each side, Daniel Davis, the Solicitor-General of the Commonwealth and Jabez Chickering of Dedham appearing for the parish, and Daniel Webster and Theron Metcalf for the church — two Republican lawyers against two Federalists. The church

[1] *A statement of the proceedings in the First Church and Parish in Dedham respecting the settlement of a minister, 1818, with some consideration of Congregational Church polity. By a member of the said Church and Parish, at the request of a multitude within and without* (Cambridge, 1819).

could have had no abler representative than Webster, for he was already at the head of the bar, and had argued, only a year and a half before, the famous Dartmouth College Case in the United States Supreme Court. It is probable that the politics of their respective counsel represented, in general, the politics of the respective parties — the members of the Church who withdrew being largely Federalist.

Meanwhile, pending the progress of the lawsuit, an actual church secession had taken place in Dedham, and the Anti-Lamsonites, or "Little Endians" as Ames called them, had left the old church building, and erected a new meeting-house just across the street from the old one. This had spurred on the "Big Endians"; and they entered into competition with the new meeting-house by entirely remodelling the old, and turning it halfway around so that it should not face its new rival across the road.[1] These movements were all quaintly recorded by Dr. Ames:

> *January 29, 1819.* Advertisement for contract for new Meeting-house, Dedham.
> *May 28.* New bell, 1692 pounds, Meeting-house. Big Endians. But sounds not much better than church bell smaller.
> *June 6.* Mr. Codman preaches to Little Endians in old House. Two bells rival in sound only!
> *June 20.* Moving old parsonage for new Meeting-house.
> *Aug. 9.* Began to raise new Meeting-house opposite old one!
> *Aug. 13.* New Meeting-house looks well. Old one trying to

[1] Dr. Lamson in his *Second Century Historical Discourses* (preached in 1838), says: "The majority of the old members did not in fact retire. . . . This I believe from a careful inspection of a very accurate list of the original members to be a fact. . . . Of one thing there can be no dispute; that is, that after the ordination there was a larger vote sanctioning the proceeding of the Parish than was ever given against them. I make this whole statement after a diligent examination of authentic documents and ample means of information and I believe that every part of it can be substantiated."

The probable fact is that the number of church members who remained and the number who withdrew were substantially equal; but that of the parish about two thirds remained and one third left.

rival it. Get materials, as if striving for handsomest road to Heaven.

Aug. 23. Steeple old Meeting-house stuck in roof in altering. Bates preached, old House.

Sept. 12. Stewart preached, old House or Little Endians! or Old Fort Church Dedham. Two Meeting-houses here striving to outshine!

Oct. 12. Tore up my pew, Meeting-house.

The controversy between the two factions was made even more acrimonious by the publication by Judge Samuel Haven of the pamphlet above referred to, describing the points at issue and attributing the blame for the whole contest to two busybody lawyers. The latter at once had Haven indicted for criminal libel; but he was acquitted, as described by Ames, who heartily sympathized with Haven's attack on the lawyers:

Dec. 3, 1819. Little Endians triumph at Cambridge Court. Sam Haven of Dedham indicted at Cambridge S. J. C. for publishing the History of Lamson's ordination at Old Dedham. Book printed at Cambridge. Found not guilty.

Dec. 8. Vast disunion of First Parish, Dedham, by lawyers leading peaceable people astray, running them into needless expense, building Meeting-house, etc., lawsuits, etc. etc.

Dec. 30. Dedication of new Meeting-house of First Church, Dedham. Full house.

Feb. 1820. Began to fix Mr. Dowse' donation of superb clock in old Meeting-house, but not soon regulated to keep time, and strikes like brass kettle struck with a stick.

Jan. 21, 1821. Mr. Burgess answers the call of the Little Endians to stay and have a house, 2800 dollars.[1]

Feb. 11. Bell in ringing cracked today, so hours of clock not heard.

---

[1] The new church was completed December 30, 1819. Reverend Ebenezer Burgess came to Dedham to preach in it in July, 1820; and was ordained March 14, 1821. See *A Centennial Discourse, November 8, 1838* (1840), by Ebenezer Burgess.

Feb. 22. All anxious for judgment, Church Case, not to be known until next Monday at Boston. Reported, 26th, against Church, in favor of Parish.

Feb. 26. Report of Judgment for Parish against 1st Church Dedham carried donation funds, all.

The decision of the Supreme Court, rendered in February, 1821, unanimously sustained the right of the parish to ordain a minister without the necessity of any concurrence by the church. The uniform practice of Massachusetts churches was thus completely overturned, the Court holding that the Bill of Rights of the Massachusetts Constitution of 1780 expressly overruled this practice by the following language: "The several towns, parishes, precincts, and other bodies politic or religious societies, shall, at all times, have the exclusive right of electing their public teachers." The Court then further decided that the church was not a corporation, and could hold no property apart from the parish; that therefore all the funds bequeathed to the church or to the deacons of the church were held for the benefit of the parish, and that the seceders had no right to the property withheld by them. Further — a still more humiliating blow — it was held that a church separating from the parish for any cause lost its existence, and that never in Massachusetts had a church a legal existence apart from a parish; hence those members of the church who remained with the parish, even though a minority of the church, still constituted the original church and had the right to choose deacons, and to bear the old name.

It is impossible to exaggerate the excitement which this decision caused in Massachusetts. "Half the towns saw their most devout Church members deprived, by a printed report of 35 pages, of their meeting-house, Parish property, Church records, communion furniture, all the material part of the Church, and compelled to begin their ecclesiastical life anew. The Bill of Rights had been converted into a lever to pry orthodox ministers and Churches out of their places." [1] So said the opponents of the Court. "On the other hand those who defended the Dedham decision urged that the Bill of Rights had been adopted when all parties were orthodox; that the framers did not allow words to creep into that Bill inadvisedly; that they knew the difference between Church and Parish, and did not accidentally omit the word 'Church.' The Church was formally and expressly excluded, in conformity with the growing democratic sentiment of that time, with a view of giving all those the right of electing a minister who were taxed for his support. And as sueing, sealing, and contracting were the badges of a corporation, no instance could be found where a Church, as separate from the Parish, had even in past times done one of those things."

Although the Dedham local newspaper, the *Village Register*, said, March 2, 1821, "On Monday last, the opinion of the Court was given in Boston by Chief Justice (Isaac Parker). The reasons were given at large and occupied one hour and ten minutes in the delivery. . . . We can only add that a number of gentlemen who attended and heard the opinion of the Court and who had expected a different result, said the reasons were sound and conclusive and declared themselves perfectly satisfied with the decision," nevertheless the decision came as a painful surprise to a large number of the bar, and as a fundamental shock to most laymen. And the minister of the seceding Dedham church probably expressed the general feeling when he said, in his anniversary sermon seventeen years

---

[1] See *Massachusetts Ecclesiastical Law* (1866), by Edward Buck; *An Historical Sketch of Congregational Churches in Massachusetts* (1859), by Reverend Joseph S. Clark; *Spirit of the Pilgrims* (1827), vol. II; *Baker* v. *Fales*, 16 Mass. 488 *et seq.*

later, "A large proportion of the people of Massachusetts have ascribed it to the bias of religious prejudice." While this charge against the Supreme Court was unquestionably unfounded, there can be no doubt that the liberal tendencies of the Justices of the Court, as shown in a line of church cases from as far back as 1811, ought to have prepared all persons interested in church affairs for the decision which was rendered in 1821. The effect of this famous case was far-reaching. As Unitarianism spread rapidly through the State, parish after parish outvoted the old church members and obtained possession of the meeting-houses and church funds, and in town after town the upholders of the old faith were obliged to relinquish their accustomed houses of worship and build new. Over fifty years passed by before the soreness and bitterness of feeling thus produced died away; and relics of it still remain in many a New England town.

XI

PERSONAL LIFE, 1796–1822

AFTER giving up the keeping of his father's tavern, at the opening of the Revolution, Nathaniel Ames, as before noted, not only practised as a physician, but also composed and published his Almanac in each year until 1775. He, moreover, engaged in farming, and was Clerk of the Court of Sessions and Common Pleas for Norfolk County for over ten years after 1794, the fees from which offices were, at times, a welcome addition to his medical income. It is evident, however, from his Diary that he found it difficult to pursue simultaneously so many activities, especially since he was confronted by considerable competition from other physicians; and his perplexities are pungently set forth in the many entries on these subjects:

> *June 6, 1796.* I cannot attend to farm, only physick and my official business which takes up all my time and keeps me slave to the public, while good part of the small fees escape me, yet am envied for getting too much!
>
> *May 6, 1797.* I find that the fatigue of riding and raising little fever often disqualifies for business and hinders that cool deliberation necessary to solve difficulties.
>
> *Feb. 25, 1798.* Dr. Goldsmith's Essays set forth that one profession is enough for one man; for if you engage in two, the world is apt to give employment to neither. But what if one profession won't maintain a man? How is he to proceed?
>
> *April 14.* Four medicasters close together. No business for either.
>
> *April 18.* Tho' not full of business, I want to think, but am constantly interrupted.

April 30. It is wonderful to see with what promptitude of heedless curiosity, the Vulgar rushes into the toils of a new adventurer or desperado come to spunge.

August 12. John Bullard deserted and employs W., my rival, to replace fractured femur. My prospect in life darkens day by day; no friend reveals the cause.

Oct. 11. If a mason for 4 minutes work and a gallon of mortar has half a dollar, what ought I to have for my services who spent thousands of dollars for books, etc.?

Oct. 17. Paid half a dollar to Marsh for four minutes' work only, plastering round chimney.

June 8, 1812. A Fellow from Stephen Whiting came and asked if I thought I could set his toe as well as Wheaton!

It is evident from the Diary that the doctor's wife did not approve of his participation in politics or other outside matters, and from hints dropped here and there it is apparent that he, at one period, sought solace away from his fireside at some of the many taverns with which Dedham, as a stage town, was amply provided. These pessimistic entries, while perhaps somewhat too personal for preservation, are nevertheless so alive with a sardonic humor that they are reproduced here in order to round out the portrait of the man:

March 25, 1792. Of all the foolish things you do, let marriage be the last — is one of the best pieces of advice I ever heard.

March 26. I cannot bear to be saddled with an insolent and rapacious B., to seize on every penny of money and do nothing to help me live — will not do the service but expects the pay of more than a maid.

April 3. Discovered worse malignity in my bosom friend than I conceived it possible to dwell in human shape! ! ! She has made it necessary that I should avoid the only houses where I could associate with mankind — and that I should drink from principle, as others do from brutish appetite! And that I should stupify my senses to become insensible of the insults and abuse I am made the butt of!! Intending to do business by means of the stage this day beginning to run

from Dedham to Boston daily, I must renounce it, because
I cannot go to Gay's [Tavern] to take the benefit of it, but
must grunt and wallow, a stupid principled drunkard, at
home to drown the sorrows I must otherwise feel. I must
also avoid J. Billings' [Tavern] which is not of so much consideration as Gay's, where I might do business.

Jan. 21, 1798. Mrs. A. hindered my going to take depositions
at Tiot, turns off my custom.

Feb. 4. Mrs. A. hinders all my business of every kind, throws
in stumbling blocks to oppose and mar everything I might
and wish to do to advantage! If I promise a patient to
visit, she hinders it!

March 14. How used is the man that has an obstinate wife to
defeat and hurt all his undertakings twice to defeat her own
purpose by burning chimney to ruin smokejack that saves
her turning spit, etc.

March 31. The world and material things appear more and
more vanity and vexation. Losing friends, and finding the
falsity of pretended ones, and malice of open enemies, make
[one] wish for better scene of existence. Even in my own
house I can find no such attachment as I hoped for in early
life. Those I most admire cannot return only by force. I
wish not to exist by mere sufferance, but with affection of
ye World!

Sept. 30. I cannot think it as obnoxious for any other inter-
rupted profession as the clerical to be conversant in politics.
Is it for a physician? Ha! Yes, says my wife!

Of his Dedham neighbors Dr. Ames wrote down his
opinions with extreme and spicy frankness. His views as
to lawyers in general, and as to the Dedham lawyers in
particular, have already been set forth above. In addition
to members of that profession, however, there were five of
his neighbors towards whom Dr. Ames appears to have
had a special antipathy — Timothy Gay, the keeper of the
rival tavern, who apparently interfered with his practice
as a physician and his income as an innkeeper; Joel Lewis;
Reverend Jason Haven, the parish parson, and his son,

Samuel Haven (later the Judge of Probate); and Deacon Isaac Bullard, one of the town's leading citizens, a selectman, a Representative in the legislature, and County Treasurer. The following entries expressed clearly and amusingly his opinions of these neighbors:

Feb. 15, 1792. Tim Gay br'ot 1 cord of old white oak wood, 16 shillings, which not half so lasting or pleasant to burn as my own! ! ! See, before pay, for future!

Sept. 16. The envious temper of Tim Gay's wife and family hindered me from earning 50 dollars of patients intending to be innoculated under my care.

Nov. 2. T. Gay's envy and puppyism spit out in helping Dr. Sprague.

Sept. 24, 1802. Tim Gay's hogs this dark stormy day let out into my corn — a pretended accident, and she says accidents will happen, but I say they sha'nt!

April 27, 1802. Sessions Court. Sundry complaints before Grand Jury and many evidences summoned, particularly to catch Tim Gay selling without license. Evaporate fumo.

June 30, 1805. Turnpike by my house making for a fortnight, plaguing the public, misspending the subscribers' money by T. Gay Jr.'s obstinate disobliged, spoiled my little horse-shed and board fence near.

Sept. 24, 1795. Joe Lewis ought to be yoked as a hog, and I wish never to go where he is till he is yoked.

July, 1793. Parson Haven by solicitation, lying and intrigue got Sam Register Probate, tho' I was recommended by the County.

Aug. 3. The meddling Priest receives some check, by Sam not getting commissioned as expected.

Oct. 31. The puppyism of Sam Haven or of his father conspicuous in engrossing law business to himself, while clerk in H. Townshend's office.

March 16, 1795. At this Parish meeting, the Minister by his presence, flattering, browbeating and false computations, gained 20 pounds to his salary, against the mind and will of many of the small party that voted for it thro fear of his sanctimonious face, tho' they had before said they would vote against raising it, knowing him to be richer than any but one in the Parish.

March 6, 1811. Sam Haven's malignant slang in Town Meeting at me shocks good folks!

January, 1796. Agents for the Town of Dedham, viz: Deacon Isaac Bullard, myself, and Deacon James Whiting to appear this Session of General Court vs. the petition of Simon Eliot and others for enlarging Mill Creek and diverting the natural course of Charles River, by which petition they offer the fairest opportunity to the meadow owners to get relieved of floods that ever offered or ever will . . . and I had spoke my passage in the stage; but finding Deacon Bullard contradicted himself often for the sake of opposing me and determined to mar, black, and bewray all I could say or do at Court, I would not go, and determined never again to be concerned with him on any occasion, if I can avoid it.

1803. Deacon Isaac Bullard, having within these few years disseized the public of two sides of the square of land on the river near his house, stopped the road through Sandy Valley, arrogated the ministerial qualifications for the Parish to excommunicate such as refuse submission to his recommendation, and thinks to guard his wood lots by fear instead of fence, has complained of my cows and brought expense on me to redeem them from the field-driver.

That the darker sides of life in a country town were naturally confided to the country doctor is seen in an entry in 1798:

This day, my neighbor, H. Mann [the local editor] in despondency, disclosed a scene of debauchery, infidelity, adultery, and villainy, among several reputable families here — almost incredible — which has destroyed his peace of mind — and if it gets vent will break up his, if not several other families! But it was communicated to me in confidence to gain consolation in my advice and keep it secret, tho' attempts on his life have, he is pretty sure, been made by poison and is in apprehension of further repetition of such attempts — and to remove the effects of such poison he applied to Dr. Warren in Boston, then to me.

The forty-six years of struggle to succeed, between 1776 and his death in 1822, did not pass, however, without many cheerful entries, for the Doctor was interested in a bewildering variety of things, and his entries give countless curious bits of information as to the daily life of the times, of which the following may serve as examples. On November 6, 1776, he recorded that he "innoculated Thomas Claggett of Newport, clock maker, who informed me that his Father was the first Person in America that ever made an electric machine, and that Dr. B. Franklin only improved upon his Father, etc., with many other curious affairs." In September, 1777, he was interested in a detailed account of mills for making sugar. In May, 1779, he described an elaborate manufacture of a gilded punch ladle, as taught by a Prussian "late a soldier in the British Army, goldsmith whom I have taken here to learn the said trade to Jeremiah Shuttleworth." In April, 1779, a Swiss gardener showed him several new methods of grafting fruit trees, which he detailed at length. In July, 1789, his interest was much aroused by "two camels exhibited here." On July 15, 1797, he "viewed a female elephant, 4 years old, larger than an ox, at Gay's stable in Dedham," and on July 17 "resort to see the elephant, who goes at night to Cambridge." [1] The scope of Dr. Ames' active mind is well

[1] Such sights were apparently perennial in Boston. The following advertisements appeared in the *Independent Chronicle*, August 20, 1803. "To the Curious! Just arrived in town, and may be seen at the Rising Sun Tavern, Marlboro Street, for this week only, That Noble Animal, the Elephant, from Bengall. Price of Admission 25 cents. Children half price." — "Live Ostriches. Arrived on Tuesday from Africa. Two large elegant Ostriches, Male and Female, and are purchased for the Columbian Museum, Milk Street. They are remarkably tame, docile, and playful to all strangers, to children in particular; they will stretch their necks to drink to the heighth of nine feet and upwards. These Birds are the largest of the feathered creation, and may justly be considered perhaps the most innocent, noble, and majestic *living curisoity* ever exhibited in this town; their Plumage may be examined by the Ladies, who may wish to gratify themselves by a close inspection. . . . Admission, as usual, 50 cents."

illustrated by the constant entries on scientific matters and improvements in agriculture, on the new manufacturing enterprises and banks then being started in the United States, on books of science and art, on the new turnpikes which were spreading like magic all over the State, and two of which were constructed through the town of Dedham. In 1796 and 1797 he discoursed on architecture and on the building of a log aqueduct thus:

> *Dec. 1796.* By favor of Capt. Edward Dowse who lent me the Travels of Anacharsis a Scythian in Greece, I finished reading the same at the end of the year with much satisfaction; in 7 elegant volumes, and an 8th of maps and charts and elegant views of Grecian architecture. The propylaea or vestibule for entrance into the Citadel of Athens is noble. The bare view of the picture thereof gives a magnificent idea of their architecture; and the history of the Greeks with views of their temples and public buildings might greatly correct the taste of our carpenters. Accordingly, I called on Eliphalet Baker, a young carpenter, to show him these plans — but I do not expect our carpenters will become architects!
> *June 30, 1797.* Calvin Whiting, authorized by Act of Court, hath brought water in pine logs to sundry families, each paying five dollars per year; but the fountain head, at about a mile off, near the Post road to Providence, is not high enough nor large enough to carry it into upper stories of our houses, nor will it be of much use in extinguishing fires.

A new method of planting potatoes, and the introduction of galvanism, were noticed by him in 1803: June 14, 1803, "Planted potatoes in grass in Hybernian manner"; June 15, "Galvanism captivating modern philosophers"; June 16, "Warren brought from England great apparatus, for galvanic experiments." In April, 1809, an invention for a noncombustible material engaged his interest:

> Since Mr. Madison's investment as President, 4 March, a Mr. Morneveck has obtained a patent for an impenetrable

stucco by fire or water for covering roofs and other purposes to secure buildings against fire which appears to possess this advantage over slate tiles or shingles. It is harder and lighter than either, is elastic, resists frost; and four of the Judges of the U. S. S. J. C. — Marshall, Washington, Johnson, Livingston have examined and recommend it. They saw an experiment upon it with aquafortis and a coal fire, neither of which seemed to have a complete power of destruction, say they! Complete power! Well, if it will resist fire and water longer than other coverings, it must be worth tryal — further — it may be made on every farm, at any time of year, at the easy cost of one cent a foot square, but its application with best effect should be in serene weather between spring and fall of year.

Illustrations of how completely the newly formed corporations of Massachusetts, and especially the banks, were organized by Federalists and Federalist lawyers are found in the following indignant comments:

> *Jan. 16, 1804.* Sundry mechanics of Dedham meet, with a Lawyer at their head, to confer on the subject of a Bank in Dedham, and subscribe, it is said, to a fund. As I am decided to take no part in conference with those who excommunicated me in December, 1802, and abused me, viz: F.[isher] A.[mes] and Deacon Bullard, and feel indignation to find the Eastern States fettered down in chains of Pettyfogism, I think I shall keep aloof yet awhile, especially as T. Gay, Jr. and J. Richardson seem the only puppets played off on this occasion by the man behind the curtain.
>
> *Feb. 1814.* Feds of Dedham petition to establish Bank! Granted. Dedham Bank Directors chosen — Willard Gay, Jabez Chickering, James Richardson, Phineas Ellis, Gen. Elijah Crane!
>
> *Oct. 2.* Eliphalet shows cloven foot. Refused to vote (for) Republican Directors, State Bank.

Other scattered personal entries of interest throw curious sidelights on the life of the time in a country town:

March 12, 1808. S. Shuttlesworth has a mare, 5 years spring coming, too mild, tame — offers for 35 dol. with my black 14 year. Let me have her. Doubts, suspense?

March 13. S. Shuttlesworth offers me a mare, almost 5 years old, light bay, white blaze in face, 3 white feet, black mane and tail; but tho' she goes well enough in chaise, seems too tame. He says she had one colt by stealth, and has been harassed and beat down low by being continually driven by women, which caused the owner to sell her to him about a month ago. He calls her good breed, and would take my old black horse 14 or 15 years old, with 35 dollars for her. I am doubting, in suspense, having offered last night 30 as utmost boot I would give. He is pertinacious to make me take her, but eternal in concluding, waiting for snow to return to Windsor.

March 16. Pd. 30 to S. Shuttlesworth, exchanged horses. Tho' to me very grateful for former services in that way!

April 19, 1810. Stage coach every day thro' Dedham sets off from Boston at 4 A.M. reaches Hartford at 8 P.M. Begins 23rd; runs it in 16 hours, 100 m., little more than 6 an hour without stop — but relays every 10 miles.

May 1. Much parade of militia. Roxbury troop of horse arunning, everybody straining to see wonder!!

Aug. About a dozen cattle having been supposed bit by a strange dog under symptoms of madness and died here, some idle fellows undertaking thereupon to kill every dog, and shooting carelessly even into houses and killing dogs under protection of owners, violently assaulting even women, robbing them of their dogs wrapped in their aprons, placing loaded guns at their breasts at same time, has excited strong sensations among the people, divided into one party maintaining the Rights of Dogs, another for indiscriminate extermination of them.

Sept. 30. Delivered Lem Gay's wife a son. Staid all day. Charmed with the verdure of his trees, russet apples and others in profusion; luxuriant cabbages, green pastures, etc., while all on the plain burned up dry!

July 5, 1811. Therm. 100 at 3 P.M.

July 6. Many people died with heat. Sleep with windows wide open several nights, and then in constant sweat![1]

March 23, 1814. Dull time for news. People meet at Court House in Dedham to suppress drunkards, but I was not notified! So I must consider myself among the drunken band.

Aug. 29. Rake hells destroy sundry gardens. Swett offers 100 dollars for discovery! Are discovered. They are Josh. Fairbanks, Ch. Mason, Ed. Jones, Jo. Underwood, Eb. Leland. They killed 16 fat chickens of Mr. Dowse and ravaged his garden, Swett's, Chickering's, and mine. Took barber's pole and placed it at Rev. Mr. Bates's.

June 24, 1815. Grand parade here of Free Masons. Paul Davenport's sermon to them, but not seasoned strong enough for some with brimstone.

Aug. 25, 1817. S. Wight steals my Sherburn apples, unfit to eat or use, and offered them to Polley, who told him he stole; but his men bought them, could not eat 'em, and my man John brought 'em home. All, old men and young, live by plunder of lots.

While the doctor's political activities declined after the war, by which time he had reached the age of seventy-five, a few scattered entries in the years between 1815 and his death in 1822 show that he still retained his contempt for the lawcraft and the manner in which the State of Massachusetts clung to its Federalist idols. In the spring of 1815 he noted: "March ends with a most depressing gloomy storm — and the morn of April 1, cheers us with rare sunshine. May the political horizon as cheerfully be cleared on 1st Monday 3rd day, of all exertions of lying, flattering delusion practiced by Fudderal Lawcraft to continue the political storm and gloom." In 1817, however, the doctor became more hopeful politically, and he re-

---

[1] It is a curious commentary on the method of life in those times that it should be thought worthy of record that in summer he slept with open windows; but he records again: "*August 7, 1813.* Sleep with windows open all night for heat."

corded, April 12, 1817: "Good news from Connecticut.
Restored to Union. Carried Republican. Governor and
House"; April 17: "Rhode Island deserts Boston rebels.
Left to set up New England kingdom themselves"; and
April 19: "Boston alone to be New England kingdom."
Two years later, in 1819, he rejoiced at the fact that "the
people annually but gradually [are] lifting the veil of Fed-
eralism with which Massachusetts has been hoodwinked
by Deacon Strong."

A visit of President Monroe to Massachusetts in 1817
was described by Dr. Ames, with still more characteristic
revival of his old hatred of the "British Junto" and the
"New England traitors":

> Among other proceedings of this pacific session [of the
> State legislature] upon rumor that the new President of
> U. S., James Monroe, is on a journey to view the North-
> Eastern States and fortifications of all our frontier, East and
> West, our Yankee Fudderalists, so lately near open rebel-
> lion and raising troops to be under command of our new
> Fed. Governor Brooks to fight Congress and set up North-
> ern Confederacy or New England kingdom, seem now slink-
> ing back, trying to recover their lost influence, and are loud
> and forward to do more than all Democrats to honor the
> President on his arrival at Boston — call forth a vast caval-
> cade to obscure and veil from the people the stain of har-
> boring British enemy and invaders of Castine, as also their
> slanders of this very Monroe; when Secretary of State,
> "that he wished and tried to introduce here the Bonapar-
> tean conscription," etc., and pretend wish to salute with
> honor him who narrowly they escaped meeting in hostile
> array, under orders of Hartford Convention or Boston
> Rebels or Conspirators! In British alliance! full, Strong.
> But alas, the Junto could not agree, flashed in the pan! and
> dispersed! So now, individual citizens must display their
> dignified superiority to slaves of the old continent in doing
> honor to their fellow citizen and Chief Magistrate or con-

fidential agent, offering without boring him their sincere salutations as men.

June 26, 1817. Vast parade of Feds for escort of President Monroe. Fudderal vinegar and verjuice is changed to oil and molasses. Gorham Parsons said to give 100 dollars to dress State Street for Presidential procession.

July 1. Great parade to receive the President Monroe, Artillery arrived from upper towns in the morning. Crane's division 1st of Militia ordered out. Cavalry to escort him upon South boundary of Norfolk to Boston. Then President reviews troops on the Great Common, near sunsetting, sleeps at Mr. Dowse's, while many are attending.

July 2. Morning, President walks from Dowse's to Polley's Tavern [in Dedham], where I was the first introduced and shook hands with him; vast many after kept him continually bowing, until General of Division orders that none offer to shake hands, but front and bow and pass by.

Then amidst cavalry and carriages goes off to review troops at Jamaica Plaine; then into Boston with vast ceremony under triumphal arch; at last retires to superb room in Exchange Coffee-house.

Aug. 28. Geo. Dean says the Rev. Mr. McFarland of Concord, N. H., violent Fudderal, got tipsey with President Monroe as he passed, taken off by his Fudderal friends, who are greatly mortified by it!

The last political event in our National history which Dr. Ames recorded was the Missouri Compromise in 1820. The good doctor was then seventy-nine years old, but his handwriting was as clear and his phrases as vigorous as when he began his Diary, sixty-two years before.

Jan. 15, 1820. Difficulty in Congress with new people, West of Mississippi, Territory of Missouri wishing to establish a government to hold fellow men in slavery! ! ! And defying Congress to restrict it, threatening to dissolve the Union, by declaring Independence; and Virginia Legislature resolves to support them against Congress attempting to restrict their extension of slavery over that vast country. We anxiously await the result.

A John Lindsey offers himself a candidate for forming a constitution for the new State of Missouri, by advertising in Missouri Gazette "that his principles are well known to be Republican and as to slavery I shall be in favor of it!" Such ignorant apes ought to be chained, blacked and taught. No wonder Western emigrants are ranked below savages.

Jan. 27, 1820. Congress, frozen by cold hearted slave holders, begins to thaw.

March 8, 1820. Congress decide for slavery in Missouri and raise Maine to sovereign State. And have as yet done nothing but combat slave-holding States who speculate in breeding slaves for the vast western territory Louisiana! ! Bidding defiance to principles of our Independence.

A year later he recorded, with characteristic humor: "*July 4, 1821.* Independence Day kept here by vast multitudes of he's and she's. Cobb, orator. Mr. Dowse gave 11 dollars rather than attend." After this date his entries became intermittent, but on the very last page of his Diary, only a few weeks before his death, his old feud with a neighbor flashed forth in an entry regarding "the pilfering of the Gay race."

Dr. Nathaniel Ames died, on July 22, 1822, at the age of eighty-one, sturdy, humorous, pugnacious, to the end — a Yankee of Yankees, a Jacobin of Jacobins.